# *Contents*

# Moving Target
## Theatre Translation and Cultural Relocation

Edited by
CAROLE-ANNE UPTON

Published by

St. Jerome Publishing
2 Maple Road West, Brooklands
Manchester, M23 9HH, United Kingdom
Tel +44 161 973 9856
Fax +44 161 905 3498
stjerome@compuserve.com
http://www.stjerome.co.uk

ISBN 1-900650-27-4 (pbk)

Printed and bound in Great Britain by
T. J. International Ltd., Cornwall, UK

Cover design by
Steve Fieldhouse, Oldham, UK (+44 161 620 2263)

Typeset by
Delta Typesetters, Cairo, Egypt
Email: delttyp@starnet.com.eg

*British Library Cataloguing in Publication Data*
A catalogue record of this book is available from the British Library

*Library of Congress Catalging-in-Publication Data*
Moving target : theatre translation and cultural relocation / edited by
Carole-Anne Upton.
     p. cm.
Includes bibliographical references (p.   ) and index.
 ISBN 1-900650-27-4 (pbk. : alk. paper)
 1. Drama--Translating.  I. Upton, Carole-Anne.
 PN886 .M68 2000
 418'.02--dc21
                          00-010132

# Introduction

TERRY HALE AND CAROLE-ANNE UPTON

Though the intimate relationship that the stage has long enjoyed with translation is no secret, neither has it been the subject of specialized intensive investigation, whether from the perspective of theatre studies, literary history, or the emergent discipline of translation studies. In this collection, translators, directors and researchers reflect on the issues surrounding translation in contemporary theatre practice.

Approximately one in eight professional productions reviewed in Britain's national press at the time of writing is a translation.[1] This is a significant statistic for it suggests that the theatre is the most receptive of all the various art forms in Britain as far as translation is concerned. In the cinema, the aversion of English-speaking audiences to dubbing and even to subtitling is proverbial. Television (except in the special case of Wales) broadcasts a negligible number of programmes originally made in languages other than English, and the publishing industry in the United Kingdom brings out fewer books in translation than any other in Europe.[2]

That the discovery of such a high incidence of translation on the British stage probably comes as something of a surprise, may be due to the fact that the translation aspect (and the translator) of a production is rarely given much prominence. To a greater or lesser extent, the dialogue, action and characters will have been quietly relocated to an idiom accessible (if not altogether familiar) to the target audience. This is arguably the goal of all translation, but in the theatre the process raises a unique set of questions, which this book sets out to explore.

---

[1] *Theatre Record* reprints from the national press all reviews of new productions in London and a considerable number outside London. In 1998, some 806 new productions of stage plays were reviewed, excluding other types of performance, notably mime and productions in languages other than English, by foreign touring companies. 577 of these productions (72%) were based in London. Some 73 London productions (12.65% of London-based plays reviewed) and 33 regional productions (14.4% of regional productions reviewed) were translations. The present writers would like to thank Ms Duska Radovitch Heaney for providing them with an initial breakdown of *Theatre Record* for 1998.

[2] Venuti, for example, has pointed out that though British and American book production has quadrupled since the 1950s, the number of translations published has generally remained between 2% and 4% of the total (Venuti 1995: 12). More recent figures for the UK would seem to indicate a translation rate of around 2% (*The Bookseller*, 20 February 1998). In Germany, which has a publishing industry comparable in size to that of the UK, some 14% of books published are translations. Translation accounts for an even larger proportion of the publishing output of other European countries: France (18%), Italy (26%), Spain (24%). (BIPE Conseil 1993).

Firstly, there are ideological questions surrounding the definition of the target audience. If the theatre mirrors the collective identity of its audience, it also creates it by re-shaping perceptions. The theatre translator therefore has a socio-political responsibility to define and address the target audience, which demands careful mediation of the source text.

Secondly, the form itself demands a dramaturgical capacity to work in several dimensions at once, incorporating visual, gestural, aural and linguistic signifiers into the translation. In the complementary consideration of all these elements, the process is closely linked to *mise en scène*, and any cultural relocation is thrown into sharp relief by the conjunction of multiple semiotic codes.

Finally, translating for performance within a given context requires a sensitivity to the various agendas in operation in both the source and target cultures – whether in terms of state censorship, cultural bias, or, at a more pragmatic level, institutional production policies. As cultural advocate, the translator may refuse to relocate the source text for fear of neutralising its cultural identity. A theatre translation has above all to function within the immediate context of performance – without annotation or editorial commentary – and alternative strategies must be developed for dealing with the seemingly untranslatable, un-saleable, or unspeakable (in all senses of the word).

A brief survey of theatre history reveals that translation has, at least since the Renaissance, always played a major role. The earliest known English version of a Greek tragedy is by one Lady Jane Lumley and dates from the middle of the fifteenth century, although whether her *Iphigeneia* is taken directly from Euripides' *Iphigeneia in Aulis* or from a Latin translation of it (by Erasmus) is uncertain (Walton 1998).

It is a well-known fact that Shakespeare, the epitome of English drama, derived most of his comic plots from the Roman playwrights Terence and Plautus, who in their turn had 'contaminated' (combined) a series of sources from Greek New Comedy. He might have been influenced by contemporary English translations of the Romans, such as William Warner's version of Plautus' *Menaechmi* which appeared in about 1594 (*The Comedy of Errors*). Stylistic parallels with the Italian *commedia dell'Arte* form bear testimony to his knowledge not only of the generic conventions but perhaps also of the numerous translations and adaptations into Italian, including several of the *Menaechmi*. Shakespeare read Latin himself, but undoubtedly also drew upon translations, notably Sir Thomas North's popular 1579 translation of Plutarch's *Lives* (*Julius Caesar*, *Anthony and Cleopatra*, *Coriolanus*) which was itself a translation not from the original Greek but from the 1559 French version by Jacques Amyot. Shakespeare might have used any of eight translations of Homer's *Iliad*, in Latin, French or English, alongside Chaucer as a source for his *Troilus and Cressida*. In fact, there is hardly a play in Shakespeare's oeuvre that does not rely, directly or indirectly, on the translation of a foreign source.

Otway's successful 1676 translation of Molière's *Les Fourberies de Scapin* was originally presented with his version of Racine's *Bérénice* and was still being revived as late as 1959.

The Prologue by the Tory Alexander Pope to Addison's *Cato*, first performed at Drury Lane in 1713, ends with the proud declaration that here, for once, is a play of British origin:

> With honest scorn the first famed Cato viewed
> Rome learning arts from Greece, whom she subdued;
> Our scene precariously subsists too long
> On French translation, and Italian song.
> Dare to have sense yourselves; assert the stage,
> Be justly warmed with your own native rage.
> Such plays alone should please a British ear,
> As Cato's self had not disdained to hear.

Clearly the sheer quantity of theatre being produced in translation in the eighteenth century was a matter of concern to some. Addison's colleague, Steele credits his director Colley Cibber (incidentally, a translator of Molière) in a preface, with persuading him to rework his translation of Terence's *Andria* and to domesticate the juvenile lead character into "an Englishman" in *The Conscious Lovers,* of 1722. The play, set in contemporary London, was a great success, and was immediately translated into both French and German. Such examples are by no means exceptional.

The nineteenth-century British stage was particularly dependent on translation, some commentators going so far as to claim that "fully half of the plays written in England during this period (1800-1850) must have been suggested by Parisian models and many were literally adapted by English authors" (Rahill 1967:115). Tom Taylor later had a string of successes at the Olympic Theatre with plays adapted from the French, including *Still Waters Run Deep* (1855) and *The Ticket-of-Leave Man* (1863), reputedly the two most popular works produced on the British stage during the nineteenth century. In 1867, a certain Francis Hitchman was lamenting "the commonness of translations and the scarcity of original dramatic writing", in a detailed study of the subject in *The Belgravia Magazine.*

Nor was the English theatre the only one indebted to such an extent to outside sources. As Lambert, D'Hulst and Bragt note with respect to French theatre of the first half of the nineteenth century:

> The translation of foreign works (Schiller, Shakespeare, the Spanish playwrights) bears all the ambiguously innovatory features of original Romantic works. Nevertheless, even Shakespeare in alexandrine guise became a revolutionary author – more revolutionary even than Casimir Delavigne or Hugo. In fact, the translations of foreign drama became the most daring plays that the French stage could offer to the public. (1985:153)

In a sense, the twentieth century adoption of such authors as Ibsen, Chekhov

and Molière into the English canon of dramatic literature (Ibsen is even represented on at least one English A-level syllabus) only continues this tradition.

However, a certain resistance to explicitly foreign works on the English-
speaking stage has been the cause of equally longstanding frustration to advocates
of cultural plurality. Even Chekhov provoked a xenophobic reaction according
to James Agate, reviewing Fagan's 1925 production of *The Cherry Orchard* in
*The Sunday Times*:

> Insularity is a good thing, perhaps, but not always as we islanders conceive it.
> "These Russians have a very un-English way of looking at things", I heard a
> lady say at the conclusion of this piece. That's our trouble. "If people are not
> English, they ought to be", puts our view in a nutshell. (Hobson 1953:119)

One might have hoped that such an attitude of cultural imperialism would be
challenged by the advent of a postcolonial, intercultural zeitgeist. Instead, according to the infamous 1977 article by *Guardian* theatre critic Michael
Billington, entitled 'Britain's Theatrical Chauvinism':

> We are still ignorant of the past riches of world drama. We see very few of
> the best new plays from other countries. And when some foreign company is
> rash enough to accept an invitation to visit London, it is usually greeted with
> a cold and patronising derision. [...]
> Anything non-English, unless it be an American musical or a solo performer,
> is regarded as some kind of cultural letter bomb. (1993:108)

Reviewing a production of Strindberg's *Miss Julie* at the Theatre Royal,
Haymarket, twenty three years later, Robert Butler in *The Independent on Sunday* was still able to congratulate the production for having "taken a Swedish
playwright whose name roughly translates as 'box office poison' and placed his
1888 classic in the grandest venue in the West End."(5.3.2000).[3] Billington's
review of the same production in *The Guardian* echoes the cry for greater receptivity: "One just wishes our theatre would range more widely over the work
of this uncomfortable genius. [...] What I would like to see is more Strindberg
staged in Britain" (29.2.2000).

Despite the theatre's age-old tendency to adopt material from other cultures,
the British sensibility has been inclined to underplay the foreignness of its inspiration. Translations and adaptations, having been thoroughly domesticated,
have entered the repertoire almost surreptitiously under the guise of British versions. Amongst those plays that are deemed worthy of the British stage, there

---

[3] Significantly, at least part of the credit for this success is given to Frank McGuinness
for his "terrific new version" which gives a "muscular immediacy" to suit the production. Predictably, however, the review makes no mention of the 'literal' translation by
Charlotte Barslund which served as the basis for Frank McGuinness' 'version', (although she is discreetly acknowledged in the programme).

remains a discernible hierarchy of acknowledged masterpieces which, even now, rarely admits of contemporary writing.

This is not to say that there has been no improvement. There are, of course, some notable pioneers of innovative theatre in translation: The Royal Court Theatre, the Gate, the Almeida, to some extent the Royal National Theatre and still to a degree the Royal Shakespeare Company, all of which consciously strive to make productions of interesting and often unfamiliar foreign drama available in translation to British audiences. Along with a number of important directors, the likes of Sam Mendes and Stephen Daldry, they seek to cultivate what Michael Billington so sorely regrets: "At the very least [...] the anthropological pleasure that comes from discovering other civilisations and ways of living: at the highest, an enrichment of the human spirit" (Ibid.:110).

The scope of the works discussed in this volume is therefore deliberately broader and more contemporary than the mainstream repertoire, and extends beyond Britain to Western and Eastern Europe, as well as Canada and the United States. Several of the contributors have had their translations staged and sometimes commissioned by the companies listed above.

Sadly though, such companies struggle to find resources in line with their ambitions. The conservatism of the English funding bodies has repeatedly been identified as a significant obstacle to the production of foreign plays, notably by Billington, but equally vociferously by Peter Hall as former director of the National Theatre. In recent years, the Gate Theatre has narrowly escaped closure, having been faced with the threatened withdrawal of its revenue funding by London Arts Board (the New Playwrights Trust was another target of the same measures). As early as 1959, Hall's predecessor Tyrone Guthrie had articulated the problem thus (although we might now wonder at the middle section of his list):

> To the official, the fund-bestowing, mind I have found the following is fairly typical rating: Shakespeare, yes. Greek tragedy and the great classics of the French and German theatre, less definitely, but still yes. Restoration comedy, very definitely no. Sheridan and Goldsmith are near the borderline. Ibsen, Shaw, Chekhov, Bridie and O'Neill are even nearer the borderline. A 'modern' play or a new play, no. A modern foreign play, quite definitely, *No*. (Guthrie 1961:128)

Among the translated plays which received press coverage in 1998, we find such works as Ron Hutchinson's adaptation of Mikhail Bulgakov's *Flight*, which opened in the Olivier, the National Theatre's biggest auditorium, on 12 February and enjoyed a run of more than three-and-a-half months. Also in the West End, Ranjit Bolt's translation of Molière's *Le Misanthrope* was well received and enjoyed a run of more than four months at the Piccadilly while Katie Mitchell's RSC/Young Vic production of Chekhov's *Uncle Vanya* in a new version by David Lan also received extensive press coverage. Outside the West

End, less than a week after the première of *Flight*, Juliette Binoche opened at the Almeida, in a new version by Nicholas Wright of Pirandello's *Naked*. If anything, the Pirandello play received even more press coverage than the Bulgakov. Later in the year, the Donmar Warehouse pulled off a similar coup, when Nicole Kidman starred in Sam Mendes' production of David Hare's adaptation of Arthur Schnitzler, *The Blue Room*. Meanwhile, a revival at the Lyric Hammersmith of Helen Edmundson's version of Tolstoy's *Anna Karenina* was welcomed by a handful of enthusiastic critics (as was a revival of Rodney Ackland's 1946 adaptation of Dostoyevsky's *Crime and Punishment* at the tiny Finborough in west London); a production of Aimé Césaire's *Une Tempête*, itself a post-colonial appropriation of Shakespeare, was considered an auspicious start for Mick Gordon, the Gate's new artistic director; and Diana Rigg enjoyed a three-month run in Jonathan Kent's production for the Almeida Theatre at the Albery of Racine's *Phèdre* in a new version, considered too self-consciously classical by some critics, from Ted Hughes.

Even now Molière, Racine, Chekhov, Pirandello and, ironically, Shakespeare provide the seemingly necessary credibility to justify British production. Viewed from this angle, the less familiar Schnitzler and Bulgakov appear bold programming choices, although neither can be described as new; the former dates from 1897, the latter was written (though not performed) in 1926-7. Notwithstanding the undeniable merits of these modern translations and adaptations, the fact remains that, more than two decades down the line from Billington's article, the range of translated material reaching professional production is still limited.

Is it mere coincidence that the two least familiar of the nine plays mentioned above should have undergone the most radical treatment in terms of adaptation? As one critic noted, Bulgakov's *Flight* was not an obvious crowd-pleaser; others noted that Ron Hutchinson's translation/adaptation was extremely free. Somewhat naïvely, the editorial of *Theatre Record* wondered whether the British public – given that this was "the first real production in England" – were being "sold a pup": "It's a great pup [...] but a pup nonetheless, in that we're not being given Bulgakov" (Issue 3, 12-25th February 1998:165). The extent of the adaptation was commented on in greater detail both by the popular press and the broadsheets with regard to *The Blue Room*. "David Hare has most freely adapted Arthur Schnitzler's *La Ronde*, once an infamous movie, propelling it into the present day and introducing such modern characters as a druggy teenage model and a naughty New Labour M.P." (Bill Hagerty in *The News of the World*, 27.9.98). "Hare's gentle comedy of sexual manners displaces Schnitzler's serious drama of sex and betrayal" (Nicholas de Jongh in *The Evening Standard*, 23.9.98). Notwithstanding a tendency for critics to exhibit their own literary knowledge, what these comments acknowledge is the process by which the alien source material has been relocated within the cultural experience of the new target audience, in terms of both dramatic form and thematic resonance. Whether such a process of domestication represents an undue betrayal of the source, or due recognition of the target is a matter of opinion.

In the case of *Naked* a number of critics draw specific parallels between the play (originally written in 1922) and a recent murder trial in the U.S. that was widely reported by the British media: "In a story with echoes of the Louise Woodward case, Binoche plays a child's nanny, Ersilia Drei, whose charge has died while in her care. She has fled from Smyrna in the Levant to Rome, attempted suicide, and is now plastered all over the newspapers" (Charles Spencer in *The Telegraph*, 21.02.98).

Curiously, the two adaptations of Russian novels received nothing but praise for the skill with which the process had been carried out. Critical response was more unpredictable in the case of the closer translations, though it is worth noting how some reviewers were obviously uncomfortable with the recreation of formal verse structures more characteristic of the French stage than the British. An unfamiliar subject is apparently more readily accepted than a foreign aesthetic or formal convention. Harry Eyres in *The Spectator*, for example, found the rhyming couplets of Bolt's *Misanthrope* "rather relentless" (11.4.98) while even Charles Spencer in *The Daily Telegraph*, who found the same couplets "vigorous" as well as "fleet-footed and funny", still occasionally found himself "longing for Martin Crimp's scabrous adaptation" of a few years previously (30.3.98). Crimp, incidentally, had relocated the action of Molière's play, stating in the opening stage directions "All characters are British, except Jennifer, who is an American. The time is now, the place is London".[4]

The dilemma over foreignization or domestication of the text is one shared by all literary translators, although the decision to relocate is arguably more consequential with a text for performance than with a text intended to be read privately. Theatre is a complex and composite medium, in which the verbal is but one element within a whole matrix of visual and aural semiotic codes. Theatrical production embodies and enacts the cultural markers within the text in a concrete physicalization which all but precludes indeterminacy. Cultural milieu is embodied in the specifics of any or all of the signifying elements (actors' physical appearance, gesture, set, costume, lighting, sound, kinesics, proxemics, etc.), as well as in the spoken word.

It is not, however, a simple question of absolutes. Rather, the wholly domestic and the wholly foreign are at opposite poles of a single spectrum of sophisticated possibilities. The very richness of this composite form gives the theatre its special capacity to juxtapose the alien and the familiar, thereby creating both distance and 'rapprochement' at the same time. It is a theatrical truism that myth,

---

[4] The published text is prefaced by a note entitled 'Re-writing Molière' in which Crimp cites Molière's assertion that comedy must portray recognisably contemporary characters. He continues:

> [I]f, 300 years later, reflecting the contemporary world has meant taking certain 'liberties' with the text, this is only in the belief that – at this distance in time – re-invention, re-writing of one writer's work by another is 'fidelity' of the truest and most passionate kind. (Crimp 1996)

for example, characteristically introduces a familiar dilemma into a deliberately remote context; a specific cultural context is established, only to be transcended in the establishment of 'universal' truths. Brecht's Sichuan, Miller's Salem, Shakespeare's Greece and Rome, all demonstrate the potential of the medium to explore domestic issues of contemporary morality with the critical distance afforded by the 'otherness' of the setting. The fact that the theatre, through such original works as these, already embodies the potential to combine the foreign with the familiar offers a rich and liberating paradigm for the translator.

The issue of cultural relocation is, not surprisingly, central for the translators in this collection. Conclusions differ; while Johnston transposes the entire milieu of Valle-Inclán's Spain to his more familiar Ireland, even changing characters' names and histories, Rozhin is adamant that the integrity of her source material lies in its very Polishness, and finds that non-verbal signifiers can provide the essential context of Polish 'otherness' that allows the linguistic text to be domesticated without being completely neutralized.

Transcultural politics prove equally controversial. Derrick Cameron presents a vision of a multiracial and multi-cultural society in which theatre translation might rid itself of the old hierarchies of Leavisite criticism and respond to a new audience with a new aesthetic, capable of incorporating non-Western, non-imperialist values into a re-working of even the most iconic Western texts. Paradoxically, such a political challenge to the bastions of conservative culture reformulates our historical tendency to domesticate the text by relocating it within a recognizable cultural context. What this approach demands, however, is a constant process of redefinition of the contemporary target culture. Similarly, Bowman and Findlay are concerned in their translations to address a community more narrowly defined by local dialect. Translation strategy, as part of a broader production approach, is determined by reception aesthetics.

Nigro, on the other hand, insists on preserving the 'otherness' of her source material, refusing what she regards as a compromise of Latin American identity to the North American hegemony. Kate Cameron explores a more subjective strategy for translating Hélène Cixous, in which a feminist agenda is relocated through the discovery of a personal, as opposed to a cultural aesthetic, in the musicality of her own voice.

While Hungarian Nagy explores the difficulty of translating context as well as text, Meech details how theatre translation strategies, particularly of domestication, proved an invaluable weapon of subversion against the communist censor under the GDR regime. Non-verbal devices (set, props, costume, mask, gesture, even sound effects) were impossible to pre-empt before they entered the public domain, and moreover, acted as a cultural bridge, highlighting parallels between some alien or mythical conflict present in the apparently innocuous source text, and the political situation in the GDR. The fundamental artistic technique of making the strange familiar and the familiar strange, has also conveniently provided a kind of alibi for subversive playwrights, practitioners and translators with limited freedom of expression.

Thankfully, the theatre, the most flexible and ephemeral of the arts, is able to embrace such diversity of approach. Drama translation provides far more than simply a 'parallel text'. More often than not, the relation between source and target in the translations analyzed here turns out to be one of asymmetry – where the original is not distorted but deliberately recrafted to address the ultimately ephemeral moment in which it is to be performed. The text, in European and American theatre at least, still forms the initial basis for most theatre production. Surely the translator, as creator of the text, should be acknowledged as a key figure within the collaborative process of production: akin to playwright, dramaturg, director? As Lindsay Bell amply demonstrates in her discussion of adapting from screen to stage, the translator's authorship of a new dramatic text implies a capacity to manipulate not just words but also structure. A translation, in rhythm, tone, character, action and setting, implicitly or explicitly contains the framework for a particular *mise en scène*, guiding director, actors, designers and finally audience towards a particular spectrum of interpretation. Batty further explores this organic relationship between translation and *mise en scène*. Through an examination of Samuel Beckett's notoriously close directorial control and meticulous self-translation, his essay sets out central issues in the relationship between translation and performance.

Beckett's dogged determination to retain control over both the translation and staging of his work is in itself an acknowledgement of the inherent instability of the performance text, as derived from the written text. The theatre is by definition protean. Its great strength lies in its very anti-literary impermanence. The repertoire, even the medium itself, is constantly being invented and reinvented with each new production. It is this fluidity of re-interpretation that allows the theatre to embrace the concept of idiosyncratic translation, in the interests of currency. Why else are new translations so frequently commissioned for classic texts, especially comedy, of which successful translations already exist (from a rough survey, there are in excess of twenty British editions of Molière translations currently available)? It is notable that the theoretical discourse of translation is full of negative metaphors of loss and interference, while theatre practice is generally governed by the creative principle. Each new translation, like each new production, involves a unique set of artistic and pragmatic choices; the result need not claim to be definitive, as long as it finds a voice in which to speak with resonance to its target audience, and at least aspire to "an enrichment of the human spirit".

The complexity and inconstancy of the performance text clearly pose an enormous (and, so far, insuperable) challenge to translation theorists. Zuber-Skerritt (1984:9) suggests that the researcher should record a single performance onto video to eliminate the problematic variables; Bassnett, in an essay symptomatically entitled 'Still Trapped in the Labyrinth – Further Reflections on Translation and Theatre' (1998:105) concludes that the theatre translator should regard the dramatic text as literature, "work with the inconsistencies of the text and leave the resolution of those inconsistencies to someone else" and that "[t]he time has come for translators to stop hunting for deep structures and coded subtexts" (Ibid.:107).

Both Bassnett and Zuber appeal for further investigation into the subject of theatre translation, and concur that the translator should ideally collaborate with the production team. A playwright is frequently consulted and involved in the shaping of the performance text through rehearsals and production meetings. And yet, the theatre translator has rarely been acknowledged as a creative figure integral to the process of production. Translation studies has paid relatively little attention to this particular role; theatre studies even less.

A number of reasons can be posited for this. Firstly, the domestication tendency has historically denied the translator credit for his/her achievement in mediating the 'foreignness' of the source, since the 'foreignness' of the original text has habitually been played down. The current practice, fairly widespread in Britain at least, of commissioning 'literal' translations to short deadlines and for minimal fees, to obtain a 'raw' text which can then be reworked into a new 'version' by a known playwright with no competence in the source language, is symptomatic of the low status in which translators have hitherto been held. Curiously, in view of the reverse hierarchy in literary translation, a 'version' or 'adaptation' in theatre seems to confer higher status on its author than does a 'translation'. Perhaps the implication has been that an adaptation requires a level of dramaturgical skill and creative vision, which, in a 'mere' translation, are solely attributable to the original playwright?[5] Playwright and translator Christopher Hampton is startlingly dismissive of the issue:

> It's a terminology problem. *Hedda* was not *translated* by me, because I don't speak Norwegian. But I don't much like "new version", because that sounds like you've altered it. The problem is that there isn't a terminology which says I haven't done anything to this play except put it in English. (Wolf 1989:36)

As these essays demonstrate, there is no such thing as a 'literal' translation. Some elements prove untranslatable (Rozhin; Nagy), while others present a wide variety of alternatives to choose between, none of them neutral within the context of the performance text (Findlay; Cameron). The concept of a literal translation of a play is as absurd as that of an 'authentic' production of Shakespeare.

---

[5] See, for example, the lexicon used in Dieter Mehl's account of *Coriolanus*, which ignores North's translation of Plutarch:

> The way he [Shakespeare] translated Plutarch's very consistent and at the same time complex character study into the scenic form of a tragedy is a particularly impressive instance of creative adaptation and dramaturgic virtuosity. This applies to his departures from the source, but no less to those many passages where he follows Plutarch with astonishing fidelity. These parallels, often practically literal quotations, suggest that he must have had an open volume of the biographies in front of him while composing his tragedy. (Mehl 1986:178)

It was the late Kenneth McLeish who declared theatre translation to be a craft and not an art.[6] This collection challenges that distinction, by exposing the creative complexities and aesthetic sensibility of the translator, whose linguistic competence is only the barest minimum of a qualification for the role, and who has at once to contend with the intricate detail of nuance and rhythm, whilst maintaining a holistic grasp of dramaturgy and staging potential as well as a profound awareness of cultural milieu. In other words, as Batty and Johnston clearly demonstrate, the theatre translator is not 'simply' decoding, but (re)creating a text for performance, with a view always to a potential *mise en scène.*

It is the privilege of the theatre translator to bring the text alive for a new audience, to release its unique energy, in anticipation of performance – in the words of George Steiner, to "make of echo a life-giving reply" (Steiner 24.10.99). In mediating between cultures, the translator has at his/her disposal not just words, but all the other elements of performance, physical and aural. The theatre translator's art is not exclusively literary.

Much has been achieved in terms of analyzing performance since the establishment of drama as an independent discipline in British universities after the Second World War. From the fundamental premise that drama is not merely a sub-genre of literature, and that performance calls for an entirely different research methodology, a theoretical framework has been developed to address processes of production and reception and to promote cultural understanding through the theatre. Few nowadays could sympathise with the view "that Greek tragedy *cannot* be discussed as achieved, created art; that it *cannot* be translated; that English readers ha[ve] *no* parallel concepts to place against the Greek" (MacKillop 1995:175). And yet, this was the pronouncement made by increasingly influential critic F. R. Leavis, who began to become interested in the subject of tragedy at Cambridge in the mid-1930s, when there was not a single university department in Britain that offered the subject. Neither would many condone the cultural naiveté of critic C. E. Montague, writing in *Dramatic Values* as early as 1910, and bemoaning the reluctance of the British theatre to stage Greek tragedy because of the perceived inaccessibility of a drama,

> [...] which asks the modern playgoer to make an enormous step out of himself and to imagine the feelings of an audience so different from himself and so vastly his superiors. What we want for our British theatre is the opposite feeling. It must be felt that the *Oedipus Tyrannus* appeals, above all, to the Greek or to the Englishman simply in his quality of discerning playgoer. The discerning playgoer is eternal... (Hobson 1953:166)

When theatre studies as a discipline finally did establish itself, the translator

---

[6] Keynote Address (September 1997) *True to Form: On Stage Translation* conference, University of Hull. Unpublished manuscript.

was not a prominent figure in the professional practice which it sought to investigate. In our subsequent attempts to engage with theatre as a cultural phenomenon and even in the recent wave of research into interculturalism, the complex and crucial role of the translator has still been largely overlooked. Theatre translation has largely fallen between the two young disciplines of theatre studies and translation studies, in much the same way as it often seems to fall between the portfolios of literature and drama as far as funding is concerned.

Even now it is still quite common for performance translation to be subsumed within the general category of Literature. This, for example, is the case in Peter Newmark's *A Textbook of Translation* (1988) where Drama occupies a total of seven paragraphs in a twelve-page section entitled 'The Translation of Serious Literature and Authoritative Statements'. Newmark, incidentally, was a student of Leavis'.

It is almost impossible not to suspect that one reason why performance translation has remained the poor relation of the translation world (at least as far as Translation Studies is concerned) is that translation theorists are generally unaware of the extent, richness and diversity of the theatrical tradition. Practising theatre translators are, by and large, similarly unaware of translation theory. In an important contribution to this book, Catalan translator-trainer Eva Espasa examines existing theory in relation to theatre translation in an analysis of 'performability' that bridges the apparent gulf between theatre practice and translation theory.

Although performance translation raises issues of semiotics, stylistics and cultural mediation, in common with literary translation, it also exploits the more anarchic characteristics of the theatre, which may appear antagonistic to translation studies. In its formal mutability, in its constantly shifting ideals, in its consideration of target audience over source text, and in its frequently ad hoc methodology, (not to mention the vexed questions of subtext and non-verbal or paralinguistic signifiers) theatre translation defies any ambition to define prescriptive norms.

The aim of this volume is neither prescriptive nor normative. Its modest goal is to provide a space for translators of theatre to reflect upon their experiences, to evaluate and contextualize their work, and to offer the reader some insight into the joys as well as the frustrations of a practice which is customarily solitary and private. The sheer range of creative strategies detailed in these essays is enough to broaden our perception of the task, and demonstrates the breadth of understanding – linguistic, dramatic, aesthetic and cultural – that is required in the translation of a text for performance. At the very least, it is a celebration of this neglected art; one that may further prove a significant early step towards a more comprehensive body of systematic research into translation for performance.

## References

Addison, Joseph (1713) *Cato*, in D.W. Lindsay (ed.) (1993) *The Beggar's Opera and Other Eighteenth-Century Plays*, London: Everyman.

Bassnett, Susan (1998) 'Still Trapped in the Labyrinth: Further Reflections on Translation and Theatre', in S. Bassnett and A. Lefevere, *Constructing Cultures: Essays on Literary Translation*, Clevedon: Multilingual Matters: 90-108.

Billington, Michael (1977) 'Britain's Theatrical Chauvinism', *The Guardian* 1 October; reprinted in (1993) *One Night Stands – A Critic's View of Modern British Theatre*, London: Nick Hern Books: 108-113.

------ (2000) 'Seduced by Miss Julie', *The Guardian* Tuesday 29th February.

BIPE Conseil (1993) *Statistical Approaches to Literary Translation in Europe, A study produced at the request of the Unit Cultural Action of DG X of the Commission of the European Communities by BIPE Conseil.*

Butler, Robert (2000) 'Crackling with Lust and Power', *The Independent on Sunday* 5th March, Culture Section: 6.

Crimp, Martin trans. (1996) *The Misanthrope,* London: Faber and Faber.

Guthrie, Tyrone (1961) *A Life in the Theatre*, London: Hamish Hamilton (Readers Union).

Hitchman, J. Francis (1867) 'Decline of the Drama', *Belgravia* II, March: 57-65.

Hobson, Harold (1953) *Theatre*, London: Burke.

Lambert, José, Lieven D'Hulst and Katrin van Bragt (1985) 'Translated literature in France, 1800-1850', in Theo Hermans (ed.) *The Manipulation of Literature: Studies in Literary Translation,* London: Croom Helm: 149-163.

MacKillop, Ian (1995) *F.R.Leavis. A Life in Criticism*, London: Allen Lane.

Mehl, Dieter (1983) *Die Tragödien Shakespeares: Eine Einführung*, Erich Schmidt Verlag GmbH and GmnH; trans. Mehl (1986) as *Shakespeare's Tragedies: An Introduction*, Cambridge: Cambridge University Press.

Newmark, Peter (1988) *A Textbook of Translation*, London: Prentice-Hall International.

Rahill, Frank (1967) *The World of Melodrama*, Pennsylvania: Pennsylvania State University Press.

Steiner, George (1999) 'Greek is the Word', *The Guardian* Sunday 24th October.

Venuti, Lawrence (1995) *The Translator's Invisibility. A History of Translation*, London and New York: Routledge.

Walton, J. Michael (1998) *Setting a Style: the Lumley Iphigeneia*, paper presented at the conference of the International Federation for Theatre Research (IFTR), Canterbury, UK. Unpublished manuscript.

Wolf, Matt (1989) 'Authorised Versions', *The Listener* 122, 23rd November: 36-37.

Zuber-Skerritt, Ortrun (ed.) (1984) *Page to Stage – Theatre as Translation*, Amsterdam: Rodopi.

# A. IDENTIFYING THE TARGET

# 1  Tradaptation
## Cultural Exchange and Black British Theatre

DERRICK CAMERON

*Abstract.* With reference to the practice of integrated casting, the re-
workings of Synge and Chekhov by the Trinidadian playwright Mustapha
Matura and the concept of 'tradaptation' (translation-adaptation) outlined
by Asian theatre director Jatinder Verma, this essay challenges some of the
traditional premises of cultural exchange in Euro-American theatre. The
black and Asian diasporas' re-working and re-imagining of the West, and
their place within it, re-fashions the Euro-American cultures' self-image –
as well as staking a claim to a reversal of that cultural exchange which
insists upon the reification of Western theatre as the pinnacle of theatrical
expression.

'**Tradaptation**' – a contraction of the terms 'translation' and 'adaptation' – was
used by the French Canadian theatre director Robert Lepage to "convey the
sense of annexing old texts to new cultural contexts" (cf. Verma 1996a:201 n1).
In turn, I want to annex the term from Lepage to the contemporary cultural
context of a multiracial and multicultural Britain. In doing so, I want to outline
the complexities of cultural exchange in black British theatre, where 'black British', for the purposes of clarity, refers to the peoples of African or Caribbean
descent. This exchange, as I hope to illustrate, is not simply between a white/
British/European theatre and its 'Others', but also an internal dialogue, debate
and exchange within and between black peoples in Britain and elsewhere.

To start with, however, I want to draw upon the writing of Jatinder Verma,
the Artistic Director of the Asian Tara Arts Theatre Company. I do so partly
because the work of the company illustrates some of the ideas in this essay, but
also because Verma himself has written the outlines of a theoretical and aesthetic rationale behind the company's work, which is useful in relation to black
British theatre (Verma 1996a; 1996b).

Verma himself uses the term **tradaptation** in relation to his productions of
Molière's *Tartuffe* (for the Royal National Theatre), and *Le Bourgeois gentilhomme* (for Tara Arts). Both plays were "[s]et in equivalent periods in India
to when Molière originally wrote the texts", and "provoked a re-perception of
the Molière classic" (Verma 1996a:196). On one level, such productions may
not seem that novel: re-locating or updating plays has been a common practice
in British theatre for decades. But the process of tradaptation (as Verma argues)
goes beyond mining a play for fashionable or 'relevant' parallels or settings, as
in modern-dress Shakespeare. **Tradaptation** here is a wholesale re-working
and re-thinking of the original text, as well as its translation and/or transloca-
tion into a new, non-European, aesthetic context. The response of audience

members and critics has occasionally been mixed, if not hostile: Verma quotes
an anonymous audience member exclaiming, "this is not Molière" in response
to *Le Bourgeois gentilhomme* (Verma 1996b:196). Another example is Irving
Wardle's neo-colonial comment:

> in the case of Jatinder Verma's production of *Troilus and Cressida* I feel an
> attack of blimpish nationalism coming on; damned outsider gatecrashing
> the club, doesn't know the rules... Eventually, if not quite yet, the club will
> have to find room for it. (Quoted by Verma, ibid.:196-197).

Such responses indicate that a British sense of appropriateness or 'authenticity' –
a 'not cricket-ness' so to speak – was being challenged by having a British
company of Asian actors 'tradapt' European playwrights – Molière, Rostand,
Gogol, even the supposedly unassailable Shakespeare – into an Indian aesthetic
and cultural context.

The key issue to note here is that such tradaptations interrupt the assumed
processes of intercultural exchange in Western theatre. Despite Patrice Pavis'
benign definition of interculturalism as "the dialectic of exchange of civilities
between cultures" (Pavis 1992:2), the more common experience has been a form
of cultural expropriation, a "borrowing without acknowledgement" (Verma
1996b:96). Critics such as Rustom Bharucha (Bharucha 1993; 1996) have perceived this as recalling and repeating the economic expropriation under colonial
rule or international capitalism. As Bharucha writes, with reference to Peter
Brook's production of the *Mahabharata*: "It seems to me that apart from questioning cultural appropriations like Brook's production, we also need to address
the larger system of power that makes such appropriations possible in the first
place" (Bharucha 1993:86). In this context, interculturalism seems less like an
exchange than an "appropriation and re-ordering of non-western material within
an orientalist framework of thought and action, which has been specifically de-
signed for the international market" (Ibid.:68). Such a relationship is far better
understood historically through the unequal power relations of postcolonialism
than through an unproblematic notion of reciprocal and mutually beneficial cultural exchange.

What Verma (amongst others) has done is challenge this process by revers-
ing or inverting it: taking the major texts of European drama and re-imagining
them in a European performance context, but with reference to Indian aesthetics, history and culture. This approach, however, is not simply a 'strategy of
reversal', whereby the formerly colonized reclaim the heights of European Literature to prove their equal status to their former rulers, thus apparently 'proving'
European culture's 'universality' even in non-European contexts. Within the
web of postcolonial power relations there is a further complexity due to what
Bharucha refers to as the "politics of location" (Bharucha 1993:240). Yet whereas
Bharucha turned to producing European plays within a "rampantly multicultural"

India (Bharucha 1996:118), the work of Tara Arts is produced in English in an equally multicultural but markedly different Britain. Bharucha eventually chose "to explore an alternative mode of intercultural research conducted in India itself – smaller in scale than the *Mahabharata*, yet more grounded in people's lives" (Bharucha 1993:240), using European texts. One example of his approach is his productions of Kroetz's *Request Concert*, where the play was re-created afresh according to the particular part of India in which the production was being staged, the intention being to convey the distinct sense of each town or city, and the life of a particular woman which was intended to be typical of it (Bharucha 1993: Part II "Transition"). He has referred to the results of such work as "intracultural": "whereby cultures within, between, and across regions can be translated, transported, and exchanged within the larger framework of the nation" (Bharucha 1996:118).

Yet, though the notion of the within/between position of intraculturalism is an invaluable insight, Bharucha's definition of it is restricted in two ways. First, there is a tacit assumption that the 'borders' of cultural exchange are limited by the borders of the nation-state, which is assumed to be a fixed and stable condition. Very few nations, especially emergent ones, can truthfully make such a claim. If Independence defined the modern Indian state, the secession of Pakistan immediately called into question the idea of fixed 'boundaries' of geographical, and therefore of cultural, cohesion. In addition, the claims of those groups who feel that they are, or constitute, a separate nation-state (for example, the Kashmiris), problematizes the issue of who is in- or excluded within the definition of 'nation', let alone who gets to define what the nation actually is. In short, Bharucha's notion of intraculturalism as limited by geographical frontiers is, at best, a constructed notion, in keeping with Benedict Anderson's idea of nation as an "imagined community" (even Bharucha recognizes the problems in a trope such as "we Indians"). At worst, it is only a better-theorized form of nationalism.

Secondly, Bharucha relies on a notion of indigeneity that cannot take account of the history of migration and the existence of Indians as migrants or indigenous citizens living and working in other parts of the world. Where would a writer such as Salman Rushdie, a playwright and novelist such as Hanif Kureishi (*My Beautiful Laundrette*, *The Buddha of Suburbia*), or an actor and writer such as Meera Syal (*Goodness Gracious Me*, *Anita and Me*) fit into Bharucha's definition of the intracultural when they are no longer living, or perhaps were not even born, within the borders of an origin(al) nation-state? Are they simply the inhabitants of 'branch offices' of the culture of the nation-state, or something different? Bharucha seems to imply that all non-indigenous productions tend towards exoticism or cultural tourism because of their lack of 'native soil' or context.

By contrast, the work of Tara Arts is inevitably informed by the "politics of location"; both of the history and culture of the Indian sub-continent and also of its contested status in the multiracial British nation-state in which it is based and

performed. Verma refers to the interrelationship of these two elements by way
of an aesthetic practice he terms ***Binglish***, and a social context he terms *jungli*.
I will deal with each in turn, before linking them to black British theatre.

Verma uses ***Binglish*** to "denote a distinct contemporary theatre practice:
featuring Asian or black casts, produced by independent Asian or black theatre
companies" (Verma 1996b:194). He distinguishes it from the multi-cultural
(which he uses to define the practice of integrated casting) and the cross-
cultural (which he defines as resulting from the differing, non-European,
perspectives of a culturally diverse production team). With *Binglish*, "[t]he attempt is directly to challenge or provoke the dominant conventions of the English
stage" (Ibid.).

Verma bases his idea of *Binglish* on a number of key components. First, the
outsider's perspective. As the term suggests, *Binglish* is "a form of spoken English as much as a *process*: Asian and black life in modern Britain is self-evidently
'not-quite-English'; and, equally, is characterized by a striving to 'be English'"
(Ibid.: original emphasis). As Verma points out, this is an "ambivalent sensibility" which lies at the heart of black and Asian identity in Britain.

Secondly, *Binglish* productions utilize 'other' texts. Verma uses the adjective 'other' to "describe a wide range of texts: existing European texts, adaptations
of such texts, new texts from Asian and black writers, texts from Asia and Africa" (Verma 1996b:195). Thus a sense of 'other-ness' traverses the 'other-ness'
of European drama for blacks and Asians; the unfamiliarity of 'tradapted' European work; the 'other-ness' of work by black and Asian authors from both Britain
and abroad to white British audiences, and so on. All these texts are characterized, Verma suggests, by what he terms "provocation". I do not feel that he
describes a deliberate offensiveness, more that the consequences of migration,
subsequent indigenization, and the economic, political and cultural life of blacks
and Asians in Britain has "provoked" a number of issues around British history,
identity and culture; a form of "colonialism in reverse" (Lewis 1978:304). The
provocation in *Binglish* productions stimulates "other ways of 'seeing'" (Verma
1996b:196) and/or introduces new themes to Britain which may or may not
have resonant parallels in this country.

Thirdly, *Binglish* productions are characterized by a 'flirtation' with the English language. Verma uses the linguistic term ***langue*** to describe "language,
accent, and mode of speech" (Verma 1996b:198). This, in a postcolonial context, is a key issue. The predominance of the 'Queen's English' as the only
correct and acceptable form of *langue*, is challenged by the diversity, richness,
and expressiveness of other forms of English from elsewhere within the
postcolonial world. Former RSC Artistic Director Terry Hands' notoriously dismissive comment that "[t]he iambic pentameter just doesn't sound right with a
strong Asian or Caribbean accent" (Lustig 1989:30) is openly flouted and rejected in the context of *Binglish* productions. As Verma explained in relation to
the cast of *Tartuffe*:

> Some of our actors are mother tongue native English speakers, who do not
> know an Indian language; others bring [their] rhythms of their mother tongue
> to the speaking of English. We have one actor from Bombay, who speaks in
> the kind of idiom Salman [Rushdie] used for *Midnight's Children*. (Koek
> 1990:15)

Lastly, the "forms of presentation" of a *Binglish* production challenge the dominant vocabulary of European staging, especially the conventions of realism and
naturalism. More crucially, they do so from the perspective of an 'insider/out-
sider', someone with both a critical awareness of those same European
conventions, and also of the cultural and artistic heritage of their own past. For
Verma, a theatre treatise such as the 4th century AD *Natya-Shastra* is:

> more detailed, more complex than anything I have ever encountered by
> Stanislavsky or Brecht. It's a most meticulous study, to the extent of defin-
> ing what are the ideal types of spaces for certain types of plays, and what are
> the ideal audiences. (Koek 1990:16)

The result is work which Verma refers to as "negotiating a foreignness" (Verma
1996b:200). He describes how "a modern white audience in Britain experiencing a *Binglish* production could be said to be oscillating continuously between
the sense of the native, the familiar and the foreign" (Ibid.). This could be on an
aesthetic level, in connection with the *mise en scène* of the production, especially when the presentational style eschews naturalism; or it could be on an
auditory level, with familiar, unfamiliar and 'foreign' accents all prevalent in
the same dramatic text. A similar experience of negotiation could be true of an
Asian or black audience, though their sense of each aspect would inevitably be
radically different.

If I now turn to Verma's concept of *jungli*, or jungle, it is perhaps best briefly
described as a metaphorical explanation of the overall social and cultural context in contemporary Britain. It is what makes the existence of *Binglish*
productions both necessary and feasible:

> I want to suggest that the Jungle, or Forest, might be a useful way to charac-
> terize modern Britain. The Forest, where borders are ill-defined, at best;
> where magic and mystery are the *sine qua non*; where, as Shakespeare re-
> minds us all too often, human beings are "translated", blessedly; where,
> above all, unconditional "play" is possible. (Verma 1996a:92)

Verma also writes that "I have in mind that the forest is *both* malevolent and the
abode of self-enlightenment" (Ibid.:98, original emphasis), drawing on both the
Christian and Indian connotations of the forest respectively. In many ways *jungli*
is an urban phenomenon, though it is not limited to this definition alone. Verma
draws on the connotations of *jungli* as a wild place, as well as its more modern
usages, as in Brecht's "Jungle of Cities". The phrase "it's a jungle out there"

from the television police series *Hill Street Blues* has passed into popular usage as a way of describing the randomness, danger and chaos of urban life, as well as having the connotations of Social Darwinist economic competition and survival to which Verma aptly and critically refers (cf. Ibid.:93). By way of a conclusion, he writes that "in the Forest, the sensibility of Binglish offers a means for the construction of rich – inclusive, consensual – pathways out of the forest" (Ibid.); that is, it is an aesthetic capable of exploring and explaining the "jungle" of contemporary British life, and providing a source of entertainment and enlightenment, rather than menace.

Applying the ideas of *jungli* and *Binglish* to black British work, there are a number of key differences, which point to a different sensibility and aesthetic, despite Verma's acknowledgement that some aesthetic elements of *Binglish* are applicable to both. Language is one example. Whilst English – of whatever kind – has to compete with a myriad of other languages in an Indian and African context, in a Caribbean one there is only the variant, or Creole English, that provides the linguistic resource with which to flirt. More important, however, is the fact that there is no formal written tradition of performance aesthetics in African or Caribbean drama which can be referred to, consulted, or used as a model or guide. This is not to say there are no aesthetic principles, but rather that they take a different, orally transmitted form. In addition, the experience of transportation and slavery (a different, more destructive and disruptive reading of 'translation' perhaps) resulted in a deformation, and subsequent reformation, of aesthetics and culture in the Caribbean, which distinguishes it from Africa. In turn, post-war migration distinguishes black Britain from the Caribbean. Despite this situation, there is a strong sense of cultural links and affinities between black peoples across the globe, as exemplified in black music such as jazz or rap.

These differences necessitate a more complex form of intraculturalism than either Verma's idea of *Binglish* or Bharucha's geographically bordered variety. Paul Gilroy's useful term of the "Black Atlantic" is perhaps the neatest way of encapsulating the relationship between geographically-scattered black peoples, who can best be understood as a diaspora (Gilroy 1993a; 1993b; 1994). A black British form of *Binglish* may largely rely on variant or Creole English for its flirtatious *langue*, but it is a *langue* that encompasses the countries of Africa, the islands of the English-speaking Caribbean, the United States and the streets of Britain. This suggests interesting and fruitful possibilities for translation and/or tradaptation work into, for example, West Indian patois, or into what Mark Sebba identifies as "British Creole", an indigenous version of its Jamaican counterpart (Sebba 1996). The Trinidad-born playwright Mustapha Matura has already done this kind of work, 'tradapting' Chekhov into *The Trinidad Sisters*, and Synge into *The Playboy of the West Indies*. As for Verma's "forms of representation", an intracultural black British theatre could utilize the performative rituals and festivals of Africa. There are also the possibilities prompted by the theatrical vocabulary of both the Trinidad and Notting Hill Carnivals, as in, respectively, Felix Cross's musical drama of personal and political independence *Glory!* (Temba Theatre Company, 1990), or Benjamin Zephaniah's dub poetry drama *Streetwise* (Temba Theatre Company, 1990).

This form of intraculturalism thus potentially encompasses the cultural practices of all the regions previously mentioned. It is an intraculturalism that transcends geographical boundaries, yet also recognizes the specificities of the cultures which are bound up within (rather than bound by) the nation-state. This, I feel, explains the diversity of "other texts" within black British theatre. The work of Talawa theatre company, for example, has encompassed C.L.R. James' *The Black Jacobins*, about the Haitian slave rebellion; productions of Shakespeare's *Antony and Cleopatra*, *King Lear*, and *Othello*; Wilde's *The Importance of Being Earnest*; the plays of West Indian writers such as Derek Walcott and Edgar White; and contemporary work from British-based writers such as Biyi Bandele-Thomas and Michael Abbensetts. This form of intraculturalism also explains why this diversity might not always result in successful work. Esiaba Irobi, in his unpublished paper 'Theatre of Elephants: Transculturation in Contemporary British Theatre', describes what he identified as one particular difficulty in Yvonne Brewster's production of Wole Soyinka's *The Road* for Talawa:

> The mask that Brewster used looked synthetic and artificial. But, in the director's understanding, it was more representative of Ogun, the god at the centre of the play, since the mask was covered all over with a shiny metal which looked more like aluminium than iron. A more awesome even if wooden mask with Ogunian configurations, I think, would have brought out the deeper meanings and mystical resonances associated with the god through the medium of the mask. Apart from this oversight which is quite understandable since the director comes from Jamaica where the cultic essence of these artefacts have been lost due to the cruelty of history, the production was powerful. (Irobi 1996:9)

In other words, an assumed homogeneity or axiomatic affinity between differing parts of the black diaspora within the Black Atlantic cannot always be presumed upon.

In conclusion, Verma describes how "[p]ostcolonial Britain, by an ironic act of symmetry, is undergoing the same uncertain groping towards defining itself as are the countries that were once colonized by Britain" (Verma 1996b:196). The legacy of colonial rule leaves its formerly colonized subjects with a far greater familiarity with the assumed, yet ultimately bogus, superiority of English culture than the citizens of the colonial state have with their supposedly 'foreign' Others. Equally, the relationship between black British culture and a wider British culture, which is falsely presumed to be homogeneously white, can be seen as part of a complex negotiation between self and other that is both inter- and intracultural. The process of theatrical tradaptation, founded on the intracultural aesthetics of an Indian or Afro-Caribbean-derived *Binglish*, and emerging from the jungle of cities, offers one way out of that particular forest. As actor Jeffrey Kissoon, one of the cast members of the *Mahabharata*, commented in an interview: "we could go beyond Brook. It's time we explored these things ourselves" (Miller 1991).

## References

Bharucha, Rustom (1993) *Theatre and the World: Performance and the Politics of Culture*, London and New York: Routledge.

------ (1996) 'Under the Sign of the Onion: Intracultural Negotiations in Theatre', *New Theatre Quarterly* XII (46):116-129.

Gilroy, Paul (1993a) *The Black Atlantic: Modernity and Double Consciousness*, London and New York: Verso.

------ (1993b) *Small Acts: Thoughts on the Politics of Black Cultures*, London and New York: Serpent's Tail.

------ (1994) 'Diaspora', *Paragraph* 17 (3):207-212.

Irobi, Esiaba (1996) 'Theatre of Elephants: Transculturation in Contemporary British Theatre', unpublished paper.

Koek, Ariane (1990) 'Hope and Glory', *Plays and Players* (March):11-13.

Lustig, Vera (1989) 'Learning to Forget a Face', *The Listener* (13 July):29-30.

Miller, Kate (1991) 'No Colours Barred', *The Stage and Television Today* (9 May):12.

Pavis, Patrice (1992) trans. Loren Kruger, *Theatre at the Crossroads of Culture*, London: Routledge.

Sebba, Mark (1996) 'How do you spell Patwa?', *Critical Quarterly* 38 (4):50-63.

Verma, Jatinder (1996a) 'Binglish: a *jungli* approach to multi-cultural theatre', *Studies in Theatre Production* 13:92-98.

------ (1996b) 'The Challenge of Binglish: Analysing Multi-Cultural Performance', in Patrick Campbell (ed.) *Analysing Performance: A Critical Reader*, Manchester: Manchester University Press:193-202.

# 2 Scottish Horses and Montreal Trains
## The Translation of Vernacular to Vernacular

MARTIN BOWMAN

*Abstract.* The subject is the translation of plays from one vernacular language to another. To what extent does the power of a vernacular language to suggest a specific culture inevitably situate the play in the milieu of the translation rather than in that of the original? What are the strategies that translators can use to ensure that their version avoids adaptation and remains firmly embedded in the original setting and culture? Is there inevitably a loss of original colour in the translated work? Other topics addressed include the translation of idiomatic expressions, the use of local details, and the question of cultural differences. The author draws upon his experiences as co-translator with Bill Findlay of Quebec plays into Scots and recent co-translation with Wajdi Mouawad of the dramatization of Irvine Welsh's *Trainspotting* for production in Montreal.

Bill Findlay and I have translated into Scots ten plays written in French by Quebec playwrights.[1] Seven of these plays have been the work of Montreal dramatist Michel Tremblay. Six of these Tremblay translations have received professional productions in Scotland, – the seventh is scheduled for 2000 – and three of these productions have been performed in North America, one in Toronto, one in New York State, and one in Tremblay's native city of Montreal (which is my home town, too). In addition, during the summer of 1997, in a long hoped-for reversal of direction, I collaborated with Montreal playwright Wajdi Mouawad on a translation into French of Harry Gibson's dramatic adaptation of Irvine Welsh's novel *Trainspotting*. This version in Montreal vernacular was produced at the Théâtre de Quat'Sous in Montreal during the winter of 1998. Wajdi and I have since translated Irish writer Enda Walsh's *Disco Pigs* for the Théâtre de Poche in Brussels where it was produced during the 1998-99 season. All of the

---

[1] The Scots Tremblay translations produced professionally are as follows: *The Guid Sisters* [*Les Belles-Sœurs*], Tron Theatre, Glasgow, 1989, 1990, 1992; *The Real Wurld?* [*Le Vrai Monde?*], Tron Theatre, Glasgow, 1991; *Hosanna*, Tron Theatre, Glasgow, 1991; *The House among the Stars* [*La Maison suspendue*], Traverse Theatre, Edinburgh, 1992; Perth Theatre, Perth, 1993; *Forever Yours, Marie-Lou* [*À toi, pour toujours, ta Marie-Lou*], LadderMan Productions, Glasgow, 1994; *Albertine, in Five Times* [*Albertine, en cinq temps*], Clyde Unity, Glasgow, 1998. In addition, the Traverse Theatre has commissioned a Scots translation of *Messe solennelle pour une pleine lune d'été*. The other plays translated into Scots by Bowman and Findlay are *The Rehearsal* [*La Répétition*] by Dominic Champagne, *The Skelfs* [*Les feluettes*] by Michel-Marc Bouchard, and *Un 'Reel' ben beau, ben triste* by Jeanne-Mance Delisle. The Delisle play was produced by Stellar Quines in Scotland during the 1999-2000 season. Neither *The Skelfs* nor *The Rehearsal* has yet been produced.

plays that I have co-translated are works written at least in part in a vernacular language and all of the translations have been into a vernacular language.

First, let me describe briefly the languages in question. Michel Tremblay's plays for the most part reflect the experience of his parents' generation. These people were working-class Quebecers, many of whom were first-generation Montrealers. Their parents had moved into the metropolis from the surrounding countryside as Montreal's industrialization developed after World War I. Tremblay himself was born in 1942 and grew up in the Plateau Mont-Royal district of east-end Montreal, a 'quartier' that was then as it is today almost entirely French-speaking. The vernacular speech of these people, heavily influenced by regional dialects and encroached upon by English, is usually characterized by the word *joual*, their way of pronouncing the word *cheval*, the French word for horse. Political correctness of recent years has called into question the appropriateness of using such a stigmatized word to identify a language. The word, however, has a vigour of its own and continues in use despite the fact that some commentators prefer a more neutral identification of this particular vernacular of Quebec French: something like Montreal vernacular French, for example.

Bill Findlay and I have brought this very particular horse into Scotland by translating Tremblay into Scots, the vernacular language of Lowland Scotland. The words used to identify these languages, or dialects, or vernaculars, disclose certain underlying assumptions about them and reveal a politico-linguistic hierarchy that posits the standard language as qualitatively 'better' than the demotic languages. In fact, the general prejudice seems to be that vernacular language is in some way disqualified from being considered a real or true or complete language. Scots, for example, is usually seen as a collection of dialects, its linguistic reputation tarnished by the absence of a standard.

Both the Scots of Irvine Welsh's characters and the French of Tremblay's represent supposedly impoverished linguistic resources. *Joual* is seen as a language of the underclass, degraded and polluted in various ways, in particular by anglicisms, mostly literal translations of English structures and the frequent intrusion of English words. Scots, although historically it has the claim to be a sister language of English, seems now very much to many people to exist in relation to standard English (since standard Scots does not exist) in much the way *joual* does to French. The original name of Scots was Inglis, or English, and Francis Begbie, the profane hard man in Welsh's *Trainspotting* would identify his language not as Scots but as English. In one scene, Begbie and his friend Mark chat up two young Canadian women on a train. When the Canadians cannot understand his question: "Whair's it yis come fae then?", he observes: "these foreign cunts've goat trouble wi the Queen's fuckin English, ken. Ye huv tae speak louder, slower, n mair posh likes. 'WHERE . . . DAE . . .YEZ . . .COME . . . FAE?'" (Welsh 1996:52).[2] Scots, in fact, would be a better name for Scots

---

[2] The version of *Trainspotting* used for the translation into Montreal French was the

Gaelic than it is for Scots Inglis. My point here is not to sort out this labyrinth of nomenclature but to suggest that even the naming of a vernacular language represents a political act. And, of course, so does translation into such a language.

Jean Fouchereaux, in an article on the translations of Michel Tremblay's *Le Vrai Monde?* in the American journal *Québec Studies*, has claimed that the act of translation reflects ideological demands that incorporate literature into politics, that the act of translation is necessarily a political act (1995:93).[3] And when Bill Findlay and I had the idea in 1978 of translating Tremblay's *Les Belles-Sœurs* into Scots, we were already aware of the political nature of our undertaking. We were looking for a Quebec text that might work in a Scots translation. From the outset, we were not interested in adapting a play into a Scots situation but of taking a play richly rooted in its world through the use of vernacular language and finding its Scots voice. We were both rank amateurs and certainly I for one had no idea of the complexities of the project. Familiar with Quebec theatre, I had the pleasure of suggesting the play we should try. There was no doubt in my mind that *Les Belles-Sœurs*, Tremblay's first successful play, would provide us with the vehicle for what we were trying to do.

Although there had been some other successful Quebec playwrights before Tremblay, no one before him had put the language of Montreal workers so vigorously and so completely on stage. The first professional production of the play, at Montreal's Théâtre du Rideau Vert, caused a furore in Montreal artistic circles, for it had dared to make art out of this stigmatized horse-language. Tremblay was later to say that he had packed into the play virtually every expression he had ever heard his mother say. So the play became a kind of monument to the language of the people who he has said would have been invisible (and inaudible) had he remained silent or written plays in a language other than his own. It seems such a startlingly simple idea now, to present people in their own language, but in 1968 *Les Belles-Sœurs* was the linguistic equivalent of hanging out dirty laundry. This was a world that should be hidden away.

Over the last thirty years, the issue has largely faded, and it is now not only accepted but also required that characters in a Quebec play speak Quebec French, which it must be pointed out is a richly varied linguistic landscape. Not that all the shame has been wrung out of this laundry by any means in terms of people's attitude to a vernacular such as *joual*, but in artistic terms at least the language has found a certain integrity. Tremblay himself no longer feels required in his texts to spell out the language of his characters as phonetically as he once did (indicating, for example, the characteristic diphthongs and elisions of Montreal

---

unpublished version of Harry Gibson's adaptation (Glasgow: Citizens' Theatre, 1995). This version differs considerably from the published version to which the references are made.

[3] Fouchereaux writes: "Traduire ici n'est pas neutre, ne doit pas être considéré comme un acte purement anodin mais plutôt comme l'expression d'une revendication, reflet d'une idéologie, le littéraire faisant corps avec le politique."

French). In rehearsal now, it goes without saying that a text set in Quebec will be performed in Quebec accents and rhythms. In fact, in recent years *joual* itself has become a language of translation.

It seems to be widely assumed that an audience must willingly suspend its disbelief to understand that a Quebec play in Scots is a Quebec play or, in the case of *Trainspotting*, that a Scots play in Quebec French remains a Scottish play. There are, for many people in the audience, prejudices to overcome before this can happen. And yet such a suspension does not seem to be required of audiences of a play translated into standard language. Audiences in English-speaking countries have no such difficulty when, to take the usual example, the characters in a Chekhov play deliver their lines in middle- or upper-class British English, or, to be more exact, in a non-regional English English of the 'better' classes. Generally speaking, audiences in English-speaking countries readily accept the 'Russianness' of Chekhov's characters. The fact that this standard register is not even the language of all of Chekhov's characters poses no problem of believability for most audiences. Somehow this is how Russians would sound if they spoke English. It is the very rootlessness of the target language, the fact that it is not connected with a particular region despite the fact that it is very much the language of a particular class, that seems to allow audiences to make this leap of their imagination.

A vernacular language is by definition specifically identified with one place. Inevitably, as a medium of translation, it seems that the culture of this language and its folk will intrude into the equally particular world of the original play despite the fact that the language is able to carry material which is not culturally rooted in its own milieu. Some kind of disjunction seems to be unavoidable between the recipient language, which declares to everyone a particular place and often a particular period, and the original text which may be threatened with the loss of its own particular identity, swamped as it were by the particularity of its new voice. If such translations cannot be effected, the question is raised as to what degree a vernacular language can be considered a language in its own right. If it cannot express a world beyond its own borders, then it must be disqualified from the world of languages. It can only be a vehicle for adaptation rather than translation. It would be impossible to translate into a vernacular language because such a language inevitably undermines the notion of translation, requiring adaptation to eliminate material that simply cannot fit into the context of the recipient language.

Of course, the practice of theatre finally rules and such theories can be discounted on the stage. There does not seem to me to be any absolute distinction that can be made between translation and adaptation. As far as my co-translators and I are concerned, however, what we have created in our work is translation rather than adaptation. The only true test of this can be found in the target audience, of course. Just as Francis Begbie does not even realize he is speaking Scots, the audience for one of our translations in Scotland should hardly notice that the language of the play is Scots. The world of the play will be so obviously different to them that they, of course, will not in any way have to be told this is not Scotland but some other place. The names of the characters, the situations, specific references to places, shops, magazines, and so on will announce themselves as other. Similarly, the French-speaking audience for *Trainspotting* should find the language to be transparent, not *joual*, certainly not Scots in *joual*, but just language. An audience, of course, is not a homogeneous entity, and places like Scotland and Quebec are hotbeds of linguistic controversy. There will be language snobs, for example, who will simply be incapable of perceiving the play translated into the vernacular as anything other than regrettable, an attempt to validate that which should be scorned. Some members of a middle-class audience in Scotland will inevitably experience a Tremblay translation into Scots as a Scottish play not because of the work itself but because of the attitudes they hold towards the language of translation. Scots-speaking members of the audience, such as my Angus cousins, however, have no such difficulty in experiencing the play as authentically of Quebec.

To whatever degree a member of the audience may characterize these translations as adaptations, clearly in the minds of my co-translators and myself, we work consistently to avoid adaptation and try to solve the many problems which arise without resorting to adaptation. We are, however, trying to use the target language fully, without reining in its resources because of fear of intruding into the original world of the play. Of course, there is a freedom that must be taken, but it is a freedom that is always calculated not to distort the original work but to find a translated equivalent. Literary style is not the issue here. Bill Findlay and I are fully confident that we have approximated Tremblay's style, for example, his use of musical elements, repetition, and choral effects.

Certain obvious features of the original work are retained although even here adjustment may be required. The setting of the play is clearly indicated in almost all the plays we have translated, and these place names are not altered even though the target audience may be unfamiliar with some of the more obscure references. Jean Fouchereaux has some difficulty with this, questioning the effect of retaining the names of towns – such as Trois-Rivières and Drummondville in *The Real Wurld?* – not familiar to Scottish audiences, but it seems to me that the retention of such names has exactly the desired effect of situating the play in its foreign location (Ibid.:88). Similarly, it is unlikely that the francophone audience in Montreal will know of Berwick and Darlington, but it will surely be obvious that these are British cities, thus reaffirming the setting of the play as beyond Quebec. With more specific cultural references, certain problems arise. Some of these references can be explained, by adding such words as 'that women's magazine' to *Chatelaine* or 'that shop' to *Kresge's*.[4] The political

---

[4] The quotations from *The Guid Sisters* are taken from our as yet unpublished revised version of the translation. *The Guid Sisters* has been published twice: *The Guid Sisters*, Toronto: Exile Editions, 1988 (released in the United Kingdom as Glasgow: Tron Theatre, 1989) and *The Guid Sisters and Other Plays*, London: Nick Hern Books, 1991.

subtext in *Trainspotting* that mentions stealing from *British Home Stores*, however, had to be sacrificed. (The anti-British material is in any case evident in Mark's monologue about his brother Billy, killed as a soldier in Northern Ireland.) On the other hand, references to *Lucozade* and *Scottish Football Today* sit comfortably in the French text and function exactly as the place names do, emphasizing the otherness of the play's world.

The names of characters have the same effect, and happily a coincidence of Quebec French and Scots pronunciation allows for virtually no adaptation. The tongue-tip trill – the rolled 'r' of the so-called Scottish burr! – of both languages allows for complete transparency. For example, Robert, an offstage character in *Les Belles-Sœurs*, has the same Québécois pronunciation in *The Guid Sisters*, the Scots version of the play. Scots performers have no difficulty in saying *Robire* and the name is obviously not that of a Scot, as translating the name as *Robert*, or *Roabert*, or *Rab* would indicate. Only rarely have we found it necessary to alter a name as in the case of the dead baby girl in *Trainspotting*. The name *Dawn* had to be sacrificed in the French version because the francophone audience would be confused by the name. My co-translator was tempted to translate the name, saying that the name *Aube* was very beautiful. However, since wee girls named Aube are thin on the ground in Edinburgh, we had to resist that temptation, settling finally on an adjustment to the name. The baby was called *Dawna* in Montreal.

Similarly, the translation of culturally specific items also affirms the world of the original play in the translated version. Radio broadcast of the rosary, for example, a daily feature of life in Montreal in the sixties, and references to mosquitoes and peanut butter, absurd in the equivalent Scottish time and place, do not disrupt the Scots fabric of a translation. Such references may be absurd in the Scottish context, but they are not problematic in the Scots language of the text. Bill and I have come over the years to realize that Scots has no trouble with these aspects of the original. Originally, we decided to translate a reference to *Coca-Cola* in *The Guid Sisters* as *orange juice*, but subsequently in rehearsal we retained the word *Coke* even though the Scots equivalent of the Montreal nonagenarian who speaks the line would never have drunk Coke in Glasgow in the 1960's. These cultural references surely also point to the impossibility of the adaptation of a vernacular world as specific as Tremblay's into Scots without losing the original work irretrievably. Such a writer might just as well write his or her own play. This does not mean, however, that all culturally specific items can be translated. For example, in *The Guid Sisters* Bill and I felt that *baloney* had to be explained as *luncheon meat*, and Wajdi and I had to drop the notion of *draftpaks* altogether, Welsh's double meaning of the term being impossible to render in a Quebec situation where the audience will have no conception of the off- licence purchase of alcohol in a pub.

---

It should be noted that the London edition underwent some editing before publication in order to make the text more readable to the English reader.

Idiomatic expressions pose another question, which I think opens up a larger issue of translatability. Not only can idiomatic expressions not be translated literally, but also they cannot always be replaced by an idiomatic expression at precisely the same moment in the text. Translators must take the measure of a writer's use of idiomatic and figurative language and try to duplicate it in their translations, but working too rigorously towards this kind of faithfulness can create its own distortions. The particular method of my collaborations with Bill and Wajdi affects the way we approach this aspect of translation. For both Bill and Wajdi, I begin by producing a literal translation, into English for Bill, into French for Wajdi. What I produce would often be incomprehensible were it not for the copious commentary that I offer alongside this word-for-word rendering of the original. What I deliberately avoid is any kind of literary interference that would get in the way of the writer responsible for making the play script itself. Once a draft is produced, there is a process of discussions, full of queries that require further explication of the language of the original. Although I could never presume to translate into Scots or *joual* myself, my familiarity with the two languages is such that I am in a position to judge, criticize, and affirm as well as to suggest alternative readings. I get to work as a sort of literary police as well, when I feel that the translation may be straying too far. However cumbersome this way of working, I know that this collaborative method has some advantages and has shed some light for us on the whole business of what translation is. For example, Bill and I have observed that in our translations of Tremblay we tend to depend more heavily than Tremblay himself on the use of idiomatic expressions. This suggests to me that a language has its own emotional laws that cannot be transgressed in the act of translation.

Although Wajdi is an established playwright and director, *Trainspotting* was his first translation. When we sat down to work together after I had produced a literal draft, the first question he asked me – and it was a brilliant one, I think – was, "What is the most powerful taboo in Scottish life?" I should explain that, despite my accent, my own upbringing in the Montreal suburb of Verdun was entirely Scots, my parents having emigrated from rural Angus when they were in their twenties. I surprised myself when I found myself replying, "The expression of emotion." It seems that the emotional landscapes of Quebec and Scotland differ considerably, particularly in the expression of love and other positive emotions. Thus Bill and I find it impossible to have a Scots-speaking character say in what would be a literal translation, "I admire you, Thérèse", and have to adopt an expression such as "Yur an angel" as an equivalent. Over and over this kind of introduction of figurative language transfigures, as it were, the original text because of demands made by the culture of the target language, which may accommodate references to mosquitoes and Coca-Cola but not simple expressions of respect and affection. The same is not true, interestingly enough, of the translation of negative and violent feelings; uncompromising bleakness seems to ring as true in urban Scots as in its Quebec equivalent. However, this kind of limitation in a language, I would suggest, is not particular to vernacular languages, but is a problem that all translators in some way surely have to confront. Jean Fouchereaux has noted the preference in French for using feminine nouns and adjectives for the expression of derision (1995:91). Such a feature surely must be untranslatable into any language that, like Scots or English, lacks gender. The presence of gender creates problems in translation into French as well. In *Trainspotting*, for example, Mark Renton refers to his veins as "Ma boys" (Welsh 1996:26). In French, however, the word for *vein* is feminine and therefore a literal translation of *boys* as *garçons* is impossible. Despite the fact that such a term is not used in *joual*, we opted for *filles*, i.e. *girls*, playing on the fact that the French words for the drug *heroin* and *heroine*, the feminine form of *hero*, are the same.[5]

There is, finally, an essential difference between French and Scots (and English, of course) that a translator in these languages must take into account. I am referring to what I would call the doubleness of these Anglian languages, the fact that their vocabulary results from two great invasions of Great Britain, creating a double lexicon of Germanic and Romance vocabulary. That English and Scots speakers prefer Anglo-Saxon vocabulary for everyday expression and resort to Latinate vocabulary for more serious discourse has been long observed. When we go from French to Scots, the translator of vernacular French must question the use of Latinate cognates that belong to a standard rather than a vernacular register. Bill and I have wrestled with this question in our translation of Tremblay's *Messe solennelle pour une pleine lune d'été*. This play is written as a secular vernacular mass and is full of words that have cognates in Scots and English, words like *apathie*, *violence*, *insensibilité*, and *dédain*. The trouble is that these words sit comfortably in a French vernacular text but jar the register out of the vernacular into standard in Scots. Yet to coin a Scots word or retrieve one from the rich linguistic heritage of Scots also disrupts the vernacular surface of the play. In this case, the original version of the play seems to require the translator to integrate into the text vocabulary that does not seem to sit comfortably with the vernacular idiom of the target language. Such problems are best solved in the rehearsal period, and so we do not yet know exactly what the resolution will be in the case of this play, which is scheduled for production at the Traverse Theatre in Edinburgh in 2000.

Inevitably, it seems that certain aspects of these vernacular plays simply cannot be translated and have to be either approximated (as in the case of anglicisms and expletive language) or abandoned (as in the case of rhyming slang in Welsh's Edinburgh Scots). Above all, since this is theatre, it is the language of the translation that must live fully in itself. Finally it is true that in such translations of vernacular into vernacular, there are two plays happening at once: a Scots play and a Quebec one. This necessary co-existence of course affirms the universal-

---

[5] The Montreal version of the dramatic adaptation of *Trainspotting* has not been published.

ity of these great vernacular writers. It has been claimed that translation implies transformation, loss, and impoverishment. From my experience, I would claim the opposite is true. Fouchereaux (1995:93) writes of the acceptance of the differences between languages and cultures. He implies that we should endeavour to perceive these differences as complements of one another, and above all as a source of enrichment.[6] My collaborations with Bill Findlay and Wajdi Mouawad certainly convince me that dramatic translation is as much an act of creativity as it is of homage. It must be so if the play is to live on the stage in its own right.

## References

Fouchereaux, Jean (1995) 'Traduire/Trahir *Le vrai monde?* de Michel Tremblay: *The Real World?/The Real Wurld?*', Québec Studies 20 (Spring/Summer): 86-96.
Welsh, Irvine, adaptation by Harry Gibson (1996) *Trainspotting. Trainspotting & Headstate*, London: Minerva.

---

[6] Fouchereaux writes:

> Il est intéressant de constater que l'intérêt et l'engouement actuels pour la traduction au Québec sont révélateurs de cette conscience aiguë de la présence de l'Autre, garant de l'acceptation de sa différence, perçue non pas comme une menace mais comme complémentarité, comme enrichissement.

# 3    Translating Standard into Dialect
## Missing the Target?

BILL FINDLAY

*Abstract.* Martin Bowman's Scottish co-translator presents a complementary and controversial essay developing a long-term exploration of dialect
translation, a process about which relatively little has hitherto been written.
This essay offers a range of rare insights into the translator's motivation and
method in rendering a contemporary play in standard French – Raymond
Cousse's *Enfantillages* – into Scots dialect. Such apparently 'asymmetric'
translation raises questions regarding the integrity of both the source and
target text, particularly in relation to dialect and social class, and dialect
and performance.

Translations of classic and contemporary plays into Scots have become a regu-
lar feature of the Scottish theatre scene today. Just as the Scottish dramatist
may choose to write in English or Scots, or in a contrasting combination of the
two, the Scottish translator can do likewise (Findlay 1996b). Although written
drama in Scots has a lineage dating back to the fifteenth century – including a
sixteenth-century translation of a twelfth-century Latin play, *Pamphilus de Amore*
(See Findlay 1998a:47-50) – the translation of drama into Scots is essentially a
twentieth-century, post-war development. The period since 1945 has seen translations of work from the historic repertoire by authors such as Molière, Goldoni,
von Kleist, Ibsen, Beaumarchais, Aeschylus, Gorki, Rostand, Gogol, and Brecht.
The translation of contemporary plays into Scots has been an even later development, only commencing about 1980, but there has since been a steady stream
of work, with translations of plays by writers such as Dario Fo, Michel Tremblay,
Enzo Cormann, Michel Vinaver, Ludmilla Petrushevskaya, and Daniel Danis
(Findlay 1996a:186-197).

The consequence of translators harnessing Scots for classic and modern work
is that modern Scottish translations for the stage are marked by diversity of
medium. In addition to Standard English and 'Scottish Standard English' (dis-
tinguished by Scotticisms in grammar, lexis, and idioms), one finds Scots
employed in a variety of forms that can be categorised as urban and rural, regional and 'standardized', historic and contemporary, literary and experimental,
colloquial and stylised. As appropriate, a translator may use any of these singly,
counterpoint varieties of English and Scots, or devise a hybrid Scots-English
instrument. Importantly, Scottish theatre audiences have come to accept as natural
the presentation of foreign plays in this range of translation media.

Since dialect translations are a relative rarity in English-language theatre
beyond Scotland, little has been written about the process of translating drama
into dialect. This essay therefore offers, from the perspective of a translator

within a theatre culture hospitable to dialect-medium writing, some insights into the dialect translator's motivation and method in, in this case, translating a source text in standard language into a non-standard medium.

Some translators are motivated in using Scots by a kind of cultural nationalism: they want to contribute, variously, to keeping the language alive, to continuation of a literary tradition in Scots, and/or to advancement of a distinctive Scottish drama. Some wish to test and stretch the creative potentialities of Scots through translation in order to demonstrate its continuing potency. Some wish to add to the still-building repertoire of Scots translations, particularly since to do so is also to add to the stock of native drama (given that translations also fulfil a role of adding to a target culture's store of dramatic texts). Other translators may not be influenced by such – small 'p' – political considerations: they may simply wish to exploit the creative flexibility afforded by a Scots-and-English resource, feeling that for certain work, Scots, or Scots and English in combination or contrast, are more effective than Standard English in rendering the letter and/or spirit of a source work.

Where all of these possible 'background' motivations share common ground is in confrontation with the source play itself, for then the decision to use Scots is narrowed to two determining factors, irrespective of the translator's more general motivations. The first such factor is linguistic equivalence; that is, just as a standard source language invites translation into a standard target one, a non-standard source one invites translation into a non-standard target one. The elevated classic German of Schiller, for example, invites translation into Standard English, whereas the Silesian dialect of Gerhart Hauptmann's *The Weavers* invites translation into Scots dialect (Findlay 1998b; MacDonald 1998). On occasion, an additional factor influencing such a linguistically determined choice is the sociolinguistic dimension to the relationship between standard and non-standard language; that is, the source language, in being either standard or non-standard, may contain within it an important signifier of social class. This, for instance, coupled with the linguistic equivalence between the east-end Montreal dialect of Québécois and an urban Scots dialect, informed the decision by Martin Bowman and me to translate Michel Tremblay's plays into Scots (Bowman and Findlay 1994:61-81; Fouchereaux 1995:86-96 compares the Scots and English translations).

The second determining factor is not concerned with linguistic equivalence thus defined, but with what can be loosely described as 'the nature of the play'. For example, in translating the standard French of Molière's *Tartuffe* into what she described as a "theatrical Scots", Liz Lochhead felt that she could better communicate the play's "sensual earthiness" and the classical but black nature of the comedy (Lochhead 1985: introduction). In such cases, the translator is choosing to draw on the distinctive qualities and creative resources of Scots for reasons bound up with the texture and spirit of a play rather than linguistic equivalency. To those who might object that there is something wrong-headed about this approach to translation, I would point out that it has become commonplace for classic and contemporary plays written originally in dialect, or in a non-standard vernacular, to be translated into a standard English, so the same latitude should be extended to those who are merely applying the same approach in reverse. I have side-stepped here the debatable issue of whether a 'literary Scots' of the kind that has been characteristic of translations of classic plays can be seen as a 'standard' medium in contrast with the varieties of demotic Scots dialect characteristically used in translations of contemporary work.

My decision to translate into dialect a contemporary play written in standard French, Raymond Cousse's *Enfantillages*[1] – *Bairns' Bothers* is the translated title – was shaped by the second category of determining factors. Before I embarked on my translation I had read and seen performed an accomplished English translation by Brian Singleton (1989), titled *These Childish Things*. Notwithstanding the proven effectiveness of that translation, I felt that a Scots translation would have its own validity for a Scottish audience: dialect would lend a texture to the play that was different from that in the English translation, placing the action in a more locally-rooted geographic, social, and linguistic context. At the level of 'background' motivation, I was attracted to the play through a general interest in identifying contemporary work capable of translation into dialect as a means of extending the repertoire of Scots play translations and of testing and stretching the creative resources of Scots.

More specifically, there were textual – and related extra-textual – reasons that I felt justified rendering *Enfantillages* into dialect. The play is set in a country village in the 1950s, and it takes the form of a monodrama with one actor playing a young boy whose background I read as working-class. Moreover, Cousse's monodramas, which he performed himself, have a strong autobiographical element, as evident in *Enfantillages*. Cousse spent his formative childhood years, from 1945 to 1959, in a country village and in a working-class home, where his father was a railwayman and his mother a farmhand (Preface to Cousse 1984:7). These autobiographical facts confirmed my sense of the play having a texture at the non-linguistic level reflecting the country location, period, and social class. A contributory factor here was my very personal response to the play as a world I intimately recognized, notwithstanding inevitable differences in cultural specifics. As someone who grew up in a working-class family and community in a country village in Fife in the 1950s, I felt a personal identity with the play's period and milieu such that, from a translation point of view, I initially 'heard' it in the Scots dialect of my own formative years. This instinctive response on first reading the play resolved into a deliberate choice once I had established the further parallels between Cousse's upbringing and my own, and once I had considered textual and extra-textual factors more fully.

The play's milieu dictated that I use a country-inflected Scots rather than an urban-coloured one. Whilst I did not seek to match Cousse's standard source

---

[1] The play had its first performance at Le Lucernaire-Forum, Festival d'Avignon, on 15 July 1984 and was published in that year.

language with a standard target one, I had nevertheless to respect the need to find equivalency in meaning, even if I had at the same time to make choices consistent with my chosen dialect usage which might have an associative effect beyond what was happening in the French. A simple example of this is my translation of *casquettes noires* (sometimes abbreviated in the play to *les casquettes*), which translates into English as *black caps* (as in Brian Singleton's translation). The reference is to headgear worn by undertakers, for which the equivalent in Scots is *lum-hats* (i.e. black hats shaped like chimneys). Because Scots and English are cognates, I could have opted for the more neutral *black hats*, but I chose to use *lum-hats* because it has greater dialectal authenticity, it has an appropriate period feel to it (its use is less current today than in the 1950s), and it conveys more tellingly the sinister visual impression that the sight of the undertakers and their hats had on the boy.

A more extended illustration of the inevitable tension between literal meaning and associative effect can be seen in the opening speech of Scene 2. I give the French first, followed by the English and Scots translations:

> Essayons j'essayais comme j'avais vu dans la cour
> du boucher les vaches les bœufs les moutons allongés
> dans la cour du boucher même les petits veaux
> (Cousse 1984:10)

> Let's try I was trying like I'd seen in the butcher's
> yard the cows the cattle the sheep stretched out in
> the butcher's yard even the little calves
> (trans. Singleton 1989:69)

> Try 'ae ah wis tryin like ah'd saw in the butcher's
> yaird the coos the stirks the sheeps lyin in the
> butcher's yaird the wee calfies even

Since, as I have said, English and Scots are cognate tongues, inevitably there is an overlap between the English and Scots translations, but where they differ does not represent in the Scots a mistranslation of the French in terms of literal meaning. *Stirks*, for example, is as direct an equivalent of *les bœufs* as standard English *cattle*; indeed, it is more so because the dictionary definition of *les bœufs* when used in the butchery trade – the context in the play – is *bullocks* or *steers*, which is the meaning of *stirks*. Standard English *cattle* does not carry this same precision, but the translator doubtless made an informed choice in using the word, with its more generalized meaning, because there might be a credibility problem in having a young boy use such exact, adult words as *bullocks* and *steers*. *Stirks* does not carry that difficulty in Scots.

However, if we look at *les petits veaux*, which in English is *the little calves* and in Scots *the wee calfies*, we find that the English is closer to the French in that it does not use a diminutive form as found in the Scots, *calfies*. On the face of it, that diminutive is redundant because of the qualifying adjective *wee*. However, the combination of the two is consistent with Scots usage; and an added consideration in opting for it was that diminutives are commonly used by children in Scots – and the speaker in the play is, of course, a boy. There was therefore a gain of sorts so far as 'texturing' the play was concerned; but, on the other hand, the Scots intensifies the pathos. In such situations there is not a loss of equivalence in terms of meaning but the dialect option can again sometimes have a level of effect beyond meaning alone.

In addition to respecting meaning in the source text so far as was consistent with dialect usage, I attempted to replicate Cousse's distinctive style and what he describes in the play's opening stage direction as "the musical unity of the text". Aside from specific language choices, Cousse conveys the 'voice' of a young boy by giving him staccato and elliptical speech. Cousse dispenses with punctuation – which omission in itself perhaps has something childlike about it – and on first reading the text one is immediately aware of the need to puzzle out a rhythm in order to establish meaning; that is, the rhythm replaces punctuation as a means of establishing sense. And that rhythm, one soon finds, is of a kind characteristically associated with children's speech, where sentences are short and often disjointed, and the delivery has a naïve earnestness and urgency, no matter the swing in emotional mood. This can be seen in this short excerpt from Scene 2 (I give the French first, then the Scots):

> Un bon coup de feu et boum les vaches les bœufs les
> moutons tout qui dégringole par terre les quatre fers
> en l'air même les petits veaux j'étais tout triste alors
> et je me disais

> *Un temps. Hésitant.*

> Je me disais je me disais qu'est-ce que je me disais
> tiens je ne sais même plus ce que je me disais ni si
> je me disais je suis triste mais j'étais triste quand
> même et je me disais

> *Se reprend, revient en avant-scène. Se rapprochant de la caisse.*

> J'étais triste et Marcel était triste aussi avec Marcel
> on était triste tous les deux mais on se battait quand
> même dans la rue pour grimper sur la brique pour voir
> dans la cour pour savoir comment ça finirait dans la
> cour  (Cousse 1984:10)

> Wan deadeye shoat and bang the coos the stirks the
> sheeps fell ower feet in the air the wee calfies even
> ah wis sair hertbroke at that an ah said tae masel

*A pause. Hesitates.*

Ah said tae masel ah said tae masel whit wis it ah
said tae masel och ah dinnae ken naemair whit wis it
ah said tae masel nor even if ah said tae masel ah'm
hertbroke but ah wis hertbroke even sae and ah said tae
masel

*Pulls himself together and returns downstage. Goes to the box.*

Ah wis hertbroke an Marcel wis hertbroke tae baith
me'n Marcel wis hertbroke even sae we fightit in the
street fur tae staund oan the brick fur tae see intae
the yaird fur tae fund oot hoo hings feenished up in
the yaird

What one also notices about Cousse's language, as reflected in this excerpt, is that he uses a quite restricted vocabulary when the boy is speaking in character, presumably reflecting the boy's stage of linguistic development. I therefore often found that in rendering a particular word or expression I had to rein in my natural tendency to ring the changes with a variety of synonymous idiomatic and figurative phrases – a tendency which Martin Bowman and I in our Scots translations of Québécois plays have found to be more marked in Scots (Bowman and Findlay, 1994). An example is Cousse's repeated use of the verb, *se fâcher*, meaning *to get angry*. (Ironically, because of Scotland's long historic links with France it is the origin of the Scots verb *fash*, meaning *to trouble* or *to annoy*, which I chose not to use because the meaning is not as strong as in the French.) I would naturally have drawn on a variety of alternatives, such as *tae loass the rag/heid, tae flee aff the haunnle, tae gan aff the deep-end, tae blaw up, tae be bleezin/bealin/ragin*, etc. Instead, I used a much narrower and less colourful range of options, which moderately ran against the grain of Scots dialect usage, but not in a manner that would strike an audience as inauthentic.

However, as with any theatre translator, the translator into dialect is not exclusively preoccupied with achieving a wholly colloquial fluency in his/her dialogue. Informed creative choices have to be made within the opportunities provided by one's medium in order to achieve a text which is also dramatically effective – that is, which has certain literary qualities shaped by the translator. An example of what I mean concerns how style-switching between registers is a reality in a Scots-dialect-speaking community, as is communication between dialect and standard speakers; hence, if one is employing a contemporary Scots dialect, then one is likely to incorporate stylistic shifts between dialect and standard, so standard options are not excluded. It would therefore be artificial to ignore these linguistic behaviours in a dialect translation of a work where contexts arise that invite them. This is not to suggest, of course, that the translator be reduced to a transcriber of authentic speech (see above); rather, one can ex-

ploit such language behaviours for creative effects consonant with the spirit of
the play.

In *Enfantillages* the voices of many other characters, both children and adults,
are mediated through the boy. Among these are the boy's pal Marcel, his classmates, his parents, Marcel's sister, Marcel's granny, the butcher and his wife,
the butcher's apprentice, the village policeman and his wife, the owners of the
stuck-together dogs, the vet, the teacher, the priest, and others. As the number
of characters shows, there is a good degree of scope for incorporating contrasting speech varieties. An obvious contrast – which was true in a Scots-speaking
village of the 1950s – is between the Scots speech of the ordinary local folk and
the English spoken by the few 'professionals' in the community: the teacher, the
priest, and the vet. I have all of these professionals speaking Standard English,
but on occasion the teacher uses items or forms – *dearie me, the belt, know full
well, stirks* – which hint that he probably more naturally speaks 'Scottish Standard English' when outwith[2] the classroom. The vet's role did not allow much
scope for 'colouring' his speech in this way; and the priest is an unsympathetic
character who is unable or unwilling to be other than 'priestly' when communicating with others, including, tellingly, children, so it sat with this 'priestliness'
to have him speak throughout in a formal standard English.

Depending on context, a Scots speaker communicating with one of these professionals may modify their speech. For example, in my translation, in Scene 4,
when Marcel and the boy are caught smoking by a teacher, who says, "Smoking
is forbidden why are you smoking", the response is in Standard English:

> Me'n Marcel said tae him We are smoking because
> the big boys gave us cigarettes to smoke so we are
> smoking them

Here the boys use English (though spoken in a slow, deliberate manner reflecting their lack of natural ease in it) because that is the language of school and
because not to do so would be to risk seeming insubordinate and/or impertinent.
However, in Scene 5, where the class as a whole are winding up the teacher by
acting thick, the boys speak Scots, which betrays their disrespect – and, to the
(now angry) teacher, probably adds to his impression of them as 'ignoramuses':

> *Anger*
>
> And how could we still eat meat ignoramuses if all the
> butchers and all the pork-butchers in the world never
> killed anyone anymore
>
> *Gradually overcoming his fear*

---

[2] *Outwith [outside]* is an example of the kind of Scotticisms, overt and covert, that
distinguish 'Scottish Standard English' (Aitken 1979:104-10).

We could still eat meat 'cause we could go an git it frae aw
the grocers in the warld 'cause ae aw the grocers in the
warld 'at sells meat in tins ye open thum wi tin-openers ma
dad's goat wan ma mither boat it fur his burthday wi a
coarkscrew at the ither end

*Aside*

The teacher's greetin ahint [crying behind] his desk

Of course, because the boy is reporting this exchange between his classmates
and the teacher, it may be that the boys actually responded to the teacher in their
'school English' but that the boy is now emboldened to have them speaking
'insubordinate Scots' because the events are safely in the past. At a more straightforward level, the contrast in registers may simply reflect how the boy recalls
events, with no guile intended. Importantly, consideration of these possible interpretations shapes the language decisions that the translator makes and helps
to justify the use of contrasting registers for dramatic effect.

In the exchanges between the boy and the priest, in Scene 7 and subsequently,
I could validly have had the boy speak Standard English by way of showing
respect to the priest. However, because the priest's condescension towards the
boys as children (e.g. he frequently uses the address *my child*) suggested that
they might feel more relaxed about behaving naturally as children with him than
they would with the teacher, who is a disciplinarian figure in a way that the
priest is not, I opted to have the boy converse with the priest in Scots. Also,
Scots had the value of investing the boy's questions about such matters as paradise and the soul with a poignant yet comic innocence in keeping with his age;
and the language contrast highlighted the boy's simplicity and directness compared with the priest's automatic tendency to obfuscate and mystify. We can see
this in the following excerpt, as well as how having the boy speak Scots allows
him to 'throw' the priest's words back, sometimes within, as it were, invisible
inverted commas because the Standard English stands out from his own dialect
speech:

Everyone has a soul ah wis happy ah said tae masel
everyone has a soul the butcher's guinea-pigs hiv a
soul tae ah really liked the butcher's guinea-pigs when
me'n Marcel went tae clap thum in thur hutch at the
butcher's
Ah ask the priest
Father div the butcher's guinea-pigs hiv a soul
That's sacrilege my child that's got nothing to do
with it
How's that goat nothin adae wi it Father
Because my child the butcher's guinea-pigs self-evidently

don't have a soul
Howcome father the butcher's guinea-pigs self-evidently
don't have a soul
The priest says nothin he his a think he only says because

*Pause. Hardening.*

Because my child if the butcher's guinea-pigs do not have
a soul it is self-evident that the Lord in his infinite
mercy did not think it was necessary to grant them one
Ah didnae ken whit mercy meant ah didnae lit oan
How father did the Lord no think it wis necessary tae grant
them a soul in his mercy
My child if the Lord hadn't thought it necessary to grant a
soul to the guinea-pigs it is self-evident that they did not
merit it
Howfur father did they no merit it
My child I am only a poor pastor I cannot know everything

An exception to the broad distinction between Scots-speaking locals and English-speaking 'professionals' is the boss of the undertakers. Because his occupation requires a kind of formal demeanour when dealing with the family of the bereaved he speaks a rather stiff English in certain contexts where he is performing his occupational role, as in Scene 9, 'The Death of Marcel', where his opening words to the family are:

Good day ladies and gentlemen we apologise for disturbing
you we've come for the box... [*To his men*] Kindly bring
forward the box gentlemen and don't forget your nails
Gaston

In choice of language, this direction to his men knowingly has as its 'audience' both the men *and*, more importantly, the bereaved family, hence its formality. However, when he speaks to his men directly his language is less affected and is the one which is more natural to him (which reveals that he is adopting a role when speaking in English):

That's us Gaston doon a wee bit oan your side
straightforrit at that

Similarly, when Marcel's sister clings on to the coffin, the boss speaks kindly to her thus:

Come on now lass you mustnae get yoursel intae a state
like this you're young you've yir haill life in front
of you

The Scots items fulfil the function of communicating his intended kindness in a fatherly and therefore more informal way. But there's still a degree of restraint here deriving from context, because he is speaking to a member of – and in front of – the bereaved family. This is signalled by his modified Scots, for more naturally he would have said, in a fuller register:

> Come oan noo lass ye mustnae git yirsel aw wrocht up
> lik this yir young ye've yir haill life in front ae ye

A similar style-switching caused by occupational role can be seen in the speech of the village policeman, where the formality of 'police language' is tipped with occasional Scots words. For example, in Scene 6, he addresses the owners of the stuck-together dogs (having copulated, the dogs cannot separate, which is causing public offence):

> Gentlemen for the present that issue is irrelevant
> first off find some way tae separate your dugs the law
> prohibits that on the public highway otherwise I'll book
> yese get going and find a vet

This commingling of 'officialese' and vernacular forms mirrors both a village policeman's ambivalent social class and his potentially uncomfortable predicament where he is both within and outwith the community. Again, in building this into my Scots I am drawing on my observation of real speech as experienced in my formative years but am making creative choices consistent with my wish to convey effectively the *spirit* of the play.

As with associative effects not present in the original, in exploiting register shifts I am adding something not in the source play because of the 'asymmetry' of translating from standard into dialect. However, I do not feel that I am betraying the integrity of that text in any substantive way, for any play translated will by definition experience a degree of acculturation because of the distinctive qualities and demands of one's target medium. In good faith, and with an awareness of the problems flowing from 'asymmetry' – as indicated by the few examples discussed above – I was trying to satisfy as best I could four guiding imperatives, which were: to respect meaning in Cousse's French as far as my chosen medium allowed; to retain something of the 'otherness' of his play by, for example, non-adaptation of personal names and other culture-specific references; to fashion a dialect text which would have the authority of authenticity for its target audience; and to create a script that would prove performable and theatrically effective. As the last imperative suggests, I had to bring a degree of 'artistry' or 'creativity' to the translation in the choices that I made, consistent with the twin demands of dialect usage and conveying the spirit of *Enfantillages*, and harmonizing these inevitably led me to depart sometimes from the strict letter of the source text, as in the use of associative effects and register contrasts.

However, one could respect a source text to the letter and in so doing disfigure the spirit of the play; that is, a purist approach might militate against achieving a theatrically successful target text and one that thereby, notwithstanding a degree of cultural relocation, seeks to honour and convey a playwright's achievements in a specific work. For there are two texts and two integrities involved: the first is self-evident; the second is the target text's 'integrity' from the perspective of its intended audience, with whom the translator is intimately familiar as a product of a shared culture. This second 'integrity' means that, for me, theatre translation, like theatre-making, is inevitably a pragmatic art, irrespective of whether a translation is 'symmetric' or 'asymmetric'; and inevitably, too, that pragmatism entails acceptance of the fact that the translator, linguistically, is in part a cultural relocator – and cannot escape being so if he or she is successfully to import into his or her culture a foreign work, in the spirit of a facilitator rather than a betrayer. Jeremy Sams[3] made a pertinent observation in relation to this when he stated that, in his opinion, it is important for a translator, as a sympathetic facilitator, to have a greater mastery of his target language than of the source language being translated; for, in the final analysis, the stage translator must make choices consistent with the nature of his or her own language and with what is theatrically effective for a target audience.

## References

Aitken, A.J. (1979) 'Scottish Speech: a historical view, with special reference to the Standard English of Scotland', in A.J. Aitken and Tom McArthur (eds.) *Languages of Scotland*, Edinburgh: Chambers:104-10.

Bowman, Martin and Bill Findlay (1994) '*Québécois* into Scots: Translating Michel Tremblay', *Scottish Language* 13:61-81.

Corbett, John (1999) *Written in the Language of the Scottish Nation: A History of Literary Translation into Scots*, Clevedon: Multilingual Matters, Topics in Translation 14.

Cousse, Raymond (1984) *Enfantillages*, prefaced by Christian Le Guillochet 'Raymond Cousse: repères biographiques', Avignon: Festival d'Avignon.

------ *Enfantillages* trans. Brian Singleton (1989) as *These Childish Things*, in David Bradby and Claude Schumacher (eds.) *New French Plays*, London: Methuen:67-91.

Findlay, Bill (1996a) 'Talking in Tongues: Scottish Translations 1970-1995', in Randall Stevenson and Gavin Wallace (eds.) *Scottish Theatre since the Seventies*, Edinburgh: Edinburgh University Press:186-97.

------ (1996b) 'Translating into Dialect', in David Johnston (ed.) *Stages of Translation: Essays and Interviews on Translating for the Stage*, Bath: Absolute Press:199-217.

------ (ed.) (1998a) *A History of Scottish Theatre*, Edinburgh: Polygon:47-50.

---

[3] In his keynote speech at the University of Hull conference which gave rise to this collection – *True to Form: On Stage Translation*, September 1997.

------ (1998b) 'Silesian into Scots: Gerhart Hauptmann's *The Weavers*', *Modern Drama* 41 (1):90-104.

Fouchereaux, Jean (1995) 'Traduire/ Trahir *Le Vrai Monde?* de Michel Tremblay: *The Real World?/The Real Wurld?*', *Québec Studies* 20 (Spring/Summer):86-96.

Lochhead, Liz (1985) *Tartuffe: a Translation into Scots from the original by Molière*, Edinburgh: Polygon.

MacDonald, Robert David (trans) (1998) *Schiller: Five Plays*, London: Absolute Classics.

# B. TRANSLATING PERFORMANCE

# 4    Performability in Translation
## Speakability? Playability? Or just Saleability?

EVA ESPASA

*Abstract.* This essay examines the changing notion of **performability** in stage translation, a concept which is analysed from textual, theatrical, and ideological perspectives. From a textual point of view, performability is often equated with 'speakability' or 'breathability', i.e. the ability to produce fluid texts which performers may utter without difficulty. From a theatrical viewpoint, the need or will to appeal to audiences usually involves a tension between foreignization and domestication. Such decisions find their way into performance as textual strategies (e.g. dialect) or audio-visual signs (e.g. body language, design, sound, and music). Performability is also determined by the theatrical ideology of the company, and is related to questions of status. Performability involves negotiation, but should not be rejected as a concept. Rather, the essay seeks to place theatre ideology and power negotiation at the heart of performability, and make speakability and breathability relative to it.

In this essay I use the term 'performability', rather than 'theatricality', to avoid essentialist questions about what is intrinsically theatrical and what is theatre.[1] 'Performability', instead, leads us to the performance, to the *mise en scène*. And anything which is performed becomes performable, even a telephone directory (Aleu et al. 1995:17). If we keep for a second within the – maybe extreme – example of the performability of the telephone directory, we will see that it would be absurd to analyze *a priori*, looking at the written text of the directory, the theatrical potential of the text. To my mind, it would be more fruitful to look at what theatre directors and performers do to the text so that it becomes performed, and then look at the criteria that have made it performable. Susan Bassnett, whose writings on translating for the stage will be analyzed below, has altogether rejected the term performability: "It seems to me a term that has no credibility, because it is resistant to any form of definition" (Bassnett 1998:95). What I intend here is to look at different definitions of performability and other related terms ('theatricality', 'speakability', 'playability') and consider their strategic value as working definitions, including Bassnett's statements as they have evolved through time.

'Performability' and 'theatricality', as well as 'theatre specificity' are often interchangeable, as Patrice Pavis has pointed out, "[t]heatricality is sometimes synonymous with theatre specificity, a notion which is aesthetically and ideologically loaded, and about whose definition it is impossible to agree" (Pavis 1983:471).

---

[1] For a lucid discussion on essentialism, with its disadvantages as well as its strategic validity, see Fuss 1989.

Pavis has also exposed the ambiguity behind the adjective 'theatrical' which –
for a naturalistic theatrical presentation style – has positive connotations of total
illusion (of the text or spectacle) or negative connotations, when the adjective
'theatrical' is applied to a performance which is considered to be too artificial,
which constantly reminds us that we are in the theatre (Pavis 1983:468). For a
Brechtian style of presentation, though, it is the contrary which would be valid.
I am well aware that the binary illusionistic/anti-illusionistic is too simplistic
nowadays and does not account for many multicultural and/or postmodernist
theatre practices. But this dichotomy has played a historical role, and theatre
practitioners, as we will see, often base their performance/translation criteria on
this unspoken duality.

Pavis admits that the concept of theatricality is "somehow mythical, too general and even idealistic" (Pavis 1983:468). So as to attempt to define 'theatricality'
more precisely, Pavis groups together the associations of the term 'theatre' in
the following three blocks. Firstly, from the Greek etymology of the term *theatron*,
theatre is equated with 'point of view', as a place from which the audience
observes an action which takes place in another place: "Only through the shift
of the relation between the look(ing) and the object beheld does [theatre] become the place where the performance takes place" (Pavis 1983:469).

Secondly, in the classical language of the 16th and 17th centuries, the term
'theatre' refers to the scene proper. Thirdly, due to a second metonymic translation of the Greek term, theatre has become synonymous with the following
concepts: dramatic genre, institution, repertoire, and the works by a specific
author (Pavis 1983:469).

It is important to keep in mind this multiplicity of meanings that 'theatre'
and 'theatricality' may have because such meanings are closely interrelated,
and also because they are usually taken into account – though not necessarily in
an explicit manner – when talking about performability.

In the above criteria, performability is analyzed either from a textual viewpoint, or from a theatrical one, in relation to the *mise en scène*. In the article
'Ways through the Labyrinth' (1985), Susan Bassnett comments on the wide
spectrum covered by the term 'performability'. This concept is usually applied to:

1. (From a textual viewpoint) the intention of underlining the fluency of the
   translated text, so that performers can utter it without unwanted effort. This
   is often equated with 'speakability' or 'breathability';

2. (From the viewpoint of the *mise en scène*) a whole set of strategies of
   cultural adaptation, such as replacing dialectal features of the source language by others of the target language, or omitting passages which are
   considered to be too rooted in the cultural linguistic context of the original
   (Bassnett 1985:90-91). Thus, from the viewpoint of theatrical practice,
   playability, or actability, are used as synonyms for performability.

From a theatrical viewpoint, the need or will to appeal to audiences usually involves decisions related to cultural adaptation: a tension between foreignizing and domestication (Venuti 1995), decisions which find their way into theatre performances in the form of textual strategies (e.g. the use of specific dialects) or the whole gamut of audio-visual signs which are interchangeable with the written text (e.g. body language, performers' external appearance, stage design, sound and music).

For example, in a Catalan production of Shelagh Delaney's *A Taste of Honey*, in the first rehearsals there was a heated debate about the domestication of songs. On the one hand, there was an overall strategy of foreignizing, in that the temporal and spatial parameters of the original play were kept. On the other, performers expressed their will to win over audiences, and therefore the need to adapt songs. The final decision was to keep the songs "as foreign as possible", but in translation. This involved a whole gamut of strategies, among which were the following:

1. Incorporating new music into the translated text;
2. Omitting the music (and incorporating its words into the drama text), due to dramatic tension/due to the lack of a stage direction specifying that certain words are a song;
3. Humming a song, or singing it to "la";
4. Creating a new song (which 'sounded' foreign, with the inclusion of English proper names):

> El meu millor amic és el little John
> però el meu tresor és l'Stevie Wing.
> Entre John i Stevie ... prefereixo en Sam,
> són ocells de camp.
> Quan els veig venir nets i clenxinats,
> amb els seus barrets tots tres tan mudats:
> John i Stevie són el meu amor,
> però en Sam és el meu tresor.

> [My best friend is little John
> but my "treasure" is Stevie Wing.
> Between John and Stevie ... I prefer Sam,
> they are "country birds".
> When I see them come, ...
> with their hats, ...
> John and Stevie are my love
> but Sam is my "treasure"][2]

---

[2] Cf. the original song in the play, which is a parody of a sentimental song of the fifties, a parody which, according to the Catalan company, would be difficult for Catalan

According to Pavis (1992:145-146; see also Mateo 1995:24-25) there are two opposite views about theatre translating. The tension between translating for the page or for the stage often involves separate distribution circuits which condition the translation strategies used. On the one hand, if the act of translating is considered as prior to and autonomous from the *mise en scène*, the translator will seek not to offer a specific interpretation of the text, thus attempting to convey the ambiguities and different readings in the translated playtext. This tendency is preferred in translations for the page, if only because of publishing policies and for financial reasons (one 'authorized' translation, which can be used for many productions, is bound to be more profitable than a translation per production). However, as Pavis points out, even though it is very important to take into account the deliberate ambiguity in a text, no reading, no translation, can avoid 'interpreting' it. The very intention of trying to maintain the indeterminacy, the mystery of a text, implies a positioning towards it, and will condition a specific reading, *mise en scène*, and reception of the text. Thus, on the other hand, translating can be seen as intrinsically related to *mise en scène*, and therefore as an operation already containing an interpretation. This view is usually defended by theatre practitioners and theoreticians: "Translation or *mise en scène*: the activity is the same; it is the art of selection among the hierarchy of signs" (Antoine Vitez, in Pavis 1992:146). I agree with this latter view, but this is not to deny the existence of translations intended primarily for the page. The page/ stage controversy is useless if the expression 'page/stage' reflects just different (sometimes compatible) distribution circuits, rather than two aesthetic, ideological practices.

In short, what is interesting in these two views on theatre translation is that they generate two different types of translation, according to two notions of performability, one, more related to the text, and the other, to the specific style of presentation of the company. The following definition by Pavis of theatricality is perfectly applicable to the views on performability which are explored here:

> Theatricality does not manifest itself [...] as a quality or an essence which is inherent to a text or a situation, but as a *pragmatic use of the scenic instrument,* so that the components of the performance manifest and fragment the linearity of the text and of the word. (Pavis 1983:471, my italics)

According to this *pragmatic* use of the "scenic instrument", we cannot talk about an abstract, universal notion of performability; rather, this will vary depending on the ideology and style of presentation of the company or the cultural *milieu*:

> Any theatrical semiotics which presupposes that the dramatic text has an

---

audiences to detect, and was therefore replaced by a different song: "I'd give the song birds to the wild wood/I'd give the sunset to the blind/and to the old folks I'd give the memory of their baby upon their knee. [...] [*She sings another verse*]" (Delaney 1959:13).

> innate theatricality, a matrix for production or even a score, which must be
> extracted at all costs and expressed on the stage, thus implying that the dra-
> matic text exists only when it is produced, seems to be begging the question.
> Those who hold that position would contend that every play has only one
> good *mise en scène* already present in the text. (Pavis 1992:26)

And this, as we will see, seems to be Bassnett's (1991; 1998) objection to
performability, if performability is understood as the impossible task of looking
for an acting subtext which will unfold in translation (Bassnett 1998:90-92).

Let us focus now on the style of presentation and its relation to performability.
It is only from a naturalistic view of theatre, which focuses on the psychological 'vraisemblance' of characters, that the concern for a translation that will
maintain this characterization is usually defended by different translators. Consequently, for Lars Hamberg, the translated dialogue, "must characterize the
speaker and thus seem genuine; [...] an easy and natural dialogue is of paramount importance in a dramatic translation, otherwise the actors have to struggle
with lines which sound unnatural and stilted" (Hamberg 1969:91, 92). Hamberg
also refers to the relation between characterization and the rhythm of the utterances. Susan Bassnett (1978), in an early article on drama translation, applied
the notions of Stanislavskian theatre practice to translation, and stressed the
importance of rhythm in scenes, which she thought ought to be transmitted to
the translation. George Wellwarth emphasizes the similarities between the translation of poetry and drama, and asserts that for both types of translation a sense
of rhythm is essential. Specifically, the translator of drama texts "must have a
sense of the rhythm of speech patterns", and in translating, one has to take into
account "speakability [...], the degree of ease with which the words of the translated text can be enunciated" (Wellwarth 1981:140). His affirmation that the
translation must not falsify the intention of the original (Wellwarth 1981:140) is
in keeping with Gogol's definition of the ideal translation, to which Wellwarth
subscribes: "the ideal translation [is] one that is like a completely transparent
pane of glass through which people can see the original without being aware of
anything intervening" (Wellwarth 1981:146). Here we can see that Wellwarth is
explicitly defending the transparency or invisibility of translation, which can be
linked to a will to be 'faithful' to the 'intention' of the original. It is from this
view that we can understand the importance which is usually given to fluid
utterance in translation. It is paradoxical that the 'ideal translation', so as to be
'good' as a translation, does not have to look like a translation but like an original; translation should remain invisible, hiding in the alleged 'naturality' of the
target language.

Thus, the tension between 'artificiality' and 'naturalism' in theatre practices
is parallel to the tension in translation studies about the fluency of the translated
text. When literary critics comment on the quality of a translation, they tend to
do so in terms of fluency. They tend to praise a fluid, transparent, invisible
translation, which hides the fact that it is indeed a translation:

> A translated text [...] is judged acceptable by most publishers, reviewers, and readers when it reads fluently, when the absence of any linguistic or stylistic peculiarities makes it seem transparent, giving the appearance that it reflects the foreign writer's personality or intention or the essential meaning of the foreign text – the appearance, in other words, that the translation is not in fact a translation, but the "original". (Venuti 1995:1)

This is one paradox of a translated text: we read it, we consider it to all intents and purposes *as if* it were the original, but to do so we have to consider it invisible, non-existent; we have to disregard it. We want to listen to the voice of the original, and yet all we have is the voice of the translation, which we decide to ignore as a voice in its own right (Hermans 1996:8-10). This paradox is especially visible in translated drama and audio-visual texts, where the audience 'suspend their disbelief' that what they are watching is not 'the real' Shakespeare but, say, a Catalan production (based on one translated text from one of many Shakespearean editions).

There are moments when the illusion is dispelled completely, as when there is explicit metatextual comment on the language of the original, as the following examples from a Catalan translation of *The Merry Wives of Windsor* show:

> FALSTAFF: [...] Breu: tinc la intenció de fer l'amor a la dona de Ford. Hi descobreixo bona disposició: xerra, talla la carn, té un cop d'ull dels que t'agafen. Jo puc traduir el pensament del seu estil familiar. El sentit menys favorable de la seva conducta, *traduït en un bon anglès*, és aquest: "Jo sóc del senyor John Falstaff". (Sagarra 1980:29, my emphasis)

> FALSTAFF: [...] Briefly, I do mean to make love to Ford's wife. I spy entertainment in her: she discourses, she carves, she gives the leer of invitation; I can construe the action of her familiar style, and the hardest voice of her behaviour, *to be Englished rightly*, is, "I am Sir John Falstaff's". (I.iii, 41-45, my emphasis)

> HOSTALER: [...] Desarmem-los i que discuteixin; que conservin llurs membres intactes i *que facin mandonguilles de la llengua anglesa*. (Sagarra 1980:73, my emphasis)

> HOST: Disarm them, and let them question; let them keep their limbs whole, and *hack our English*. (III.i, 71-72, my emphasis)

These metatextual comments were kept in a 1994 Catalan production of the play, and were laughed at by audiences, since the *mise en scène* did not aim at 'vraisemblance' but at comedy, and favoured anti-illusionistic techniques.

Going back to the speakability of the translated text, Maryse Pelletier, a theatre translator, stresses the need for 'musicality' in translation. However, she is aware that such musicality is not an absolute value but is conditioned by the musicality of the original and the peculiarities of the target language: "the translator must hear the characters, [...] give them speech that is harsh or smooth if it is harsh or smooth in the original – all of this, of course, within the limits of the second language" (Pelletier 1988: 31). More importantly, Pelletier subordinates the accuracy of the translation to its theatrical impact:

> What is important in the theatre is not the exactness of the words but the effect they create in the context in which they have been placed. If an actor has to sustain an intention or a change of intention on a certain word, I would prefer that the word be strong rather than exact, vivid rather than correct. (Pelletier 1988:32)

Therefore, all the above considerations – sound, rhythm, 'naturalism' – will be important when translators want to recreate specific sound effects, rhythm or characterization, either because they read them into the original, or – especially – because such criteria are highly valued in the theatre conventions and ideology of the company, and the target culture. Thus, from a Stanislavskian viewpoint, the performers may try and identify with the characters they are interpreting; and they will seek that characterization reflected in the translated text, or they will amend it accordingly. From a Brechtian perspective, however, performers will more probably distance themselves from the character, from the translated text, from the performance, and favour strategies which will break the illusion of representation and lay bare its artificiality. Thus, translation does not have to be a vehicle for the illusion of theatre, but one more instrument, among the scenic signs, which exposes the artificiality of theatre.[3]

There are other practical aspects of theatre production which may influence the treatment a translation receives in its transposition to the stage, all regarding time, such as the overall performance time and the relative length of monologues, which may lead to omissions, as Mateo (1995) has rightly pointed out. If a usual performance nowadays lasts 90 minutes approximately in Catalan and Spanish playhouses, it is not surprising that, for example, present-day Shakespearean performances, both in English and in translation, do not usually present the full text. And Bassnett has pointed out that different expectations regarding the length of performance, across cultures and theatre practices, are "bound to have an effect on translation strategies" (1998:106).

So far we have seen that 'performability' is firstly conditioned by textual

---

[3] An anecdote by a Catalan actor may illustrate this. When I asked his opinion about a specific translated text, he told me about a theatre director he had worked for, who was using a Latin American Spanish translation in his production. The performers wanted to replace certain words and idioms by others which are more common in Peninsular Spanish. The director did not find this necessary, because he was interested in the interpretation work that started from the text, rather than in the translation itself. This anecdote may show how translation is subordinated to specific theatre practices.

and theatrical practices. Besides, the duality of the written/performed text allows for the combination of at least two acting styles. Even if the translated text is of a specific style, the *mise en scène* can show a different tendency (Törnqvist 1991:174; Aaltonen 1996:71). We have also seen that "the problem of performability in translation is [...] complicated by changing concepts of performance" (Bassnett 1980:122-123), variable through time and space, as is especially visible in translating texts which were written many centuries ago in far-away cultures. Now, it is crucial to consider *who* has power in a theatre company to decide *what* is performable – and what is ruled out as unperformable. Thus, performability is shaped by the question of status.

Susan Bassnett has denounced the low prestige associated with translating: "translation has been perceived as a secondary activity, as a 'mechanical' rather than a 'creative' process, within the competence of anyone with a basic grounding in a language other than their own; in short, as a low status occupation" (Bassnett 1988 [1980]:2). Within theatre practice, the consequences of the little prestige accorded to translating are the subordination of the translation to other production factors. This need not be negative in that it implies the insertion of the translation into the production process. But if this is positive from a theatrical point of view, from an ideological point of view of power, of decision-making, this can be negative. Susan Bassnett, in three articles published in 1985, 1991 and 1998, revises her former views on theatre translation (Bassnett 1978; 1988 [1980]:120-132; 1998):

> Some years ago, in an early article on problems of theatre translation [1978], I suggested that there might be a gestural language distinguishable within the written text. This theory was based on work in theatre practice, where directors and actors distinguish physical signs to follow from off the written page. I raised the question as to how this gestural language might be discernible, suggesting that it might exist in a manner similar to the Stanislavskian sub-text that is decoded by the actor and encoded into gestural form. Now, with hindsight, the idea of gestural patterning in a text appears to be a loose and woolly concept: it may be all very well for monolingual actors to speculate on the gestus of a text, but where interlingual translation is involved other solutions must be sought. (Bassnett 1985:98)

In this article from 1985, 'Ways through the Labyrinth: Strategies and Methods for Translating Theatre Texts', Bassnett questions the validity of the term 'performability', since it has been used from different viewpoints, textually and theatrically, but it has not been defined (Bassnett 1985:90-91; see also 1998:95, quoted above). The author argues that performability is not a concept that has to be added *a posteriori*, in the analysis of the translated text, but it has to be taken into account throughout the process of translation and production. One means of incorporating performability into this process is 'collaborative translation'. For Bassnett, this requires that two people work together – two natives of the source and target language, or one source-language native working together with the theatre company that will stage the translated playtext. This method is parallel to the collective creation of a show and has the advantage that 'performability' is not an extra element but something that appears when the written and the oral text are worked through simultaneously. Thus, the process of translating includes a series of questions directly related to the *mise en scène*, such as different theatre conventions and styles of presentation in the source – and target – milieux (Bassnett 1985:91).

In her article 'Translating for the Theatre: the Case Against Performability' (1991), as the title shows, Bassnett goes one step further and altogether rejects the notion of performability, as she does in 1998. But in her 1991 article she very specifically critiques the connection between performance and theatre financial policies. She argues that the concept of 'performability' has been used as a pretext so that the status of translation is considered inferior to that of theatrical writing. Bassnett gives the example of the translation policies of the National Theatre, in which a translator is commissioned to undertake a so-called literal translation, and then this text is handed to a well-known, often monolingual, playwright, who adapts the text for the theatre, so as to make it performable. For Bassnett, under this alleged 'performability', there hide economic policies: the name of a well-known playwright can attract more people; that is why he or she is granted the authorship and a substantial amount of the translation benefits (Bassnett 1991:101). For Bassnett, the separation between the written and the performed texts has a direct consequence for the status of the translator. I quote her argument extensively, because I will go on to comment on it:

> *Performance*, which means inevitably interpretation, *interrupts the relationship between writer, text and reader*, and imposes an additional dimension which many writers have found undesirable. [...] Pirandello's vision of the playtext is that it belongs primarily to the writer and that performance is a form of attack on the writer's intentions. Bernard Shaw [...] does take inordinate care in his lengthy stage directions to *control* even the physical appearance of his characters. In other words, what post-naturalist theatre demands is a high degree of fidelity to the written text on the part of both director and performers, and once that idea of fidelity was established, it was imposed on the whole gamut of theatre texts regardless of their quintessential difference. *The implications for the interlingual translator gradually emerged: if performers were bound on a vertical master-servant relationship to the written text, so also should translators be*. The power of the written playtext changed completely in the nineteenth century, and methods of training actors changed accordingly, as did their status. The key figure to emerge in this new concept of theatre is *the director, yet another link in the chain separating the writing process from the performance*. Bound in this servile relationship, one avenue of escape for translators was to invent the idea of "performability" as an excuse to exercise greater liberties with the

text than convention allowed. That term has then been taken up by commentators on theatre translation, without regard for its history, and has entered into the general discourse of theatre translation, thereby muddying the already murky waters still further. (Bassnett 1991:104-105, my emphasis)

Thus, the more elements there are in the theatrical communication chain, the more the translator will be subordinated to the rest of the people involved in the *mise en scène*. Bassnett's argument is certainly valid in that it shows the influence of status in the question of performability: who decides what is performable? The person(s) with more power in the theatre company. In this article, Bassnett hits the nail on the head regarding the connection between status and performability which exists in the well-known tandem playwright/unknown translator: the more visibility is granted to a well-known playwright, the more invisible the figure of the translator remains.

But this criticism is completely opposite to Bassnett's prior belief in collaborative translation, which she defended in 1985. The following opinion of Burton Raffel, about collaborative poetry translation, is perfectly applicable to theatre translation: "The central fact about collaborative translation is that only rarely is it between equals" (Raffel 1988:129). A collaborative or collective translation *perforce* involves (unequal) negotiation among the agents interpreting the text, from the point of view of translating, directing and acting alike. But this does not necessarily entail rejecting 'performability' altogether. It can prove an elucidating practice to trace the history of the term 'performability', so as to see *how* performability has been constructed over time and in different theatre practices. And, as for the distance between the dramatic and the theatrical text, the mediation of a complex chain of participants, this need not be an obstacle to translation – as Bassnett seems to suggest – but it is a specific feature of theatre, as a density of signs, even though, or precisely because it implies a process of negotiating the production of translated playtexts. Rather, this negotiation has to be included as an explanatory factor of performability. Ultimately, I would argue for putting theatre ideology and power negotiation at the heart of performability, and make such textual and theatrical factors as speakability and playability relative to it.[4]

"A study of the figurative language used by translators in their statements

---

[4] This poses questions which are comparable to Diana Fuss' work on essentialism:

> The question we should be asking is not 'Is this text essentialist (and therefore 'bad')?' but rather, 'if this text is essentialist, *what motivates its deployment?*' How does the sign essence circulate in various contemporary critical debates? Where, how, and why is it invoked? What are its political and textual effects? (Fuss 1989:xi)

Joan W. Scott makes a similar claim about the strategic use of 'experience' in research projects on history:

about their work can tell us about the status of translation as a textual act."
(Bassnett 1994:xiii). In her preface to the revised edition of *Translation Studies*,
Bassnett summarizes with these words a suggestive field of study in translation
studies, "the systematic study of statements about translation made by translators and linguists in different times and places" (Bassnett 1994:xiii). In her
writings on theatre translation, Bassnett applies her labyrinth metaphor to her
own research in the field:

> a long, tortuous journey that started in the mid-1970s and is still going on
> even as we come to the end of the century. Over the years I have revised my
> views several times, though I still find that the image of the labyrinth is an
> apt one for this most problematic and neglected area of translation studies
> research. (Bassnett 1998:90)

Bassnett uses this image for her research, rather than for translation practice,
but she does conflate both in her own comments on other images for theatre
translation:

> Patrice Pavis has talked about the 'crossroads' of cultures, where theatre
> traditions and practices meet and mingle, and this is a useful image, imply-
> ing as it does a process of exchange in the encounter between cultural systems
> (Pavis, 1992). Significantly, the image of the 'crossroads', like the image of
> the labyrinth, implies a plurality of possibilities and rejects any notion of
> closure. (Bassnett 1998:106)

Even though Bassnett sees the image of the labyrinth as open and plural, when
we apply it to the activity of translating, we might picture a lonely translator,
trapped in a labyrinth with restricted binary possibilities, of trial and error, which
could easily suggest an either/or approach towards translating, of having to learn
only through the experience of repeatedly coming up against blind alleys.

However, Bassnett is right in explicitly pointing to the metaphors for translation and their connotations. She does comment on Pavis' image of translation
as crossroads (Bassnett 1998:106, quoted above), which might remind us of
Jacques Derrida's 'switch points', glossed by Diana Fuss as "those linguistic
levers which insure that words and letters never reach their final destinations"
(Fuss 1989:88). It might remind us especially of Houston A. Baker Jr.'s "translation at the crossing" (Baker, in Fuss 1989:87): "the crossing sign is the antithesis
of a place marker. It signifies, always, change, motion, transience, process"

---

> Given the ubiquity of the term [experience], it seems to me more useful to work
> with it, to analyze its operations and to redefine its meaning. This entails focus-
> sing on processes of identity production, insisting on the discursive nature of
> 'experience' and on the politics of its construction. [...] Experience is, in this
> approach, not the origin of our explanation, but that which we want to explain.
> (Scott 1991:797)

(Baker, in Fuss 1989:88), which he proposes for Afro-American critics, and which can apply to any translation practices that challenge Eurocentrism: "The task of present-day scholars [...] is to situate themselves inventively and daringly at the crossing sign in order to materialize vernacular faces" (Baker, in Fuss 1989:89).

Another suggestive image proposed by Pavis is that of the hourglass (1992: 4-5) where he suggests that each grain/element of the source culture has to be turned upside down in order to arrive at the target culture:

> [The hourglass] is a strange object, reminiscent of a funnel and a mill [...] In the upper bowl is the foreign culture, the source culture, which is more or less codified and solidified in diverse anthropological, sociocultural or artistic modelizations. In order to reach us, this culture must pass through a narrow neck. If the grains of culture or their conglomerate are sufficiently fine, they will flow through *without any trouble*, however slowly, into the lower bowl, that of the target culture, from which point we observe this slow flow. The grains will rearrange themselves in a way which appears random, but which is partly regulated by their passage through some dozen filters put in place by the target culture and the observer.
> The hourglass presents two risks. If it is only a mill, it will blend the source culture, destroy its every specificity and drop into the lower bowl an inert and deformed substance which will have lost its original modeling without being molded into that of the target culture. If it is only a funnel, it will indiscriminately absorb the initial substance without reshaping it through the series of filters or leaving any trace of the original matter. (Pavis 1992:4-5, my emphasis)

This image, like the one of the railway crossing, is dynamic and open, and at the same time acknowledges the negotiation processes involved in any transcultural transaction. One might wonder about a transference process "without any trouble", which would imply a lack of resilience on the part of one culture towards acculturation. The second paragraph of the quote, though, makes it clear that such transference is not free from trouble, and aptly focuses the metaphor on the filtering frame (the hourglass, the funnel/mill) rather than on the grains which are filtered. This focussing on the frame is similar to the framing devices which are the railway lines, the switch points or the crossroads, even the fixity of the walls in a labyrinth, and which are reminiscent of the institutional and ideological framings of translation activities.

One way of retaining the labyrinth metaphor, as applied to translating for the stage, is to consider creative possibilities of escaping from the labyrinth, as in the Greek myth of Ariadne. Ariadne, in love with Theseus, helped him in his escape from an intricate labyrinth after he had killed the Minotaur – Ariadne gave Theseus a long thread which guided Theseus on his way out of the labyrinth.

Thus, another possibility for imagery in theatre translation is to follow the thread of desire, as above, and as can be exemplified with the following anecdote. When I was doing research for my doctoral thesis, I asked for permission to attend rehearsals, to observe the changes to translated texts as they were acted and produced. A theatre director rejected my petition, on the grounds that rehearsals were like a love affair between him and the performers, and he did not want voyeurs. Indeed, theatre analysts, and especially translators, are voyeurs in that only on rare occasions are we explicitly invited, taken into account in the writing and performance processes on stage. Translating for the stage, then, can be compared to a paradoxically voyeuristic experience: both secret – not necessarily ratified by the writer of the source text – and public – offered to a different audience. Finally, I would just like to mention another related image which is embedded in the very name '*play*ability'. Like all games, theatre translation derives at least as much pleasure from learning the rules of the game as from subverting them.

## References

Aaltonen, Sirkku (1996) *Acculturation of the Other. Irish Milieux in Finnish Drama Translation*, Joensuu: University of Joensuu Press.

Aleu, M. Lluïsa, Minerva Álvarez and Aurèlia Esteve (1995) *L'art del teatre*, Barcelona: Empúries.

Bassnett, Susan (1978) 'Translating Spatial Poetry: An Examination of Theatre Texts in Performance', in James S. Holmes, José Lambert and Raymond van den Broeck (eds.) *Literature and Translation. New Perspectives in Literary Studies*, Leuven: Acco:161-176.

------ (1985) 'Ways Through the Labyrinth: Strategies and Methods for Translating Theatre Texts', in Theo Hermans *The Manipulation of Literature: Studies in Literary Translation*, London: Croom Helm:87-102.

------ (1988 [1980]) *Translation Studies*, London: Routledge.

------ (1991) 'Translating for the Theatre: The Case Against Performability', *TTR* 4 (1):99-111.

------ (1994 [1991]) *Translation Studies*, revised edition, London: Routledge.

------ (1998) 'Still Trapped in the Labyrinth: Further Reflections on Translation and Theatre', in Susan Bassnett and André Lefevere, *Constructing Cultures: Essays on Literary Translation*, Clevedon: Multilingual Matters:90-108.

Delaney, Shelagh (1959) *A Taste of Honey*, London: Methuen.

Fuss, Diana (1989) *Essentially Speaking. Feminism, Nature and Difference*, New York: Routledge.

Hamberg, Lars (1969) 'Some Practical Considerations concerning Dramatic Translation', *Babel* 15 (2):91-100.

Hermans, Theo (1996) *'Translation's Other'*, An Inaugural Lecture delivered at University College, London.

Mateo, Marta (1995) 'Constraints and Possibilities of Performance Elements in Drama Translation', *Perspectives* 1:21-33.

Oliver, H.J. (ed.) (1971) *The Merry Wives of Windsor*, The Arden Shakespeare, third series, London: Routledge.

Pavis, Patrice (1980) *Dictionnaire du théâtre: termes et concepts de l'analyse théâtrale*, Paris, trans. Fernando de Toro (1983) as *Diccionario del teatro: dramaturgia, estética, semiología*, Barcelona: Paidos. All references in the text have been translated from the Spanish by the author of this essay.

------ (1992) trans. Loren Kruger, *Theatre at the Crossroads of Culture*, London: Routledge.

Pelletier, Maryse (1988) 'Theatre and the Music of Language', in David Homel & Sherry Simon (eds.) *Mapping Literature: the Art and Politics of Translation*, Montreal: Vehícule Press:31-32.

Raffel, Burton (1988) *The Art of Translating Poetry*, Pennsylvania University Park: Pennsylvania State University Press.

Sagarra, Josep Maria de (trans) (1980) [1942-43] *Les alegres casades de Windsor,* Barcelona: Institut del Teatre.

Scott, Joan W. (1991) 'The Evidence of Experience', *Critical Inquiry* 17 (4):773-797.

Shakespeare, William (ca. 1597) *The Merry Wives of Windsor*, in Oliver, H.D. (ed.) (1971) The Arden Shakespeare, third series, London: Routeledge.

Törnqvist, Egil (1991) *Transposing Drama. Studies in Representation*, Basingstoke: Macmillan.

Venuti, Lawrence (1995) *The Translator's Invisibility. A History of Translation*, London: Routledge.

Wellwarth, George (1981) 'Special Considerations in Drama Translation', in Marilyn Gaddis Rose (ed.) *Translation Spectrum. Essays in Theory and Practice*, Albany: State University of New York Press:140-146.

# 5    Acts with Words
## Beckett, Translation, *Mise en Scène* and Authorship

MARK BATTY

*Abstract*. Issues of written text translation as an act of destruction or preservation are considered as mirroring issues raised in the construction of a performance 'text', taking into account the roles of director, designers and actors in positioning the dramatic text within a proposed *mise en scène*. An analysis is offered of how the two processes, both involved with the construction of signifying systems for the stage, may be allowed to inform one another, specifically in considering the authorship of a performance from or through a dramatic piece of writing. References are to the stage work of Samuel Beckett, his collaborators, translators, interpreters and defenders, including the attitudes of the author and his estate to the 'manipulation' or 'abuse' of his work in a variety of cultural contexts.

Samuel Beckett was notoriously protective of the manner in which his work for the stage ought to be presented. Famously, his firm resolve with regards to the performances of his works could lead on occasions to legal action barring specific performances where a director's interpretation strayed, in his eyes, unacceptably too far. Since his death, the Beckett Estate has continued such action with equal verve. And yet, if so much energy and determination had been put into a defence of a very personal vision as offered by his writing for the stage, why had there never been a similar preciousness applied to the theoretically far more damaging practice of translation of his work into languages other than those already provided for by Beckett himself? Is it not accepted that, for those to whom the original language texts are inaccessible, any author's reputation and the assessment of his/her literary achievement lies, to some extent, in the hands of translators?

Clearly, the consequences of such thinking are neither practical nor desirable. Nevertheless, Samuel Beckett, as a bilingual writer, self-translator and director of his own plays, provides in his body of work an obvious opportunity to attempt to relate the complexities of translation of text to those of performance of text, including the impossible notions of fidelity and infidelity to an author's intentions, and to do so within an understanding of what might constitute the parameters of authorship. Such an investigation might also offer a perspective on the operations of effective authorship that both translation and *mise en scène* represent.

That Beckett both translated his own plays and directed them can be considered as symptomatic of a very particular artistic impulse that views a text as fluid and incomplete, as necessary failure; a linguistic construct that perpetually seeks its most complete form of enunciation; "Saying is inventing" as the character Molloy declares in the novel bearing his name (Beckett 1955:41). Certainly,

Beckett's fiction reflects a process of desperate enquiry, of the self seeking absolute expression, and it is interesting to note that, as Enoch Brater points out in his book *The Drama in the Text*, much of this material often makes more sense when spoken and heard than when simply read and silently digested. David Watson in his *Paradox and Desire in Beckett's Fiction* describes how Beckett's prose works "inscribe a 'theatrical' element of performance [...] onto the space of the narrative novel. But what is performed is the very act or process of enunciation" (1991:83). This impulse towards articulation and performance, towards demonstration and the comfort characters might elicit from repetition, led Beckett naturally to playwrighting and following the proven success of *En attendant Godot* in 1953, a sustained attempt to create with his subsequent plays precise scores for dramatic events.

As a result of the greater involvement necessitated by the shift from fiction to drama there seems to have been a gradual realization in Beckett that his authorship of a piece of dramatic writing need not end with the written text. When writing his first plays, Beckett openly flaunted his lack of knowledge in all things theatrical ("I have no understanding of the theatre, I know nothing about it, I never go, it's appalling",[1] he claimed in 1952). In addition to this early acknowledgement of his practical inexperience in the theatre, he would insist, when quizzed, that there was little or nothing he could do to assist with the rehearsal of his plays. His maturation from such confessed ignorance of the ways of the theatre and apparent indifference towards the interpretation of his work to his markedly increased interest in overseeing productions during the sixties, culminating in his decision to direct his plays personally, is not just incidental. Taking this step he was recognizing how he might extend the effectiveness of his authorship beyond the simple completion of a typed manuscript. This concern is paralleled in the self-inflicted chore of translating the great majority of his own material from French into English or vice versa, and in his engagement with the translators of his works into other languages, most notably Italian and German. Indeed, for Beckett, directing a text always involved a process of re-translation and revision of that text. Indeed, these tasks might very well represent two parts of the same impulse.

At the simplest level, engaging with works long since 'finished', either as translator or director, provided Beckett with an opportunity to tidy up perceived faults and weaknesses. When asked once if he saw anything new in his plays when he returned to them he replied "Yes. Mistakes." (Quoted by Clancy Signal in McMillan and Fehsenfeld 1988:182). Indeed, the relationship between Beckett's 'translated' texts and their sources was always quite dynamic, with the results of a new language version often instigating changes in the original version.

Beckett considered his first play, *En attendant Godot*, particularly undisci-

---

[1] Beckett, Samuel, preamble to extracts from *En attendant Godot*, recited by Roger Blin, broadcast by the O.R.T.F., January 1952. My translation.

plined. When he witnessed its original rehearsal process in Paris in 1952 he was flexible to all suggestions. The French director Roger Blin was left with a free rein to do as he felt necessary and the surviving prompt copy of the production attests to a number of substantial cuts applied to the first published version.[2] The most significant of these are a striking out of two whole pages in the first act and two thirds of a page and then a further page and a half in the second. The omission of these sections of the play met with Beckett's approval and they did not subsequently make the transfer to the English or later French editions of the printed play. Significantly, Blin's directorial decisions replicate the kind of editorial decision made by Beckett himself when cutting whole pages of *Mercier et Camier* from his English translation to hack away lingering passages and avoid unnecessary repetitions. They relate not to practicalities of length or narrative weakness, but to the thematic needs of the play's dramatic substance. For example, the first significant cut of two pages in Act One was of a passage in which Pozzo attempts to explain, amid interruptions and appeals to continue from Estragon, that it is uncertain whether or not Lucky will carry out the requests he makes of him. Its loss speeds up the approach of Lucky's speech, coming sooner after the dance than originally permitted. This section was to be further reduced in Beckett's own production at the Schiller-Theater in Berlin in 1975 where the whole conversation following Pozzo's "The Net. He thinks he's entangled in a net" was cut (See Knowlson 1993:38 and 130-131).

This ready acceptance of a director's decision to cut segments of his drama following a response to the text in the rehearsal room shows perhaps Beckett's willing recognition of a sharp learning curve. As the first example of how the stage incarnation of one of his written works influenced Beckett's subsequent translation of that work, it marks the beginning of the point at which Beckett the translator and Beckett the director merged. In his acceptance of Blin's cuts he was recognising not only the dramatic potentials of this one text (and how they needed to be released from stifling inadequacies of the written text), but also accepting a new authorial position in relation to that text that was to inform his developing dramatic language.

Given that both translation and *mise en scène* provide metatextual commentaries on a source text, Beckett's own reworking of his writings, either as their director or translator, can be viewed as his greatest body of commentary upon his own work. When examining this commentary one begins to appreciate the manner in which, engaging in the functions of director or translator, Beckett sought not only to clarify but also to sharpen. Steven Connor, reviewing Beckett's self-translated fiction points out that his "excisions seem to have a thematic as well as a cosmetic purpose" (Connor 1989:28) and there is a similar emphasis in the translations he crafted of his dramatic works where his concern was not simply to improve, remove or add to the linguistic elements of the texts, but to

---

[2] A photocopy of the prompt copy is kept at the Beckett Archive, Reading University Library.

do so in order to reinforce the thematic currents and the dramatic impetus available to actors and directors. A notable example exists with the play *Krapp's Last Tape* where the line "but I suppose better than a kick in the crutch" was first rendered faithfully into French as "mais sans doute mieux qu'un coup de pied dans l'entre-jambes" but then improved to assert Krapp's status as isolated in self-inflicted loneliness in the German "immerhin etwas besser als zwischen Daumen und Zeigefinger" [but somewhat better than between thumb and forefinger]. In the case of *En attendant Godot*, to offer further example, there has been a documented analysis of the way in which Beckett sought to increase the humour in his translation into the English version, *Waiting for Godot*, and emphasize it further in his own German production of *Warten auf Godot* in 1975. Thus, for example, the original French "Un Anglais s'étant enivré" [An Englishman having got himself drunk] became "An Englishman having drunk a little more than usual" in both English and in German ("Ein Engländer, der etwas mehr als gewöhnlich getrunken hat"). The simple "J'écoute" [I'm listening] becomes the sarcastic "I find this really most extraordinarily interesting" and Estragon describes his foot in English as "swelling visibly" as opposed to the more factual French "il enfle" [it's swelling]. Elmar Tophoven's German translation was thoroughly revised for the Berlin 1975 production which Beckett directed, with many sections cut back and reduced where it was felt they interfered with the necessary rhythms of particular sections. Tracing Beckett's relationship to his Godot texts from its French original manipulated and cut by Blin, to his own reworking into English and his meticulous redrafting of the German text for actual production, one can see the development of the play from a loose collection of dialogues to a tighter, much reduced and more refined dramatic study of waiting.

Further examples of the increased dramatization of a text through translation can be provided by examining the transition of *Fin de partie* to *Endgame* and Beckett's work on the play in its German incarnation, *Endspiel*, at the Berlin Schiller-Theater in 1967. Again Beckett did not consider *Fin de partie*, once published, as a definitive text until it could be tried and tested in performance. That it at first failed fully to live up to Beckett's formalistic goals meant that once again the processes of direction and translation were necessary operations for him in discovering the play's true voice. When preparing the English translation he had the experience of having involved himself in its French première behind him. In this grimmer piece, the function of the humour was more acerbic than in its predecessor, and such playing on words as "Voilà ta gaffe. Avale-la" and "T'occupe pas de mes moignons"[3] being anyway untranslatable, the Eng-

---

[3] In French, 'swallowing one's gaffe' is equivalent to the English 'kicking the bucket', adding vindictively to Clov's striking of Hamm with the gaffe as he suggests Hamm swallows it. The similarity of the words *oignons* [onions] and *moignons* [stumps] provides for a twist of the common French expression which translates directly as 'Never you mind my onions'!

lish version is less rich in puns and word play than the original. This proved appropriate to the more desperate and claustrophobic atmosphere required of the play in performance, where the bickering couple can vent more spleen in English with a smaller fund of sarcasm to fall back on. Accordingly, in Beckett's own *mise en scène* of the piece much of the comedy was further eroded, including a reduction of Clov's opening mime and the loss of the *lazzo* of the dropped telescope. Additionally, following a difficult rehearsal period in Paris with Roger Blin, Beckett's concern was to mark the musicality of the text more prominently in his English version, allowing his formalistic goals for the piece to be more evident, and this becomes more apparent in his revision of Elmar Tophoven's German text. He was concerned with reinforcing echoes in the translation that strengthen the dramatic structure of the play in performance by setting up a series of compelling resonances. Hamm's *calmant* [painkiller], *Pillen* in Tophoven's translation, he changed to *Beruhigungsmittel*; the *remontant* (the tonic, given by Tophoven as *Tropfen*) to *Stärkungsmittel*, permitting a final echo in the cruel retort "you're on earth, there's no cure for that!" in his revision of it to "dagegen gibt es kein Mittel!".[4] He also set about establishing a series of leitmotifs, for example, around phrases to do with leaving and employed the facility provided in the language of alliteration and repetition in the forms of the verb *'to go'*: *'Gehen'*, *'ging'*, and *'gegangen'*.

Beckett later passed on some of his own discoveries about the play in a letter to his Polish translator in 1981:

> Herewith corrected copy of *Fin de partie*. The cuts and the simplifications are the result of my work on the play as director and function of the players at my disposal. To another director they may not seem desirable. Three however I strongly recommend. 1) The inspection of the audience (p.45). 2) The vision of the boy (pp.103-105). 3) The song (p.107).[5]

In other words, he sought to bring it closer in line with the standard English text, where some of these things had never appeared. Clov's sighting of the child through the window in *Fin de partie* was severely abridged in *Endgame*, omitting all dialogue from its being spotted to Clov's decision to go out supposedly to exterminate it. Clov's song had also been taken out. In the German version for performance Beckett went further and wanted Hamm's interruptions ("Articule" and "Assez") to be removed, leaving a single long diatribe from Clov following Hamm's desire to hear a few words from his heart. These changes are in recognition of a dramatic progression that proved irresistible in rehearsal and allow the play's resolution – Clov's threatened departure – to arrive more swiftly. Hamm's lack of interest or concern at the arrival of the child and his

---

[4] Detailed consideration of the German translations of his works and the processes involved in their being constructed and revised, is offered in Garforth 1996:49-70.

[5] Samuel Beckett, Letter to Marek Kedzierski, quoted in Knowlson 1992:xviii. Beckett's page references are to the 'Les Editions de Minuit' publication of *Fin de partie*.

slackening insistence on control over Clov (as originally manifested by his interruptions) facilitate a more subdued, defeated Hamm that an actor might build
towards, or rather wane into, by the end of the play.

Implicitly within these few examples given, and within the comments of the
letter to his Polish translator, there is a significant connection made by Beckett
between his work as a director and that as reviser and translator of his own texts:
not only does the written text dictate the shape of the dramatic event but the
processes leading to a dramatic event informs its written text. A creative loop,
or spiral, was being established through which a text was permitted to strive
ever closer to its most suitable form of enunciation. This placed Beckett as author in-between written text and performance text, facilitating a filtering of the
impulses of the one into the fabric of the other and tailoring according to the
specific circumstances of each theatricalisation.

Conventionally, however, the playwright's authorship of the theatrical event
ends with the production of a written text and s/he is subsequently reliant upon
groups of interpretative artists to complete the work and produce the performance text. The ultimate control over the manner in which the performance text
will achieve its utterance lies, of course, in the hands of the director, and it is s/
he who authors the play as it is offered to the public. A director, then, usually
stands in-between the written text and the performance text as a sort of surro-
gate author; his/her role is analogous, therefore, to that of the translator. Most
commonly, the playwright only provides the material for a first register in performance (that of the imaginary; the narratives and messages embedded in the
linguistic structure of the text) but relies upon others, through a translator-like
operation, to find and apply a second register (that of mimesis; the collection of
symbolic structures that contain and aid the transfer of information from stage
to auditorium) and it is usually considered the director's task to find an appropriate balance between the two registers. Looking at the work of Samuel Beckett,
and with specific consideration of his attachment to the evolution of his dramatic texts through translation and *mise en scène*, one begins to realize how he
might be treated as a special case, and one which might be used to inform the
practical relationships between other writers and their translators and directors.

As his own translator and director, Beckett placed himself in a privileged
position by being on such intimate terms with the text to be dramatised, facilitating an effective flowback where what the artist learns as a director can return
to improve the work of that artist as writer/translator. Consequently, and most
significantly, Samuel Beckett's dramatic works under scrutiny show themselves
to have been crafted and revised with the utmost attention to the material of
their second register, of the manner in which they are to be performed. As with
the fiction, which always demonstrated a tendency towards vocal enunciation
as part of its thematic goal, the drama is constructed to allow *how* it speaks to
inform *what* it speaks. In his constructs, action is text and text is action; his
dramas are a series of veritable acts with words.

Of course, Samuel Beckett was one artist amongst many and as much as one might seek to make a theoretical exception of him, he is likely to be treated according to the rule. Accordingly, directors world-wide have been tempted to 'translate' his dramas onto the stage following their own impulses and creativity. Straying too far from Beckett's own models for performance, however, is to court the controversy Beckett purists are prone to ignite. There are many examples of such controversy. A production of *En attendant Godot* directed by Joël Jouanneau in 1991 had its stage constructed to represent a disused factory or warehouse, with Beckett's tree replaced by the shell of an old electricity generator. The production raised questions about the extent to which one can abuse an author's work by imposing extraneous images and implying relationships and situations alien to the original material. Jouanneau's rendering of *Godot* involved the application of what Patrice Pavis refers to as an ideotextual *mise en scène,* (Pavis 1992:36-8) one which mediates between the text as written and the social context of its reception. Similar examples of this mode of thought applied to Beckett are JoAnne Akalaitis' controversial 1984 production of *Endgame*, set in a disused and derelict New York subway station and Susan Sontag's 1994 production of *Waiting for Godot* in Sarajevo for which she cut the entire second act of the play, provided three Vladimir/Estragon couples, two trees and a set including beds, chairs, crates and sandbags. It was Godot reduced to metaphor, but strikingly real to those that witnessed it in the war-ravaged city under siege.

This utilitarian, or humanist, approach to the work of art might very often be guilty of neglecting the work's own specific functions, or even make a virtue of this. And yet, of course, to some degree all *mises en scène* need to be ideotextual, for a dramatic text is of necessity the product of a specific culture, or subculture, at a specific time in its history. Any act of enunciation of a non-contemporary or foreign play will always involve, therefore, the act of finding equivalencies for the intended and encoded thematic and dramatic material in the arena of the target audience's cultural vocabulary. But to what degree does any necessarily ideotextual *mise en scène* pervert the intentions of the playwright, where these might ever be satisfactorily defined? Where Beckett is concerned, or any author like him, how far can one afford to divorce content from its proscribed and inscribed form? Certainly, as translators, we seek to transcribe a dramatic work into a target language by finding linguistic equivalencies to the material of the source text and attempt to group these in a manner that evokes the same or similar theatrical potential of the original. Out of necessity we are producing an original work of art, as does each director, but the relationship with the original author is complex; both intimate and remote at the same time. If we produce an adaptation of the original work we feel the obligation to make that clear. Should this not be the ideal starting point for any director who wishes to engage with a text which has evolved its written form through a process of discovering its own manner of stage enunciation?

Another example which will help to focus attention is that of Deborah Warner's production of Beckett's *Footfalls* in London in 1994. The director strayed so far from the written text and its intended performance text that the Beckett

Estate intervened, insisted on certain changes, stopped a European tour of the production and forbade Deborah Warner from ever directing a piece of Beckett's again. Her 'crime' had been to give fragments of one character's text to another, to relocate the main actress twice during the performance, having her perform the first and third segments of the triptych on the stage and the second, the mother's speech, on a platform constructed above the audiences' heads in the theatre's front circle. That the key character of M had been 'rationalized' and portrayed as clinically disturbed or insane was also seen as a two-dimensional interpretation of the situation of the drama.

Where does one begin to justify such harsh restrictions of an artist's creative intent? To what extent is an author's right to have their work presented as 'intended' enforceable? We can perhaps only go a short distance in trying to reconcile the different responses provoked by such questions as, looking briefly at the different domains within which author and directors usually claim to have most leverage, we come again to a splitting of responsibilities over register. It seems that where the actual written text is concerned there is little difficulty in placing an argument. Deborah Warner agreed to having the mother's words taken out of the daughter's mouth but not to relocating the actress upon the stage within Beckett's proscribed lighting. Similarly, Mike Nichols, the director of the infamous Broadway *Waiting for Godot*, who permitted Robin Williams as Estragon to improvise and adjust Beckett's text where comic potential dictated, was prepared to admit to having perverted Beckett's work in that manner, but not by having located it so overtly in an American environment (the stage being littered with a skull, a tyre and bones). Warner claimed she wanted to "release Beckett for a new generation"; "I have to carry with me the history of my time" she justified (Gussow 1996:103). Nichols argued that "There is no point for Americans to put on English accents or do all the staging that Roger Blin did in Paris. Why?... What we attempted to do was to express Beckett's ideas for acting by Americans" (Ibid.:96) and, of course, they are both correct in these intuitive responses. The difficulty arises when, moving on from these standpoints, a kind of logic dictates that the work of art ought therefore to be freely manipulable, completely distanced from its point of origin. In the words of JoAnne Akalaitis, "when a playwright licenses a work, especially if it's not the première of the play, it's licensed to a director and in a sense it is given over. It's gone" (Oppenheim 1997:137).

This qualifying 'in a sense' does not carry the full weight of the argument. It seems instead to be an avoidance of complexities that the argument might raise. What is certain is that whereas directors are prepared to concede over matters of the printed text, the sculpting of the matter of the second register, the results of their confrontation with the text in the pre-verbal and pre-gestural arena, is construed as being the exclusive territory of the interpretative artist and it is upon this territory that the greater part of the debate in this area has taken place.

Might not some response to the debate be found in consideration of the act of translation? Whereas the translator focuses simultaneously backwards into source language and forwards into target language to give form to his preverbal conceptualisation of the source text, many directors, it seems, pursue a single-direction dynamic away from the written text. Consequently, the manner in which a play is to achieve its expression, through manipulating the forms available within the imaginative vocabulary of a specific culture's theatrical tradition, is often considered very much the concern of directors, scenographers and designers. And yet theatricality can be defined as the successful integration within the spectator of the two described registers, thereby providing a total appreciation of the drama that has unfolded before them. It can be demonstrated that Beckett came quickly to appreciate this phenomenon and more carefully inscribe in his works the manner in which they needed to be presented, to more fully capture the essence of what he strove to express through greater experimentation with theatrical form, with the subject, with the narrative, with presence and absence.

Beckett's plays tackle repeatedly the question of human identity and endeavour. In doing so they offer a critique of the processes of constructing meaning, very often within systems in which enlightenment is related to power, the fragmented human identity being the location of the struggle for tangible knowledge and permanence. It is by foregrounding the theatre's means of generating and investing value in meaning that he in part succeeds in making his artistic statement. In other words, by inscribing the techniques for the second register of formalistic structure within his work, he manages to portray the dilemma and ambiguity of the human struggle to create order within chaotic existence. If you eliminate, undermine or disregard the significance of one side of this equation you dilute or eradicate the other. The plays cannot speak if you alter the voice and, like a house of cards, the delicate balance, if disturbed, flutters to nothing. It is understandable then that Beckett, and his Estate after him, held such a strong grip upon the manner in which his works were to be performed. Not only are his plays precisely constructed expressions of specific concerns, hardly lending themselves to other agendas, but they also contain, within the black ink on white paper of their written texts, the patterns and frameworks for their performance texts. To work against these, it could be argued, is an act of either ignorance or arrogance, let alone disrespect which rarely anyway holds any currency in the theatrical contract. Where form is so artfully integrated into content, where italicized description sits so earnestly alongside the text to be recited in a written work, the place of the director can, arguably, only be one parallel to that of the translator whose function s/he anyway parallels; a sharply receptive artist, a communicator, a transmitter and renderer of thought.

## References

Beckett, Samuel (1952) *En attendant Godot*, Paris: Les Editions de Minuit.
------ (1953) *Warten auf Godot*, Frankfurt am Main: Suhrkamp.
------ (1955) *Molloy*, New York: Grove Press.

------ (1956) *Waiting for Godot*, London: Faber and Faber.

------ (1957a) *Endspiel*, Frankfurt am Main: Suhrkamp.

------ (1957b) *Fin de partie*, Paris: Les Editions de Minuit.

------ (1958) *Endgame*, London: Faber and Faber.

------ (1959a) *La dernière bande*, Paris: Les Editions de Minuit.

------ (1959b) *Krapp's Last Tape*, London: Faber and Faber.

------ (1974) *Das Letzte Band*, Frankfurt am Main: Suhrkamp.

------ (1976) *Footfalls*, London: Faber and Faber.

Brater, Enoch (1994) *The Drama in the Text*, Oxford: Oxford University Press.

Connor, Steven (1989) 'Traduttore, traditore: Samuel Beckett's Translation of *Mercier et Camier*', *Journal of Beckett Studies* (11 and 12).

Garforth, Julian A (1996) 'Translating Beckett's Translations', *Journal of Beckett Studies* 6 (1):49-70.

Gussow, Mel (1996) *Conversations with (and about) Beckett*, London: Nick Hern.

Knowlson, James (ed.) (1992) *The Theatrical Notebooks of Samuel Beckett – 'Endgame'*, London: Faber and Faber.

------ (ed.) (1993) *The Theatrical Notebooks of Samuel Beckett – 'Waiting for Godot'*, London: Faber and Faber.

Oppenheim, Louis (1997) *Directing Beckett*, Michigan: University of Michigan Press.

Pavis, Patrice (1992) trans. Loren Kruger, *Theatre at the Crossroads of Culture*, London: Routledge.

Signal, C. (1988) 'Rehearsal Diary', in Dougald McMillan and M. Fehsenfeld (eds.) *Beckett in the Theatre*, London: John Calder.

Watson, David (1991) *Paradox and Desire in Beckett's Fiction*, London: Macmillan.

# 6    'Priest' from Screen to Stage
## An Adaptation of Jimmy McGovern's Screenplay

LINDSAY BELL

*Abstract.* This essay offers an examination of the adaptation process begun after writing, workshopping and producing a stage adaptation of *Priest* at the University of Alberta in 1996. Aspects of the adaptation/relocation process immediately raise parallels with translation theory: questions of (film-theatre) equivalences; finding solutions to adapting filmic structure and treatment of events into theatrical conventions and narrative techniques; transposition versus adaptation/adoption; justification of artistic/aesthetic choices – the screenwriter's versus the adapter's; freedom to create versus the integrity of the original source; and the issue of ownership. The essay presents an analysis of the challenges and solutions that were discovered in the process, and offers an opportunity for further discussion in applying translation theory to this adaptation process.

What follows is a discussion which stems from my stage adaptation of *Priest*,[1] and the critical challenges discovered in the adaptation process. First of all, I will address the intent and nature of the adaptation: why I was doing it, what was the goal of the project, and what were the major challenges I faced in writing the adaptation. The second critical issue has to do with the challenge of justifying someone else's work and their decisions; do I assume or accept their justification as part of the template I am working from, or do I manipulate the work and discover new justifications that are suited to my adaptation? The third issue, and probably the most difficult to overcome and realize, was the challenge in claiming the work as my own – the process toward owning the work. This latter point elicited further questions regarding the word ***adaptation*** itself; what exactly is an adaptation? Is it a reproduction of a piece in a different medium or language, with everything from the original relatively intact? Or is there room to play and freedom to create in the process of adaptation?

Before I delve into these issues, I will provide an overview of the story-line of the original screenplay *Priest* by Jimmy McGovern. Essentially, *Priest* presents ethical and moral dilemmas, the question of forgiveness and acceptance, and the dichotomy between Christianity and the Catholic Church. There are seven central characters: Father Greg, the protagonist and a young, gay priest, who has just arrived at his first parish; Graham, his lover; Father Matthew, the senior priest at the parish; Maria, the rectory housekeeper and Father Matthew's lover; and the Unsworth's, a prominent family in the parish – Phil, Mary, and their

---

[1] *Priest*, original screenplay by Jimmy McGovern and stage adaptation by Lindsay Bell, was workshopped and performed under the direction of Paul Gelineau at the Department of Drama, University of Alberta, Edmonton, Alberta, February 1997.

fourteen year-old daughter, Lisa. It is revealed that Lisa is a victim of incest. The two central conflicts of the story are: firstly, Father Greg's conflict within himself as a gay man and a Catholic priest, and secondly, the inner struggle he faces when he is obliged to honour the sanctity of Lisa's confession, during which she discloses that she is sexually abused by her father. The first of these conflicts collide when Father Greg and Graham are arrested for what amounts to public indecency, and Father Greg is consequently transferred to an isolated parish in the country where he will 'no longer be a disgrace to the Catholic Church.' In the midst of these events, Mary comes home unexpectedly and discovers the sexual abuse, and later accuses Father Greg of knowing about the abuse and doing nothing to help Lisa.

Throughout *Priest*, Father Greg is caught between his duty as a Christian and the regulations of the Catholic Church. In addition to this, Father Greg's relationship with Father Matthew is divided between two opposite interpretations of the word of God and the role of the priest in society. His initial judgement of Father Matthew and Maria's relationship is later paralleled with the judgement that is cast upon himself by the congregation when his homosexuality is made apparent:

> FATHER MATTHEW [*to the congregation*]: How dare you turn your back on this man [Father Greg]. How dare you do this and call yourselves Catholics. If you are so adamant about judging him, why haven't you judged me all these years? Why?[2]

At this point, Father Greg has returned from the country parish, on the brink of being at peace with himself as a gay, Catholic priest, and seeks forgiveness and acceptance from the congregation. The congregation overtly rejects him and we are left with the final image of the two priests – Fathers Matthew and Greg, and the congregation forming a line to receive communion from Father Matthew. Father Greg stands alone, with an entire congregation refusing to accept him as a priest or communion from him. After a moment, Lisa, in an act of pure forgiveness and acceptance, moves forward to receive communion from Father Greg.

What developed from this original framework was an adaptation that: maintained a majority of the original dialogue; reduced the number of characters and locations and focused mainly on the journeys of the central characters; manipulated and made time and space malleable with dramatic conventions; and changed the setting from Liverpool, England to New Brunswick, Canada. A reduction in the number of characters resulted in a redistribution of dialogue among the remaining characters and the relocation of some of the key events of the story. This process solved some adaptation strategies, such as tapering the scope of the stage version, but problematized others in terms of characters taking on

---

[2] Dialogue from the stage adaptation.

other characters' dialogues, which in turn affects their journey and function in the telling of the story. Through various stage conventions and techniques, the adaptation manipulates time and space in an attempt fully to capture the central conflicts and to find theatrical equivalences. Focusing on the journeys of the central players and exploring the primary conflicts at the heart of the story was the initial step towards constructing the spine of the play. Changing the setting of the story from Liverpool, England to the eastern Canadian city of Fredericton, New Brunswick, provided a familiar foundation from which the adaptation could develop. Fredericton was chosen as it offered several parallels to the setting of the original screenplay as well as presenting an opportunity to explore cross-cultural elements. The relocation of the adaptation invites ensuing shifts in social, political and cultural structures as well as a shift in reception to a Canadian theatre audience. However, I no longer believe that Fredericton was a strong choice, as it does not have the politically or religiously charged environment to support the events of the story. But in saying this, there are no specific geographical signifiers in the play, other than the fact that the dialogue has been 'Canadianized' to a certain extent, and specific British cultural references have been omitted or, in some cases, a Canadian equivalent found.

Addressing the first of the critical issues of my experience in adapting *Priest* for the stage begins with the intent of the adaptation itself. Was the point of the exercise merely to translate the events and characters of the film into another medium? Was the goal to put the film's specific aesthetic on stage? No. Definitely not. So, how was the stage adaptation achieved and through what methodology? The adaptation process from screen to stage hinged upon three key objectives: to reduce the panoramic scope of the film to its essential relationships and conflicts – those to which I referred earlier; to develop a suitable and appropriate structure and aesthetic for the stage; and to exploit the *theatrical* potential in terms of character development (as it differs from film).

Excizing the extraneous material and getting to the heart of the story to locate its dramatic core and the source of the dramatic tension was the primary goal. However, more often than not, a particular character or element of the story-line that was originally thought extraneous, at some point in the process revealed itself to be quite the opposite. Some concerns that arose at this point ultimately questioned the intent of the adaptation. How do you keep the critical elements of the story but exclude the character or characters that elicit that particular part of the story? Is it possible to preserve the *entirety* of the original in the adaptation process, whether it be from novel to film, play to film or film to play? Or, is it inherent in the process of adapting that the end result inevitably fails to capture, to translate, the *original whole* – as though it were a chemical reaction where something is lost in the process. It was a constant struggle to keep the adaptation manageable for a stage production, discovering its possibilities as well as its limitations, apart from the panoramic elements that film can provide. Ultimately, there proved to be a surplus of story elements in the film – pools and eddies of story-lines that I considered vital and necessary for the stage adaptation. It became impossible to include all of them, nor was it the intent of the adaptation to do so.

Starting at a different point in the story than the film does, was the first window I opened within the performance text. Framing the stage version with a collage of elements that are incorporated throughout the play and are a distinct departure from the film established a sense of autonomy. The film begins with a community-wide preparation for Father Greg's arrival in the parish. The stage version takes a step backwards in time, to Greg's ordination and introduces four characters – Lisa, Mary, Phil, and Graham – who are to be the most profoundly affected by his role as a priest. These four characters are not physically in attendance at the ordination, but rather, they are symbolically present and they embody the knowledge and experiences they will have acquired by the end of the play – who they become in relation to Greg as a man and as a priest: Lisa, in a state of grace and forgiveness; Mary, unable to forgive; Phil, convicted sexual offender; and Graham, his lover. The Prologue then, introduces the beginning and the end, the present and the future, which meet and share the same space. It also introduces Father Ellerton, who is retiring and is replaced by Greg in the parish.

## PROLOGUE

*Opening music: Gregorian Chants*
*GREG's ordination: FATHER GREG lies prostrate on the floor of the sanctuary, arms outstretched, in the shape of the cross. The BISHOP presides. The music fades and a collage of four voices (GRAHAM, MARY, PHIL) begin to recite the Lord's Prayer as they enter; leading these voices is a young girl singing the prayer (LISA).*
LISA: (*Entering, singing*) Our Father, who art in heaven, hallowed be thy name. Thy kingdom come, thy will be done, on Earth as it is in heaven. Give us this day, our daily bread, and forgive us our trespasses, as we forgive those who trespass against us, and lead us not into temptation, but deliver us from evil. For ever and ever.
*GRAHAM, begins the prayer after LISA's "hallowed be thy name." MARY, and PHIL follow in a similarly staggered manner.*
*As the prayers begin, the BISHOP begins the ceremony.*
BISHOP: That you bless these elect. We beg you to hear us. That you bless and sanctify these elect. We beg you to hear us. (*Chanting*) That you bless and sanctify and consecrate these elect. We beg you to hear us.
GREG: (*Kneeling*) Lord, have mercy. Christ, have mercy. Lord, have mercy.
*The BISHOP places both hands on GREG's head for a moment, signifying the 'transfer of power'.*
BISHOP: My brethren, let us implore God the Father almighty to multiply his heavenly gift in this servant of his whom he has chosen for the office of

the priesthood. May he fulfil by his grace the office he receives by his goodness; through Christ our Lord.

BISHOP *and* GREG: Amen.

*LISA repeats the song once, GRAHAM, MARY, PHIL repeat the prayer, again in a staggered manner, as they recede and exit. GREG kisses the BISHOP's ring. The BISHOP exits.*

GREG: (*Praying*) Lord, make me an instrument of your peace: where there is hatred let me sow love, where there is injury let me sow pardon, where there is doubt let me sow faith, where there is despair let me give hope, where there is darkness let me give light, where there is sadness let me give joy.

*The lights come up on FATHER ELLERTON, who is on the cross.*

GREG: (*Continuing.*) O Divine Master, grant I may not try to be comforted but to comfort, not to be understood but to understand, not try to be loved but to love. Because it is in giving that we receive, it is in forgiving that we are forgiven, and it is in dying that we are born to eternal life. Amen. (*He reverently removes his vestments as he exits.*)

*A primal scream erupts from FATHER ELLERTON as he collapses.*

As the scope of the play was tapered, the structure of the adaptation began to settle into place, which at first sounds advantageous, but problems quickly surfaced. Scripts with fast, short, cinematic scene structures have always captured my attention – such as Sally Clark's *Moo*,[3] or Judith Thompson's *I Am Yours*[4] – and as a result, I found the adaptation taking on a similar structure. The cinematic scene structure of *Priest* was the very thing I was trying to adapt, and yet, it was appearing on the page. As a result, the 'filmic' structure remains the central criticism of the adaptation despite my efforts to create a 'stage' structure in which the play would live without the residue of its progenitor. Discovering and incorporating dramatic conventions as possible film-theatre equivalences, and manipulating time and space were two of the strategies employed to overcome some of the cinematic structural influences of the film. More exploration, or metamorphosis, is needed, however, to cast off the remaining cinematic influences.

One example of the manipulation of time and space strategy is what I called a *trialogue* – in which there are two different points in time and space presented simultaneously on stage, with one character (Greg) linking the two separate dimensions. Greg functions as the fulcrum, and Graham and Matthew are at opposite poles. This section operates through an interchange of questions asked in one time/space and answered in the other; it provided a useful segue and introduced an aesthetic element.

---

[3] Clark, Sally (1989) *Moo*, Toronto: Playwrights Canada Press.
[4] Thompson, Judith (1989) *I Am Yours*, in *The Other Side of the Dark: Four Plays*, Toronto: Coach House Press.

*A few hours later, early morning at the rectory. GREG enters the rectory and is somewhat agitated and dishevelled. GRAHAM's presence/existence still lingers in GREG's mind such that GRAHAM remains where he was at the end of the previous scene.*
MATTHEW *enters.*
MATTHEW: You switched the light off in the hall.
GREG: Yes?
MATTHEW: Yes, well, I always keep it on at night – "At my window a little light will keep burning, All may come in, The arms of a friend are waiting."
GREG: Tammy Wynette?
MATTHEW: It's John 23, actually.
GRAHAM: Are you a Catholic?
MATTHEW: Do you want to talk?
GRAHAM: It takes one to know one.
GREG: No, thanks.
GRAHAM: Do you want to stay?
GREG: Maybe another time. I'm kind of tired.
MATTHEW: Are you sure?
GRAHAM: Yeah, maybe another time.
GREG: Thanks, though.
MATTHEW: Of course. OK. Good-night. (*Exits.*)
GREG: Good-night.
GRAHAM: Good-night.

The characterization in Jimmy McGovern's original film initially captured my interest in tackling this project. However, I found it necessary for the adaptation to take some of the characters a step further, psychologically, than what is seen in the film. Specifically, I explored some possibilities for four of the central characters: Father Greg, Father Matthew, Graham and Lisa. Realizing their potential created an expressionistic telling of Father Greg's story. This is demonstrated most clearly in the adaptation's 'nightmare scene,' which is a collage of characters and voices that taunt, distort, and magnify Father Greg's mental and emotional state. The combined effect on Father Greg of knowing Lisa's situation, not knowing what to do about Father Matthew's relationship with Maria or his own relationship with Graham, augments the dramatic tension and the nightmare became a focal point for several conflicts to collide. Fragments of dialogue gather momentum until they become disconnected from their original speaker, and the characters begin to appropriate dialogue from each other, which further distorts the telling of the story.

*The lights dim. There is an indiscernible eeriness. GREG is sleeping.*
*LISA enters.*
LISA: He makes me do things.
GRAHAM: I came here to see you.
MATTHEW: Are you judging me?

PHIL: That's my girl.

NAOMI: We love each other.

MARY: It could be an adolescent thing.

LISA: My dad.

*MATTHEW enters.*

MATTHEW: When I was in South America, you had to have a woman.

*GRAHAM enters.*

GRAHAM: Are we going to see each other again?

*MARY enters.*

MARY: Apparently it happens to kids her age.

*NAOMI enters.*

NAOMI: If you're going to judge, you should know all the facts.

*PHIL enters.*

PHIL: Hey, you OK?

*ELLERTON enters.*

ELLERTON: Nobility, even in defeat.

LISA: He makes me do all sorts of things.

MARY: If I'm not with her, Phil is.

MATTHEW: That's what made me become a priest.

NAOMI: I seduced him, he didn't seduce me.

PHIL: What brought it on?

GRAHAM: Are you a Catholic?

*Pause.*

*Their voices begin to overlap until they are speaking all at once, building in momentum and intensity.*

NAOMI: He makes me do things.

LISA: I came here to see you.

GRAHAM: That's my girl.

MARY: Are you judging me?

PHIL: We love each other.

MATTHEW: It could be an adolescent thing.

GRAHAM: My dad.

NAOMI: Apparently it happens to kids her age.

ELLERTON: When I was in South America you had to have a woman.

MATTHEW: Hey, you OK?

MARY: Are we going to see each other again?

LISA: Nobility, even in defeat.

PHIL: If you're going to judge, you should know all the facts.

ALL: I came here to see you.

MATTHEW: That's my girl.

NAOMI: My dad.

MARY: He makes me do things.

LISA: We love each other.

GRAHAM: Nobility, even in defeat.

PHIL: It could be an adolescent thing.
ELLERTON: Are you judging me?
LISA: I seduced him he didn't seduce me.
NAOMI: He makes me do all sorts of things.
MATTHEW: If I'm not with her, Phil is.
MARY: What brought it on?
GRAHAM: That's my girl.
PHIL: Are we going to see each other again?
MATTHEW: Greg, are you alright?
*Isolated from the other voices.*
LISA: Incest is human. It's the most natural thing in the world.
*Waking up, a primal scream erupts from GREG. Blackout.*

Father Matthew's character in the adaptation is developed a step further to reinforce and solidify his socialist beliefs. As a result, we gain a clearer justification for Father Greg's decision to return to the parish at the end due to the persuasive argument put forth by Father Matthew:

FATHER MATTHEW: When are you going to realize that you can't be that idealistic priest you want to be until you start facing some truths about yourself. How long are you going to deny who you are underneath those pristine vestments of yours? Until you stop denying who you are, you will stay out here in the middle of nowhere, getting a dollar for every mass you say and not being allowed out after dark.

The character of Graham and his relationship with Father Greg was difficult to develop beyond what is established in the film. The importance of their relationship to each other by the end of the film is not apparent, I would argue, nor is it justified by the preceding events. In a conversation with Jimmy McGovern shortly after the production of the stage version, I learned that the film director, Antonia Bird, while shooting, found a more committed relationship between Father Greg and Graham than that which existed in the original screenplay. This *found* relationship between Father Greg and Graham no doubt contributed to my own, and the actors', struggles to justify their relationship throughout the writing and workshopping of the play – it was not the original intention of their character development or their relationship, it wasn't part of the initial psychological make-up, but was imposed upon them part-way through their journey. To partially remedy this and provide an indication of the strength of their relationship, the adaptation includes a 'good-bye' scene between Father Greg and Graham, during which Graham asks a resonating question: "Tell me Greg, is it wrong for you the man, or wrong for you the priest? How can it be wrong to love?" With Graham voicing his love for Father Greg in this scene, their relationship acquires and demonstrates a greater emotional investment and serves to support their actions and motivations throughout the rest of the play.

With respect to Lisa, her character seemed more open to possibilities of development than did the others. The addition of Lisa's monologue to the stage adaptation gives a psychological dimension to Lisa's reality as a victim of sexual abuse and of epileptic seizures. This monologue and the nightmare scene represent the largest steps I took away from the original film. The idea for the monologue was inspired by Canadian playwright Judith Thompson, who speaks openly about her history of epilepsy. What I found most intriguing was how she remembered the seizure, as opposed to blacking-out, which tends to be more common. Many of the primal fears that she reveals so vividly in her plays find their origin in what she remembers experiencing during her seizures. In terms of Lisa, I found that her own seizure-world was worth exploring. Much like Father Greg's nightmare scene, Lisa's monologue becomes a window into her emotional, mental, and physical trauma, and through this window, the horrific and devastating reality of her situation is unveiled. The monologue reinforces the dilemma Father Greg faces – the conflict between his natural impulse to help Lisa versus the rules and regulations of the Catholic Church, which forbid his interference. By this point in the play, Lisa has told Father Greg of the incest in confession, but she has denied him permission to tell anyone. Later, in her religion class at school, taught by Father Greg, she has a seizure. The following monologue occurs immediately after she comes out of the seizure:

> LISA: I ... I don't blackout ... like I'm supposed to ... I don't tell the doctors though ... I let them think I'm ... that I'm ... normal ... when it happens ... I remember everything ... and it's ... it's always ... the same ... kinda like a dream world or something ... a place that I just ... end up in ... somehow ... and he's ... he's always there ... I mean it's all black ... and I can't see anything ... but he's there ... somewhere ... in the darkness ... I don't know how I know that he's there he just is and I try to run away but I can't move ... and I want to scream but nothing comes out of my mouth ... but ... other times ... it's weird 'cause other times ... I can move ... and I run and ...and all I can think of is Hide! Hide! Now! ... and then it ... then it just gets worse ... and it feels ... feels like I'm underwater and it's dark ... even darker than before ... and I'm near the bottom ... way down deep ... near the bottom and everything is in slow motion or something but I still feel as though he's there ... in the black water ... and I can't work my way through the water to get away ... 'cause I'm not strong enough ... and the water ... the water ... it isn't like water somehow ... it's more like thick-wet-cement or something ... so I have to stay where I am ... and this is when ... if I look up ... up through the water ... I can see a faint light ... it's blue ... a faint blue light ... way up ... up above me ... and I think ... if I-could-only-get to that blue light everything would be ok and I begin to feel like I can breathe again – like it all washes over me and goes away ... but sometimes ... it's like ... it's like I don't want to get to the light ... like I don't want to come up for air ... I just want to stay there ... and let him catch me ... 'cause then ... I mean ... if he did catch me it would be all over ... wouldn't it? I would be dead ... right?

Another difficult aspect of the adaptation process I encountered has to do with justifying someone else's work and their decisions – in this case, the writer Jimmy McGovern's, and the director Antonia Bird's. I have already mentioned the struggle to justify Father Greg and Graham's relationship, and how their relationship was discovered while shooting the film and not part of the original screenplay. Taking the film as a template and working with the relationships, character motivations, and situations as they were in the film, often presented a challenge to justify these decisions – not only to myself, but to the director, the actors, and ultimately to the audience as well. So vivid is the original film, the actual *development* of the adaptation was – in terms of character, structure and dramatic tension – hindered, restricted, and overshadowed by the potent original source. In many instances, the remedy was in evoking and adhering to the *theatrical* potential of the piece rather than adopting, conceding to, or assuming the justifications of the original work. Employing my own aesthetics, and inevitably my own prejudices in the 'translating' process, the process became one of questioning the film as a reliable source to tell Greg's story, and finding alternative methods, avenues, currents, colours, tempos, through which to tell the story in a stage performance.

Closely related to the struggle to justify character actions and motivations was my struggle to *own* the work – to claim it as mine. I think the premise of adapting is both liberating and confining at the same time. It provides a playground, but it can also debilitate one's imagination to play within that ground. Considering the overwhelming visual impact of the film, adapting from screen to stage presented enormous barriers to my imagination as I searched for my own aesthetic – sequence of events, rhythm, narrative, performance issues. When I was finally able to create, outside the scope of the original, when I was out from under the shadow of the film and was able to take the characters in a new direction, add a new dimension and flesh out their story – only then did I claim the work as my own. I played with dramatic conventions and concepts of time and space as a solution to film-theatre equivalences – often overlapping these devices and creating an expressionistic world in which to show the audience Father Greg, his thoughts and his nightmares. The additions or embellishments in character development, as with Lisa, helped me to claim the adaptation as something beyond the film and different from it. However, I think there is still much ground to be discovered including endless possibilities of theatrical potential.

All this said, there are a series of questions that have been left somewhat unresolved regarding the adaptation process itself – textbook answers to which I am not sure exist. If the original work is considered a template, how much freedom of creativity exists in the actual adaptation/translation process, or must one resign oneself to the confines and the scope prescribed by the original work? Is that first step away from the template, to discover and uncover new ground, warranted? What parallels can be drawn between the director's concept of a play and the adaptation process? Are not all 'acts of theatre' actually acts of adaptation/translation – from written text to performance text? How many steps is the adapter (director, translator) allowed to deviate away from the original and still remain within the realm of adaptation or, how many steps does it take before it ceases to be an adaptation and becomes something else? Is there a specific point at which the integrity of the text is in jeopardy? Is there a line? What or who governs this line? How do you know when it is violated? Or is it merely a matter of critical opinion versus artistic licence?

At this point, after the performance of the adaptation, and with a much wiser retrospective view, I see adaptation as a process of opening windows – finding windows of opportunity in the original work to create, to play, and to discover the freedom that I think adaptation into a different medium deserves. And I say this with the utmost respect for the integrity of the original work. I regard the film as a template, but I think it governed, restricted, and inhibited the direction of where I wanted the play to go – which is perhaps, the most significant challenge and also the inherent trap in the adaptation process.

## Acknowledgements

Canada Council for the Arts, and Alberta Foundation for the Arts for their finantial support to participate in the *True to Form: On Stage Translation* conference. Special thanks to Paul Gelineau, Jimmy McGovern and Leah Schmidt.

# 7    Valle-Inclán: The Meaning of Form

DAVID JOHNSTON

*Abstract.* This essay draws upon the experience of writing versions of three plays by Ramón del Valle-Inclán for very different productions on stage and radio: *Bohemian Lights*, *The Barbarous Comedies*, and *Divine Words*. It considers decisions taken at verbal level to accommodate the demands of different production styles. More importantly, it examines strategies used in all three adaptations and productions, chiefly of radical relocation to an Irish milieu, to re-create the form and impact of Valle's highly distinctive *esperpento* form. The conclusion is that while verbal adequacy and theatrical appropriateness are at odds, it is still possible across a variety of productions to remain faithful to the spirit and form of Valle's innovative and eminently challenging vision, through a process of 'transubstantiation'.

It is now commonly accepted amongst those who translate drama that the translator has a responsibility for enabling the play to be reconcretized as a play rather than for solely translating the words as text.[1] This is a loyalty that is clearly experiential and dramatic rather than primarily linguistic and literary, and it marks a general professional move away from a closed authorially-dominated view towards translational activity being understood in terms of the functioning of a reception aesthetics. My adaptations of Lope, Calderón, García Lorca, for example, no less than my stage version of *Don Quijote*, where one might have expected to encounter a higher degree of second-writer visibility, have all been written on that basis. I have been led, almost inexorably, to the view that there is no reasonable basis from which to assert, either theoretically or practically, the translatability of the playtext.[2] Where performability is an informing objective of the exercise, some measure at least of adaptation is inescapable. Such transubstantiation of the literal original will clearly arise from the need to negotiate culture-specific icons, motifs, discourses, speech-patterns, and the like, but also, perhaps more intangibly, from the requirement to ensure that the impact and range of meanings implicit in the original, and which are only fully decoded through performance, may be similarly decoded in English-language performance. Given the current flurry of terminology coined latterly to describe

---

[1] Our first approach to the play is, of course, through the verbal text. But subsequently all too often it is the verbal text which is allowed to stand for the play as a whole. This approach is widespread in the work of drama specialists in Modern Languages and English Studies especially (See Short in Carter and Simpson 1989:141).

[2] Newmark attempts to make a cut-and-dried (but still influential) distinction between translation and adaptation when he writes that "when a play is transferred from the source to the target-language culture, it is usually no longer a translation, but an adaptation" (Newmark 1988:173).

different views of translation, I should perhaps confess that I use the word 'transubstantiation' with tongue somewhat in cheek, although the theological implications of turning the accidentals of one experience into the essentials of another is perhaps a good way of describing a dynamic approach to culture-specific terms. Moreover, it reminds us that if there is any ultimate truth in what we are about, it lies in the here and now reality of a theatre audience, its perceptions cleansed and directed towards that otherness of experience which is the play. The truth resides in the experience of theatre, which is in itself open to constant revision, and not in a process of translation which all too often can be easily ascribed to mechanistic notions of the relationship between source and target languages.

In 1993, as London's Gate Theatre was casting about for ways of enriching its already considerable repertoire of European plays, I suggested to the then-Artistic Director, Laurence Boswell, that we should consider the possibility of producing Valle-Inclán's *Bohemian Lights* (written in 1920 but denied its first two professional productions even in Spain until 1972 and 1988).[3] It is a play which, as a Hispanist, I knew to be both startlingly innovative and linguistically demanding. As a translator, therefore, I found myself in the presence of a dramatist whose use of language was not simply original or demanding. It was the defining element of his theatre; it was what gave his theatre both meaning and form. The richly imagistic language of Federico García Lorca's theatre, for example, is of course a defining element of his plays. His work is expressed through a highly cohesive grammar of images, and preserving the integrity of this in translation becomes the prime linguistic responsibility of his translator. But this linguistic responsibility is still subservient to the experiential loyalty of re-creating the extraordinary complicity which, more than language itself, is the defining element of Lorca's emotive tragedies – the verbal fidelity of some readily-available translations of these plays provides ineloquent confirmation of this view.[4] The complicity which derives from Lorca's tragic sense will, in performance of course, be confirmed through audience experience – empathy, enrichment, catharsis. All of this, however, remains much more difficult to assess in the world of Valle-Inclán, in terms both of generic labelling and of audience engagement. His greatest plays – among them *Bohemian Lights*, the trilogy of *The Barbarous Comedies*, and *Divine Words* – freewheel between tragic nobility, melodramatic pathos and macabre humour. Their energy derives from mutually competing discourses, registers and character motivations that are frequently operative even within the same speech, and which confound any attempt to empathise wholly with the characters, or for that matter to be totally distanced from them. I found that draft upon draft of my *Bohemian Lights*, while

---

[3] For a brief performance history of Valle-Inclán's theatre, see Zahareas and Gillespie 1976. In the event, the authors' optimism as to Valle-Inclán's immediate prospects on the English-language stage was to prove, at the very least, premature.

[4] See, for example, the 1998 special issue of *Donaire*, dedicated to translations of Lorca.

picking its way through the maze of culture-specific references with some relative success, still clunked with the dull woodenness of 'translationese'. In other words, *Bohemian Lights* required not solely cultural mediation and theatrical reconcretization; its very intelligibility as a piece of theatre depended upon finding an appropriate texture and context for its highly distinctive language use. If cultural relocation is a useful recourse in that it enables the translator, or second writer, to develop a coherent working metaphor for the dramatic body of the play, the human truths and conflicts which underlie the clothing of the verbal text, in the case of Valle-Inclán such a transubstantiation seemed to me to be the only way of ensuring the coherence of the tones, counterpoints and dissonances of Valle's carefully orchestrated verbal music.[5]

Valle is, perhaps above all, a writer who remains one of the most disruptive and experimental of Spain's twentieth-century dramatists. In his most innovative pieces, the *esperpentos*, he subjects the syntax of stage language to a degree of fragmentation that is immediately suggestive of the fractured discourse of the theatre of the absurd and the problematic speech of characters like those of Edward Albee. This is a language which emphasizes disfluency. In common with much of the dialogue of Ionesco or Arrabal, it foregrounds primal speech organized more through rhythmic patterns than discursive strategies, so that in the final analysis the Spanish-speaking spectator of a Valle play, in particular of the *esperpento*-type plays, is aware of presencing a major linguistic event in which the energy of the piece derives more from its linguistic clothing than its deeper dramatic structures or the interaction of its characters. These are plays which generate linguistic fireworks rather than verbal illumination.

Critics have tended, with some justification, to describe the *esperpento* in terms of a formal aesthetic, as announced by the blind and dying poet Max Estrella in the seminal Scene Twelve of *Bohemian Lights*. Traditionally denoting a person of abnormal appearance or an absurd or foolish thing, the word is used here to coin a new aesthetic which, in the style of Goya's *Caprichos*, *Disparates* and *Black Paintings*, emphasizes the grotesque and the de-formed (here the hyphenation is absolutely valid).[6] The *esperpento* is a looking-glass which is itself distorted and which, in consequence, like a concave fairground mirror, creates an image that is a systematic de-formation, or satirical caricature, of whatever is revealed within. But Valle's view of the *esperpentic* in human affairs is most fundamentally rooted in his sense of the huge mismatch between the lowly depths of human motivation and the outer reaches of our linguistic pretensions. In *Bohemian Lights* Max Estrella and his disreputable crony, Don

---

[5] It is one of the central propositions of this article that through this richly polyphonic stage language, Valle-Inclán is not only questioning the apparently unified nature of any given lexical culture, but is also adumbrating the broadened and increasingly destabilized concept of what constitutes the performative (Introduction to Campbell 1996: esp. 3-4).
[6] For a detailed analysis of the genesis and range of meanings implicit in the idea of the *esperpento*, see Lyon 1983, and Keown and Warner 1991.

Latino de Hispalis, wend their drunken way through a Madrid 'alive with hunger and strife', a labyrinthine world of tall-talk, flaring rhetoric and inflammatory discourse as richly evocative of the vicious circularity of Spanish history and politics as is Flann O'Brien's *The Third Policeman* of Irish life.

Both *The Third Policeman* and *Bohemian Lights* are centrally concerned with portraying the limitations of established discourses in the face of the onslaught of life at its most un-formed and chaotic, arguably at its most real, certainly at its most invasive. In the case of the Irish novel, it is the discourse of the rational which is first satirized and then pitilessly destroyed, in great part through the device of the footnotes which the narrator appends to his magical-realist story. In the Spanish play, it is the discourse of the classical, the voice of the aristocrat of letters Max Estrella, with his initial faith in the redemptive and ennobling power of art, which shatters under the pressure of a modern experience strung between the twin poles of rage and powerlessness. The naming of the *esperpento* in Scene Twelve of *Bohemian Lights* clearly creates a very complex problem of stage translation. It marks the most explicit moment at which language mirrors formlessness, just as in O'Brien's novel the Policeman's explanation of the molecular energy which constitutes the essence of sheep reflects most acutely O'Brien's sense of the meaningless whirl which is the human condition.[7] For Valle-Inclán and O'Brien alike there were always the compensatory attractions of bohemian living. But their artistic legacy is a language as jagged and contradictory as human life, as resonant and as ultimately dishonest as our pretensions to understand or make sense of any of it. *Bohemian Lights* is therefore much more than an *ars artis*; it is Valle-Inclán's nostalgia-tinged declaration that the dreams of the old order are dead and that language should no longer suggest spurious arrangements of experience or mimic non-existent patterns in our living, but should instead re-create both the energy of life and its drift, its contradictory condition both as free talk and as mirror of the determinant forces of our history and geography.

The *esperpento* therefore refers to a sort of framed activity, in which the foreground is occupied by the dislocations operative in characters' lives while the background is set by an instantly recognizable, if caricatured, history (much in the way, for example, that we at the turn of the millennium might talk about the Thatcher years). If we accept such dislocations, therefore, as being the idiosyncrasies inherited from a particular time and place, Valle's characters are foregrounded as caricatures of their moment and culture, consciously modelled stage-creations in the dualist way that such a phrase might be understood in Ireland if applied to characters like Captain Boyle and Joxer Daly. Indeed, this male double-act in *Juno and the Paycock* functions in a similar way to that of Max Estrella and Don Latino de Hispalis in *Bohemian Lights*, in that it establishes dialogue as central to and not solely descriptive or creative of the dramatic

---

[7] See Johnston 1998a. This earlier piece can be read as preparatory in several ways to the present article.

action (this was one of the reasons, among others, that I eventually chose to set my version of *Bohemian Lights* in the Dublin of 1915, just one year before the Easter Rising, the moment at which Irish modernity is born through violence, subsequently to be maintained through caricature).[8] The multiple truths and un-truths of any situation are presented simultaneously in the dialectic established between the double-act, distracting attention from any character interaction in terms of psychology and leading us instead into a Beckettian world of language games, the shadow talk that fills the gap between individuals' inadequacy and the disproportionate demands made upon them by history or culture. The other groups of characters who surround Max and Don Latino, and who in the Galician *esperpentos* function Synge-like as an ageless community voice, serve to high-light the historical, social and cultural context within which such language games operate, but in the foreground is Valle-Inclán's love of the word, the word as sound, stripped of virtually all conceptual meaning, and orchestrated through the surrounding patterns of fortune-telling canaries, talking parrots, barking dogs, squeaking mice and ultimately, in *Divine Words*, the pathetic grunts of a hydrocephalic child whose grotesque fate it is to die of alcoholic poisoning.

What does this mean for the putative translator of Valle-Inclán's *esperpentos*, plays which foreground problematic speech as the correlative of a dysfunctional society, an intrusive history and a grotesque culture? Firstly, the translator has to find a way of re-creating the tensions along which this dialogue functions. On one hand, it is the shared language of a community – in *Bohemian Lights* of post-Bolshevik Madrid, in plays like *The Barbarous Comedies* and *Divine Words* of a Galician community spatially rather than temporally defined (in the manner of Synge's depiction of the West of Ireland). On the other hand, that shared language is not comfortably familial, but through its bewildering range of com-peting discourses and its recourse to a whole series of disruptive devices – from simple literary and philosophical echoings to deviant usages and neologisms – it reflects a community internally divided along the fault lines of history – in *Bohemian Lights*, dispossession and empowerment, in the Galician *esperpentos*, feudal religion and superstitious paganism.

In this way, the stage language of Valle-Inclán's later plays is a poetry lo-cated in the extremes of humour and despair, a Beckettian 'speaking slabber' free of all immediately recognizable attachments. Yet it also contrives to con-tinue a dialogue between the individual seen as a Bosch-like repository of unchanging sin and as a creature ruthlessly determined by time and place. Re-turning to the notion of stage-audience complicity, this means that Valle's *esperpentos* are, in terms of their emotional exactment, in part high drama as individuals push beyond the frontiers of their inherited morality, in part mere shadow or puppet shows as the same characters are tossed helplessly on the tidal waves of tradition, history and moral expediency. It is precisely in this way

---

[8] Press criticism was interestingly divided as to the validity of such a recourse (For an overview, see Johnston 1996).

that the *esperpentos* mount their concerted assault on the conventional grammar of engagement, without seeking to be wholly distancing either (although some critics have indeed seen Valle as a sort of precursor of Brechtian epic style). Seamus Heaney, writing of talk round the family table in County Derry, describes the effect which the translator of Valle might wish to achieve. Here, when community identity is threatened by inappropriate use of language, the speaker will re-think 'and decently relapse into the wrong grammar which kept us allied and at bay'. The Spanish audience of a Valle play is allied through the dramatist's ear, tuned to the linguistic codes of the instantly recognisable traditions and forces of national life, but is also held at bay by the fracturing of these codes and the distortion of these traditions.

It is precisely this goal of the very specific mapping of cultural identity through language which leads Valle-Inclán to assert the uniqueness (and therefore untranslatability) of theatre.[9] What strategies can the translator adopt to cope with this very complex orchestrating of a language so organically expressive of a cultural identity in which the individual is both located and dislocated, an expressiveness that is in every way emblematic of the *esperpentic* vision? In the case of Lorca, for example, once the translator recognizes the emotional force upon which the stage-audience complicity of plays like *Blood Wedding* depend, it is a relatively simple matter to forge a coherent voice for Lorca in English (Johnston 1998b). With Valle's *esperpentos*, however, in which the complicity sits astride a difficult and at times uncomfortable tension of simultaneous engagement and distance, the translator must develop a stage language which will enable the audience to feel 'this concerns me after all' without allowing elements of distancing to be experienced as merely puzzling.[10] In other words, although Valle's stage language is driven by internal contradictions, and assaulted and battered by stylistic violence, audiences do not experience it in a piecemeal way. It is a new, indeed unique, stage language; but it is also a coherent one.

This essay has thus far centred upon the translator's analysis of how the language of Valle's *esperpentos* provides their central form. Language is not simply a vehicle. It is foregrounded both as aesthetic and as dramatic action. Consequently, the audience's experience of the play comes centrally through language, and more specifically from the disconcerting and jarring variety of discourses employed in any one scene. Valle's stage directions are an integral part of this language experience. These are essentially pieces of poetic prose in which the dramatist, largely resigned to the perceived unperformability of his

---

[9] Both Lorca and the Spanish philosopher Ortega y Gasset were voicing similar doubts as to the possibility of translation (in terms of the search for semantic equivalence) at around the same time.

[10] This is an adaptation of Gabriel Marcel's famous aphorism that "it is through the emotions that we discover that 'this concerns me after all'". It has always seemed to me an absolutely perfect defence of Aristotelian theatre, if such a defence is called for.

plays, is doing two things: firstly, he is linguistically framing the action (and through that, incidentally, attempting to set down the performance conditions for a new theatre), and, secondly, he is engaging in his creative imagination with the new challenges of the visual language of cinematography. In all of the versions of Valle-Inclán plays I have written I have therefore tried to incorporate some of the stage directions into the audience's experience of the play. In *Bohemian Lights* (1993:35), for example, members of the cast themselves delivered parts of the stage directions, creating from the outset the sense of a choral Dublin voice. Here is an example taken from Scene Four in which the drunken Max Starr (Estrella) and his outrageous companion Don Latino (in my version Captain Sweeney) search for a late-opening bar in trouble-torn Dublin:

> *Night. Maximus Cornelius Starr and Captain Sweeney stagger arm in arm along a lonely street. The smell of violence lingers on the air, signs of it are all around: smashed bottles, windows and doors closed and boarded-up. A weak greenish light shivers from those few lamps still lit, while the moon shines onto the tenement roofs, plunging one side of the street into darkness. Every now and then the road rumbles, as though with the approach of a train, as yet another patrol or armoured convoy passes nearby. Shadows of soldiers and of police. Archetypal. The sense of centuries' violence. As the swing doors of the Palace Bar open and close, a triangle of yellow light spills onto the pavement. Max and Sweeney, drunk under the moon, scholars staggering along a line of streetlights, are drawn irresistibly towards it.*

In the case of *Divine Words*, which is set in Galicia, and which was commissioned by BBC Radio Drama, the need to render these elements linguistically visible was even more pressing. By developing a character in the play into a narrator, I tried to develop a device which would not only re-create the potent sense of the oral tradition (with its implicit idea of language in self-conscious performance) from which much of Valle's work derives, but which would also further immerse the listener (in this case) in Valle's language-rich world. Here is a very simple example taken from near the beginning of the play. The first quotation is from Maria Delgado's published translation (1993:10), which follows the original with a high degree of fidelity. The stage directions at the start of Act One, Scene Two read thus:

> *A clump of trees at the side of the road. There, half-hidden amongst the shadows, with her flowered handkerchief open, JUANA LA REINA can be seen begging. Her idiot son LAUREANO, smothered in the cart's straw mattress and patched blankets, groans and grimaces in his accustomed manner.*

My version reads thus (the direction 'close' refers to the quality of voice necessary for distinguishing the narrator from the other characters):

BASTIAN *Close*: That's when I saw Juana. There she was, sort of slumped under a big tree at the side of the road just outside the town, with her flowery handkerchief lyin' open in front of the idjit boy, him with his big jelly head poking out from the cart pullin' faces. And her the colour o' death.[11]

Working for radio encouraged a virtue to be born out of necessity. In this oral tradition the language of narration is presented both as memory and as performance. The final line 'and her the colour of death' has not been gratuitously appended, but rather serves to bathe this and subsequent scenes in a situational pathos which is instantly undermined by the harsher edges of a language more concerned with performance than empathy. The rhetorical juxtaposition of "him with his big jelly head poking out from the cart pullin' faces" with "And her the colour o' death" is an example of a stage voice which vies simultaneously to distance and to engage.

This strategy of verbal visibility required considerable adaptation of the opening scene of the play, as the following examples will show. Once again, the first quotation is taken from Delgado (1993:5):

*San Clemente [...] A village church [...] Under the Romanesque portico PEDRO GAILO, the sexton, is snuffing out the burning candles. He appears a funereal old man [...] He shakes his fingers, attempting to blow off the gathered soot on his fingertips, and then finally wipes them on the pillars of the portico. His gestures are awkward, his speech is at times incoherent, and he can be frequently seen talking to himself.*
PEDRO GAILO: They come and just throw themselves on the road, staring at the altar, wandering from one place to another, lazy blighters! I wouldn't wipe the floor with them! A bunch of good for nothings. Causing havoc wherever they go! Look where they've planted themselves! Scum of the earth! People who don't work and spend their lives on the road! ...
*PEDRO GAILO wipes his forehead and the four remaining hairs on his head stand on end. His squinting eyes look out towards the road where two travellers are resting; a man and a woman with a small child, the fruit of their lust [...] The woman is known by different names [...] Although her partner's true identity is another enigma, she calls him Lucero [...]*
LUCERO: As for that brat, we'd be best off dumping him at the next place we kip for the night.

The various verbal strategies employed in this opening scene of *Divine Words* – ranging from the evocation of the ancient stone church (the cultural framework in which action and characters are located) to the lyrical intensity of Pedro's dislike for the beggars, expressed in a flow of imprecation for which Valle thought Spanish to be particularly well suited (the functioning of a dislocation, in this case, a caste mentality) – require careful negotiation so as to avoid fragmenting

---

[11] First broadcast on BBC Radio 3, 15 March 1998, directed by Kate Rowland.

the language world so richly evoked by Valle. Here is my version of the opening scene. Once again, verbal visibility is a paramount consideration.

> *A Latin mass, echoing between ancient stone walls. It fades.*
> BASTIAN *Close*: That's how it started, I remember that. God knows, I don't know how I've managed to forget so much ... after all, some of it was me own doing, God forgive me ... but it was a long time ago ... a lifetime ... *Music fades in and out as he speaks.* I can still see Pedro Gailo though. Muttering his way round San Clemente after mass, snuffing out the candles and wiping his fingers on them big stone columns. Jasus, he was a peculiar man even then. Everyone always knew him for a cantankerous auld shite... but afterwards there was them that thought he should have been made a saint. Him a saint. They even asked me to speak to the Bishop. I wasn't having any of it but.
> *Resonant footsteps drawing near. Muttering.*
> BASTIAN: Is that you finished for the day Pedro? It's as well for some.
> PEDRO: God almighty! You scared the divil out of me! What are you doing here Bastian, hanging around an empty church when every God-fearing soul in the town's away on home?
> BASTIAN: Ach, I was just sitting thinking.
> PEDRO: Well, in answer to your gratuitous remark: a Sacristan's work is never done.
> BASTIAN: Neither is a village mayor's, Pedro, believe you me.
> PEDRO: Then you'd be best getting home to do it. I have to clear away them beggars from out of the doorway before I lock up. Wasn't the church robbed not a spit ago? I'll walk you out to the door.
> *Footsteps and the sound of a large door creaking open.*
> PEDRO GAILO: Would you just look at them, cluttering up the doorway, making good Christians look away, with their antics and their stumps and bits sticking out all over the show. I'll take me leave of you, if you don't mind, Bastian. Some of us have work to do.
> BASTIAN: God forbid I should get in the way of the Church's business, Pedro. I'll be off then.
> PEDRO: Right. Good luck. *Loudly, his voice echoing under the stone.* Away to hell with yous. Get out of here, go on shift yourselves. Away and get yourselves some decent employment, instead of planting yourselves like gorse bushes under our Lady's feet. Bloody tinkers and gypsies. I wouldn't piss on you if yous were dyin' of thirst *To himself.* Ah Jasus, I've gone and left the candles on the altar burning. *Loudly.* That's your fecking fault so it is.
> *Footsteps away.*
> SEVENTH MIAU *Whisper*: The coast's clear. He's gone back in to get his sticky fingers into the St Vincent de Paul.
> BASTIAN *Close*: The Seventh Miau, right enough. He was there. I think he was. He used to come and go like the wind. Nobody knew too much about him. Except that he was as hard as nails.
> *A child whimpers.*

SEVENTH MIAU: For the love of God, Alegria, can you not get that chiselur to quit his whingeing? If he doesn't give my head peace, I'll swing for him, I swear I will.

I have tried to define the *esperpento* as the mapping of cultural identity, in this case Galician, onto a stage language whose primary authenticating conventions are not drawn from the wider social world, in which dramatic activity is normally embedded, but from the fairground mirror of the *esperpento* itself. In other words, the authenticating conventions of Valle's theatre are not the social norms, modes of conduct and action which underpin our everyday social existence and which in turn form the basis of our understanding of the speech and actions of the fictional characters in the world of the play. His are the rules of *esperpentic* distortion.[12] This means that the translator must bring not just the normal linguistic and communicative competences to the language, but also a specific cultural strategy to cope with the performance texture of the language. In terms of complicity – and it seems to me that this is always the first line of interrogation to which the putative translator should subject the original play – the strategy should surely be one of fluency and disfluency, the harmony of a single cultural discourse set against the dissonant tones of an individual who is in constant linguistic performance and whose performance is in turn mirrored through the grotesque prism of the *esperpento*. Moreover, given that a domesticating approach to translating Valle would not only smooth out the jagged edges of his dialogue, but would also dissipate the sense of otherness that a Galician writer holds for a Madrid audience (for whom Valle was essentially writing), I felt that I had to develop a dramatic strategy which would enable an audience in London, for whom I was essentially writing, to recognize the issues at play in the *esperpento* without allowing them wholly to appropriate the frame of reference. By using Irish voices for the Galician plays and, in the case of *Bohemian Lights*, an Irish setting, I could achieve a variety of desired effects. Irish culture (in the broadly anthropological sense) remains predominantly oral, meaning that spoken language retains a greater performance element: moreover, with the importance of the oral dimension, Irish speech is more richly infused with those elements and registers which might in other cultures be more exclusively reserved for the written page. In this way I have intended my versions of the Galician *esperpentos* to function not simply as translations but as exercises in intercultural activity.[13] The grotesque images which Valle holds up in his distorting mirror can be re-energized in the new context of the English-language version, being meaningfully contrasted by the English spectator against a more

---

[12] These rules are described by Max as being implacably mathematical, although also filtered through "the bottom of a glass" (Johnston 1993:44-45).
[13] Intercultural in terms of the incorporation of otherness into essentially native assumptions, rather than mindlessly multicultural, which all too often results in productions which are simply linguistic versions of an international foodfest (Johnston 2000).

recognizable norm (the grotesque patently requires an immediate counterpoint within the spectator's own knowledge if it is to be recognized as the meaningfully de-formed and not simply dismissed as the irredeemably foreign). The quirks and injustices of Valle's specific historical moment, the folds in the fabric of his particular cultural tradition, thus find their linguistic equivalents in a moment and a tradition which are both familiar and other. Finally, I was playing to one of my own strengths. I am at home with the rhythms and lexis of Irish speech, just as I am all too aware of the hidden seams and darknesses of the Irish character and of Irish life.

The dysfunctional family is a frequent device in both Irish and Spanish drama, speaking not only of a nexus of unfulfilled and unfulfilling relationships, but also of a culture which lays inordinate emphasis on the weight of tradition. In *Divine Words* the hapless Pedro Gailo is being harried by village gossips with their unrelenting tales of his unfaithful wife. Convention demands a Calderonian response. He must kill her so that his family honour and male pride may survive intact. Valle's treatment of the honour code is characteristically caustic, but it can at least be readily culturally located by a Spanish audience. However, as Pedro drunkenly tells his daughter that her mother's days are numbered, an incestuous dislocation, the deep truth perhaps of the matter, begins to assert its presence. The scene gives an insight into Valle's writing at its best. A repugnant but widely accepted culture (in this case, machismo as a bulwark of family power structures) is viewed through a satirical prism which both deconstructs it and holds up its monstrous face to the audience:

> PEDRO: See this knife, see that whore your mother, well I'm going to cleave her head from her fecking shoulders ... and I'll take it to Bastian ... and d'you know what I'll tell him ... I'll tell him to arrest me there and then. In situ. This is the head of my lawful wedded wife. In defence of my self-respect, I was forced to sever it from her body. I trust that in your infinite wisdom you will ensure I receive just chastisement ...
>
> SIMONIŇA: Aw da, me blood's running cold in me body to hear you talk ... it's wicked gossip, every last word ... evil biddies without a drop of good for anyone.
>
> PEDRO: It's better for you this way ... what sort of example does a mother set for a young and impressive ... impressionable ... daughter abandoning her husband in the eyes of man and God ... what's the best such a jezzabel can expect ... The knife ...
>
> SIMONIŇA: Aw da, these are wicked thoughts ... cast them out.
>
> PEDRO: It is written in the scriptures ... she shall pay for her whorish ways ... her head upon a silver salver ... you'll be an orphan ... Mind you, I'm not that sorry for you ... you're a wee shite most of the time ... now get out to hell ... I've me own business to attend to ... would you look at that knife, God you could slice a blade of grass with it. [...] You're a lovely girl. You'll have a drink.
>
> SIMONIŇA: Brandy?

PEDRO: Go on ... just a mouthful, enough to wet them lovely lips of yours ... Shame on the harlot that abandons her home.

SIMONIŇA: Finish it off, and push them black thoughts out of your head.

PEDRO: A wife belongs to her husband and a husband no less to his wife. They give their bodies to each other according to the law of the Holy Sacrament of Marriage.

SIMONIŇA: If all you're looking for is another woman ... you're not exactly a total wreck and there's a bit of life in the auld dog yet ... as long as you don't have them traipsing through here ... I'm not doing the bidding of any new ma ...

PEDRO: Ah, but what about tonight ... what'll I do if I'm seized by temptation in the dark of the night? Man is born of weakness and the devil strikes the weak at their weakest moment.

SIMONIŇA: Use your Latin to drive him away.

PEDRO: I'm not making meself clear ... what if he commands me to sin, with me own daughter like?

SIMONIŇA: Oh da!

PEDRO: Pull your shawl up around your shoulders, will you ... I can feel the devil stirring inside me ...

SIMONIŇA: Finish your drink and get away to your bed.

PEDRO: You've got great big legs on you, Simoniña.

SIMONIŇA: With my weight, I'd look strange with skinny ones.

PEDRO: And such lovely white skin.

SIMONIŇA: You're me da! You shouldn't be looking at me white skin, lovely or not.

PEDRO: Make yourself dacent and we'll dig her grave together.

SIMONIŇA: Da, get a hauld of yourself!

The honour code and its bloody consequences, so readily understood by a Spanish audience, is assimilated by the audience of *Divine Words* through the imperative of other-directed and easily outraged decency, still operative in Irish rural life, although perhaps less so in London. However, the setting of this *Divine Words* remains firmly Spanish. Irish voices and speech patterns are simply a theatrical sleight of hand, a linguistic peg on which a largely British audience can hang its understanding of the functions and dysfunctions of sexuality in a male-dominated inquisitorially Catholic culture. This strategy allows some scope of freedom when dealing with culture-specific items, so that these may be either mediated, Nida-style, into the target culture through a process of seeking a dynamic equivalent or else translated literally (as is the case here with brandy, when whiskey would be more usual in Ireland) in order to reinforce at certain unobtrusive points the primary foreignness of the play. But, even so, the translator should not forget that such culture-specific items are very often, in turn, parts of a linguistic code as much as they are essentially colourful motifs. In the case of Valle, the linguistic code, the verbal performance, of which the item is a part, must be prioritised over its ability to maintain the intercultural dialogue between stage and auditorium. A simple example of this occurs in Scene Ten of *Bohemian Lights*. Now a great deal drunker than when we saw them entering the Palace Bar at the start of Scene Four, Max and Sweeney (Don Latino) find themselves in the company of prostitutes in a city park. Maria Delgado's version (1993:151) reads thus:

> AN OLD HEAVILY MADE-UP TART: Handsome! Oi! ... Handsome! Wanna join me in here for a bit?
> DON LATINO: I might consider it if you put your teeth back in.
> AN OLD HEAVILY MADE-UP TART: Gissa fag then!
> DON LATINO: I'll give you *The Spanish Correspondence Magazine* instead so that you can educate yourself. There's a letter in it written by Maura.
> AN OLD HEAVILY MADE-UP TART: He knows where he can stuff it.
> DON LATINO: Jews don't like to stuff anything anywhere.

Clearly there is a joke going on here. In the original Spanish the old prostitute's reply to Don Latino's reference to Maura (a Jewish politician) is literally "May they give him black pudding", to which Don Latino replies "It's against the Judaic rites". Delgado's dialogue is already weighed down by the title of the magazine, and the joke falls flat because it makes no sense either in the cultural context of the characters to which an English-speaking audience is privy, or in its own terms. In his version, John Lyon (1992:133) endeavours to retain the cultural specificity of the black pudding:

> PAINTED TART: He can stuff a sausage up his arse!
> DON LATINO: It's against his Jewish religion.

This is what the late Ken McLeish would have called a 'politician's joke'. It has laboured to set itself up, and anything sufficiently seen is simply not funny. The problem here is that neither of these translators has seen this as a linguistic problem, but have instead considered the translation of 'black pudding' from the perspective of that part of theory which deals with approaches to the translation of culture-specific motifs and items. The joke, like the rest of Valle's language, can work only if it has linguistic coherence. In the mouth of Don Latino, as in Dublin bar-room banter, the frame of reference for all such utterances is performative, and external reality is really only a pretext upon which the speaker may hone his or her expressiveness. My version (1993:43) reads:

> OLD WHORE: Hey! Yous! Good lookin' pair of young bucks yous are. Are yous game?
> SWEENEY: If you put your teeth back in.
> OLD WHORE: Yous wouldn't have a farthing, would yous, just for a drop o' gin? To warm me young bones, like.
> SWEENEY: I'll give you a copy of *The Irish Volunteer*. That'll do you more good. There's an article in it by Citoyen Connolly himself.

OLD WHORE: Up his arse for a start.
SWEENEY: He's from Scotland. A notoriously tight-arsed nation.

No more politically acceptable, perhaps, but at least the tone of banter, the sharp edge of language in self-conscious performance, has been preserved. In the final analysis, this is exactly what the objective of the translator of Valle-Inclán's *esperpentos* should be. In a way, of course, this emphasis on language as the locus of, rather than vehicle for, performance makes this author, who died in 1936 just as the Spanish Civil War was flaring, central to the post-modern exploration of performance theory. Given the constraints of space, it is not the purpose of this article to open up a new debate in this respect. And most certainly not in this brief conclusion given the complexity of the issues which emerge from the widespread cultural shift that prioritizes enactment over action. But these closing remarks might begin to point to a new perspective from which the later theatre of Valle-Inclán may well be fruitfully considered.

In the words of Steven Connor, "Ours is a world, it is commonly said, of widespread and pervasive simulation, in which the traditional means of separating off instances of performance from instances of the real seem to be compromised, if not wholly superseded" (1996:109). Both *Bohemian Lights* and *Divine Words* close with examples of language considered solely as enactment. In the final scene of *Bohemian Lights*, Sweeney appropriates not the artistic and political perceptions which inform Max's coining of the *esperpento* but, more crucially, his naming of it. Sweeney's swaggering use of a word he does not understand draws the glowing approval of the resident bar-room drunkard who salutes him as possessing "A brain like a bloody planet!"(Johnston 1993:48) Thus is enactment rewarded. In *Divine Words* it is the less than pure Pedro Gailo's intonation of the "divine words" of the Latin version of "let he who is without sin cast the first stone" which pacifies a mob bent on exacting a cruel revenge on his wayward wife, immediately after they have howled with derisory laughter at the same words delivered in their own native language. In both cases, it is the performative and talismanic rather than the referential and locutionary aspects of language which are highlighted as being of impact. Language has become sound. The speaker is performer and the interlocutor becomes the audience. Valle-Inclán would, of course, have seen this as a dangerous shift towards non-communication. But he was also alive to the ways of the world, and it is precisely that quality of "aliveness" that should inhabit any translation of his plays.

# References

Campbell, Patrick (1996) *Analysing Performance,* Manchester and New York: Manchester University Press.

Connor, Steven (1996) 'Postmodern Performance', in Patrick Campbell (ed.) *Analysing Performance*, Manchester and New York: Manchester University Press:107-124.

Delgado, Maria trans. (1993) *Valle-Inclán. Plays One*, London: Methuen World Classics.

Johnston, David (trans) (1993) 'Bohemian Lights', *Plays International* 9 (2):32-48.

------ (1996) 'Text and Ideotext: Translation and Adaptation for the Stage', in Malcolm Coulthard and Patricia Anne Odber de Baubeta (eds.) *The Knowledges of the Translator,* Lewiston, Queenston and Lampeter: Mellen Press:243-258.

------ (1998a) 'Valle-Inclán: The Mirroring of Esperpento', *Modern Drama* 41 (1):30-48.

------ (1998b) 'Translating García Lorca: the Importance of Voice', *Donaire*, London: Education Office of the Embassy of Spain, 11:54-60.

------ (2000) 'Translation for the Stage as Intercultural Activity', in Christopher Shorley (ed.) *Reading Between the Lines*, Dublin: Royal Irish Academy.

Keown, Dominic and Robin Warner trans. (1991) *Valle-Inclán. The Grotesque Farce of Punch the Cuckold / Esperpento de los cuernos de don Friolera*, Warminster: Aris & Phillips.

Lyon, John (1983) *The Theatre of Valle-Inclán*, Cambridge: Cambridge University Press.

------ trans. (1992) *Lights of Bohemia/Luces de Bohemia*, Warminster: Aris & Phillips.

Newmark, Peter (1988) *A Textbook of Translation*, Hertford: Prentice Hall.

Short, Mick (1989) 'Discourse analysis and the analysis of drama', in Roland Carter and Paul Simpson *Language, Discourse and Literature*, London: Unwin Hyman.

Zahareas, Anthony N. and Gerald Gillespie trans. (1976) *Ramón del Valle-Inclán: Bohemian Lights*, Edinburgh: Edinburgh University Press.

# 8    Performing Voices: Translation and Hélène Cixous

KATE CAMERON

*Abstract*. A sense of ownership of the written word is diffuse in theatre, and giving voice to others may literally mean letting the performers put the text into their own words through devising or improvisation. Many involved in contemporary performance practice argue that the very notion of a playwright or script is redundant, since it prioritizes word over body, text over visual, written over spoken. In this context, the dramatic and theoretical work of Hélène Cixous is examined, with the suggestion that the emancipated voice in performance represents a feminine counter to the masculine tradition of (written) literature. Voice and song are key concepts; the idea is that speech is closer to the unconscious than writing and in theatre creates a liberating force within a political agenda. In following an improvisational strategy, the translator is therefore mediator not just of the musicality of the text, but also of the political agenda behind it.

Hélène Cixous' most recent play, *La Ville parjure ou le réveil des érinyes* [*The Perjured City or the Awakening of the Furies*] has as yet no translation. While working on the translation, I have come up against some interesting and challenging points, which illustrate some general issues for the translator of theatre, as well as ones specific to this author. I will show how this play functions as 'performance writing', and particularly as a performative example of Cixous' theory of ***écriture féminine***[1] (which translates rather clumsily as 'feminine writing'). I will develop this in terms of the response that this writing demands of its translator.

I have selected three short extracts from the play to illustrate particular aspects of *écriture féminine*, and to highlight my response as translator of these features. The first extract deals with poetic inter-textuality, the second with song, and the third with improvisation.

As a first principle of translation, some background and context are required. Hélène Cixous is a French contemporary writer and theorist. In Britain, she is probably better known for her theory and critical writing, whereas her plays are mostly unknown; few of them have been performed here, and even fewer translated into English. As a playwright, Cixous is famous in France for her collaborations with the Théâtre du Soleil in Paris (who have also published her plays in conjunction with their productions). She has a close association with their artistic director, Ariane Mnouchkine, and is always involved with the productions of her plays.

---

[1] *Ecriture féminine* is the term Cixous uses in her seminal work *La jeune née* (1975), which exposes the veiled structures of language and society, writing and gender; ideas which I have referred to in my study of this play (Cixous and Clément 1986).

Cixous' plays are highly stylized, both in their writing and their productions. Her writing moves fluidly between poetic language and slang. Her most recent plays are epic in proportion and in style. They are many hours long, and usually involve a huge cast. The influence of classical theatre, of both Greek tragedy and Shakespeare[2] is clear in Cixous' texts, as it is in Mnouchkine's *mises en scènes*. Cixous talks openly of following in Shakespeare's footsteps; she often refers to his plays by quoting from them within her own play texts. The epic quality is also reminiscent of Brecht, in the use of alienation devices such as the treatment of voice, where the main protagonists address the audience and proclaim the injustices done to them by the social machinery.

Produced in 1994, *La Ville parjure* is based on a real life tragedy in recent French history. '*Le scandale du sang*' ['blood scandal'], involved the death of haemophiliac children who were given transfusions with blood which was infected with the HIV virus, blood which was given although it was known to carry a risk of contamination. The play takes place after the death of two children, Benjamin and Daniel Ezechiel, and is set in the cemetery where they are buried, on the outskirts of a mythical city. The mother of the children, known simply as *La Mère* [The Mother], returns to the cemetery in mourning for her dead children, turning her back on the city which has killed them, and seeking revenge for the crime. She is guided and helped by several mythical characters who live in this place of the dead: Aeschylus, also known as The Guardian of the cemetery, Night, The Chorus and The Furies, Greek female figures of vengeance who traditionally haunt the perpetrators of murder. The ghosts of her children are also present.

The perpetrators of the crimes are the doctors and their lawyers, who come to the cemetery to persuade the mother to accept money as compensation for the death of her children, and thus avoid a public court case which would fuel an uprising in the city. The Furies, awakening after thousands of years, realize that there is still no justice in the world and take matters into their own hands by capturing the doctors and bringing them to trial in the cemetery.

The play ends like all good tragedies, with the death of the protagonists. A military dictator overthrows the monarchy and orchestrates a massacre, flooding the cemetery by sabotaging the bursting dam above it (the sound of the

---

[2] Cixous refers to Shakespeare as much in her plays as in her writing on theatre, and there is no doubt as to the huge influence his work has had on her play-writing. She has said:

> My type of writing for the theatre one might situate in the line of Shakespearian historical plays. I've always loved them, I've always read them, but I've never considered these plays as giving me a political message. [...] History is the daylight or stage light in which human beings are steeped. (MacCannell 1990:201)

This play in particular could be regarded as a contemporary equivalent to Shakespeare, in its reworking of historical events in conjunction with metaphor and poetical allegory.

breaking dam is a motif throughout the play). However, there is a final scene set in a paradise after-life, where the victims look down on the world from the vantage point of death, where they can celebrate and laugh, free from the sufferings and injustices of the city.

Several aspects of this play are consistent with Cixous' other historical plays and illustrate her ideas on theatre and her writing theory in general. Some of these are more pertinent to the translator, as I will show. Others contribute to an understanding of her work. For example, the return of the dead and the setting of the play in the cemetery confirm Cixous' belief that death is an important feature of theatre, that we go to the theatre to experience death, to face our mortality, our humanity.[3] The splitting of characters into several roles, the playing of the same character by several different actors, is also a recurring theme. In the case of *La Ville parjure*, this occurs most obviously with The Chorus and The Furies; but almost all the other main protagonists, apart from the Mother, Aeschylus and The Night, appear in pairs: two children, two lawyers, a King and a Queen, a General and his Lieutenant. In the case of the doctor, this is taken one step further, by an interesting device of splitting his character into two adversaries, known simply as X1 and X2, who have conflicting views on what he has done. This pairing of characters reflects Cixous' interest and acknowledgement of 'the other'[4] in everyone: the shadow, the opposite, the projected. Theatre offers Cixous the opportunity to challenge the traditional binaries of identity, since when we watch a play and relate to the different characters, we experience all aspects of humanity – the good and the bad, the murderer as well as the murdered: "We are all victims, but we are also executioners" (Cixous 1987:257, my translation). Cixous explores the multi-faceted nature of identity within the characters she writes. She sees theatre as a place to give voice to others, to male and female, to rich and poor, to powerful and exiled; a place where writing can move away from the author and towards the 'other'; giving voice to the 'other' literally, through the dramatic realisation of the play. She talks of theatre in terms of:

> The scene, the land, where the 'I' remains imperceptible, the country of others. That is where their (spoken) words, their silences, their cries, their song can be heard, each according to their own world and in their own foreign tongue. (Cixous 1987:253, my translation).

---

[3] Cixous has written of theatre as the place we go to face our own mortality: "La tombe est là pour nous rassurer. Car en la touchant, en posant nos lèvres sur son marbre, c'est aussi notre mort que nous affrontons" [The tomb is there to reassure us. Because by touching it, by placing our lips upon its marble, we also confront our own death] (Cixous 1987:250, my translation).

[4] This is another key term from Cixous' theoretical writing, explored in *La jeune née*, a term also used in Hegelian and psychoanalytical theory in describing the hierarchical and dialectical models of identity she challenges and reinterprets.

Such a view is particularly pertinent for the translator who is equally involved in responding to the plurality of languages, and the need for things to be expressed by people, to people, in their own language. Cixous' use of multifarious and layered voices – a striking feature of this play – as well as the mixing and changing of registers, creates a particular challenge to the translator. Heightened poetic language is juxtaposed with slang; prophetic, declamatory speech sits alongside humorous rhyming and punning; song forms are followed by everyday speech. With these radically different voices and shifts in register between the poetic and the mundane, the oral and the written, Cixous appears to be challenging our expectations of one form or another, by crushing these binaries, by refusing to divide them one from another but rather seeing them all as aspects of one. The challenge of this text for the translator is thus how to embrace its differences, how to deal with the difficulties presented by the clashing of registers and the anarchic mix of voices.

The model of Greek tragedy, influential in her other plays, is here even more prominently fore-grounded in several ways: by the central presences of Aeschylus, The Chorus and The Furies; by the mythical context in which the historical story is set; and by the written form. In its use of blank verse, this play differs from her others, and moves closer to the classical roots of theatre. The use of verse also serves to highlight metre, assonance and rhyme, which shifts the language more strongly towards the aural and requires even more of any translator.

In terms of stage directions, there are none, apart from "she enters", "he exits", etc. There are no references to any visual elements or action. The only directions are auditory: there are references at key moments throughout the play to the sound of the cracking dam (which later causes the apocalyptic flooding of the cemetery), as well as indications as to how some elements of the text should be voiced – in some instances these are sung. This reflects one of Cixous' concerns with theatre – to shift the emphasis from the visual to the auditory: "If the stage is a woman, it will mean ridding this space of theatricality... it will therefore be necessary to work at exploding the confines of the stage, lessening our dependency on the visual and stressing the auditory" (Cixous 1984:547, my translation).

Because Cixous is a theorist as well as a playwright, writing about writing, about women's writing, I attempt to enter into that double theory/practice, writing/performance utterance. I look at the text on the page. I'm looking for clues in the shape of the writing. I'm looking for rhyme and reason. It appears to be written in verse, by the short, capitalised lines. What is the metre? I begin counting. Sometimes it scans, then it doesn't. Sometimes it rhymes, then it doesn't. The rhyme falls at the end of the line, but more often it falls in the middle point. There's assonance, then none. It's in blank verse, then for no apparent reason and sometimes within the same speech, it goes into prose. I begin to wonder what's going on. I try to work out the strategy, the pattern, convinced there must be some hidden scheme of things. Do certain characters speak more poetically than others, rhyme less or more? Do the 'good' characters differ from the 'bad'? There are tendencies, but no more. There's no consistency, no adherence to any rule. The text is a puzzle, and just when I think I've solved it, it contradicts me completely. I can't help feeling there is no hidden agenda, except to keep the whole thing open, dynamic, and playful. Not to bind the characters or limit the language to any model. To refer to one, but then to leap off in another direction. To set up a rule, only to break it.

I try speaking it aloud. I discover that it is pleasurable, in the mouth, to the ear. The rhymes, although they do not fall in conventional places, do exist. The metre, although fitful, does exist. And the assonance can be plainly heard. This orality is not bound to conventions of rhyming couplets or alexandrine metre, though Cixous is teasing with form. There is a playfulness in the enjoyment of sounds, in the proximity of assonant words and the auditory effect this creates, as well as playfulness with meaning, through puns, homonyms and polysemy. The language feels enjoyable and spontaneous, both in its execution and its result. The process of writing is manifest. It reminds me of rap and improvisation.

I wonder if the rules matter, if the writing isn't in fact about enjoyment, playing with form, and taking pleasure in breaking rules. I remember a word Cixous uses: *jouissance*[5]. The expression of joy, spouting forth, ebullient and unrestrained, motivated by desire. And I realise that this is *écriture féminine*, the 'oral-written'. It is subversive and does not play by the rules. But it knows the classical rules and it refers to them while subverting them. I realize she is rebelling against the very notion of my attempts to work out how things run, even though I must go through the process of working this out, since she sees this as part of what she has described as "masculine anxiety and its obsessional relationship to the workings [it] must control – knowing how it runs in order to make it run" (Cixous and Clément 1986:96).

Her writing thus defies the formulaic translator, who, like a mathematician, seeks logic by using logic, for this text is a trick, a riddle. I feel foolish. The answer is much simpler, but stranger because of its simplicity. The thing you can't see because it stares you in the face, because it hits you in the ear.

As her translator, I choose to follow her lead, to take this language into my own mouth, my own mother tongue, hear it, feel it, savour it, make it my own. If I am a slave to the original, dissecting it, pulling it apart and trying to reassemble it, I betray it by denying its intention, which is to fly, unbound by any law. The word Cixous uses is "*voler*", which is French for both 'to fly' and 'to steal'. The polysemy is no coincidence in her use of the word: "To fly/steal is a woman's gesture, to steal into language to make it fly" (Ibid.:96).

As her translator, I too must improvise – understand the form and play with it. I cannot stand apologetically on the sidelines of the original. I must possess

---

[5] This is a key term in Cixous' theory of *écriture féminine*. The word means 'joy', 'pleasure', as well as referring to the female orgasm, therefore a complete 'letting go', a sexual pleasure. Gender is implicit in her use of this term.

it, rewrite it, so that the text comes alive, so that it breathes, finds its own rhythm, its own sound.

How do I do that? I speak it aloud, I feel it in my mouth. I hear the play with sound, with polysemy (which is more attainable in French than English). I try to preserve the openness and spontaneity of Cixous' form by the principle of improvisation, where structures are created and played with. Once I understand the game, then I can play too. Once I have tuned my ear to the musicality of her writing, I can create this music in my own tongue.

The act of translating from one language into another is a transformation, yet too often it is thought of as transmission, from A to B. But A in Cixous does not equal B. As words in one language do not equal words in another. Even the notion of 'equivalence', a common strategy in literary translation, is apologetic, suggesting a reduction in value, a making-do. Not only must difference be acknowledged, it must be embraced and celebrated.

This point is especially pertinent to Cixous' text. It is a tendency of translation to homogenise, to stultify the original by incorporating it into the target language to such a degree that the translation becomes imperceptible, the translator 'invisible' (Venuti 1995: Introduction). A fluency is achieved which gives an illusion of originality. This strategy would be totally at odds with the spirit of Cixous' writing, precisely because she is using shifts in register and idiom consciously and to effect, and is particularly attuned to resonances from the classical past. It is in the context of this reverberating theatricality, with intertextual references to Racine and Shakespeare, that I highlight my first extract taken from the opening scene. After a long monologue by The Mother, Aeschylus enters. His identity has not yet been revealed, and at this point he is known simply as The Guardian of the cemetery.

1      LE GARDIEN: Alors, vraiment tu t'en vas?
       Et où iras-tu?
       LA MERE: Je vais … Je veux … Je ne sais pas encore.
       J'entends mes enfants m'appeler, mes enfants morts.
5      Je veux vivre près de mes fantômes.
       J'ai pensé habiter dans le camp de mes bien-aimés
       Qui s'étend sous ta garde.
       Un logis dans ta cité des morts,
       Ce serait naturel. Qu'en dirais-tu, gardien?
10     LE GARDIEN: D'un côté, je dirais, sois mon invitée,
       J'ai un bon caveau à te proposer.
       Un appartement d'argile, c'est ce qui convient
       A la mère qui refuse la fatalité.
       Mais de l'autre côté, je dois te le dire,
15     Sais-tu que ce cimetière, qui était magnifique hier,
       Habité qu'il était par les plus vénérables des morts,
       Hantés par les plus nobles spectres,
       Squatté par une vaste avant-garde d'amis de la liberté,

Camarades de la mort, amants du grand air, arriérés prophétiques.
20  Toute une gloire humaine rebelle au pouvoir de la cité menteuse.
Sais-tu qu'il est aujourd'hui très sévèrement abandonné?
(Cixous 1994:14-15)


1  THE GUARDIAN: So, are you really leaving?
And where will you go?
THE MOTHER: I'll go … I want … I don't know yet.
I can hear my dead children calling me, my dead children.
5  I want to live close to my ghosts.
I've thought about living in my darlings' camp
Which stretches out under your guard.
A dwelling place in your city of the dead,
Would be appropriate. What would you say, Guardian?
10  THE GUARDIAN: On the one hand I'd say be my guest,
I've a nice vault where you could rest.
A clay apartment would be very suitable
For the mother who refuses the immutable.
But on the other hand, I must tell you,
15  This cemetery, which yesterday was very grand,
Inhabited as it was by the most venerable dead,
Haunted by the noblest spectres,
Squatted by a vast avant garde of liberty's friends,
Comrades of death, lovers of fresh air, prophetic fools,
20  A glorious humanity rebellious against the power of the treacherous city,
Do you realise today it is almost deserted?


The style shifts readily between everyday speech and a more heightened poetic language, plays with rhyme and assonance, and shifts in and out of classical alexandrine structures of metre and rhyme. Where I have lost rhyme, for example with the 'é' rhymes in lines 10, 11 and 14 of the original, and with *'cimetière'* and *'hier'* in line 15, I have found alternative places for rhymes in my translation: in lines 10 and 11 with 'guest' and 'rest', lines 12 and 13, with 'suitable' and 'immutable', and with the rhyme of 'very' in line 16 to echo 'cemetery' earlier in the same line. I have been unwilling to force rhymes into the same positions which they occupy in the original, since this would contradict the overriding gesture of the writing which is playful. There is a sense that the rhyme is where it is because that is where it occurred. And in the same spirit, as translator, I have *found* rhyme and assonance, rather than having to create them through will and artifice.

My second extract, from Scene IV, demonstrates Cixous' interests in writing for theatre and the possibilities she sees in its relationship to the body, to speech and to the unconscious. She considers the unconscious to be closer to oral language, and particularly to song, a device she uses in this playtext in the voices of the children, whose speeches are all sung.

The voice sings from a time before law, before the Symbolic took one's breath away and reappropriated it into language under its authority of separation. The deepest, the oldest, the loveliest Visitation. Within each woman the first, the nameless love is singing. (Cixous and Clément 1986:93)

1    DANIEL *(chantant)*: Lève-toi, petit frère,
     Dresse-toi sur tes guiboles de squelette,
     C'est l'heure de la guerre, je piaffe,
     Je crache le fer, je crache le feu,
5    J'aiguise mes canines
     Je fais des boulettes avec mon sang noir,
     Je coupe les vers en quatre
     Tu tardes ou tu vis encore?
     BENJAMIN *(chantant)*: Je vis encore, je veux encore,
10   Je veux rester avec maman
     Son cœur est mon appartement
     Enfant de l'air, enfant du vent,
     J'ai peur de l'or, j'ai peur du sang.
     Je vis encore avec maman.
     (Cixous 1994:47)

1    DANIEL *(singing)*: Get up, little brother,
     Get up on your skeleton pins,
     It's the hour of war, I paw the ground,
     I spit metal, I spit fire,
5    I sharpen my teeth
     I make pellets with my black blood
     I cut worms into pieces
     Are you staying behind or are you still alive?
     BENJAMIN *(singing)*: I'm still alive, I still want,
10   I want to stay with mummy
     Her heart is my home
     Child of the air, child of the wind,
     I'm scared of blood, I'm scared of gold.
     I still live with mummy.

In this short extract, the ghosts of the dead children, Daniel and Benjamin, awaken to avenge their own deaths and their mother's grief. The language begins very rhythmically and with strong rhyming patterns, although these do not follow classical structures. Often the rhyme is internal, falling at the beginning or middle point of the line. As with the previous extract, Cixous refers to the rules, but breaks them almost immediately. The rhymes and repetitive vowel and consonant sounds differ between the eldest boy and his younger brother. In the French, the younger boy's text is full of nasal *'an'* sounds, especially linked with the French word for mother, *maman*. These early infant sounds reinforce the neediness, the babyishness of the young child torn from his mother. His brother's text is more punctuated, more aggressive, controlled and confident. Somehow these qualities need to be recreated in English. In the case of the older boy I chose hard consonants and short syllabic structures. With the younger boy my solution was to choose '*mummy*', and generally emphasise '*m*'s', '*o*'s and '*um*'s', open vowels, like the first sounds a baby makes.

In translating this passage, again I had difficulty in maintaining the frequency of rhyme in the original, while also remaining faithful to the actual words. I decided that what was important was the overall scheme of things, finding the rhyme when and where I could, without forcing the text into the same pattern as the original. I concentrated on the sounds, the assonant qualities, and the rhythms, which define the characters of the two boys and the song-form of their speeches.

Referring to her plays, Cixous states: "I write by ear: my ear leaning towards the music of the heart. I listen and I translate" (Cixous 1987:262, my translation). Particularly pertinent to translators of theatre, the ear rather than the eye will be chiefly attentive to the musicality of language, to the oral and the aural. The translator must attune ears and mouths to the qualities and differences in the original language and their own tongue. Just as in performance, the actor's body and breath can liberate the text and uncover other aspects which were hidden in the writing, so my task as translator is one of revelation, to release the potential of the original text: not trampling it, not imposing something else onto it, but touching it lightly, to transform it so that it can sing in another tongue, to allow its presence as breath and voicing to be heard. Cixous' language incorporates the performative, the sense that all utterance is made by the body, by breath, by the very heartbeat which gives us life, rhythmic.[6]

This quality can be described as evanescence. It highlights the moment of live speech, performance, this movement between sound and silence – improvisation, the most transient and instantaneous of all forms, which invents itself as

---

[6] This idea connects with Luce Irigaray's theory of language's relationship to the body. In her essay 'Flesh Colours', she writes: "The shapes taken by meaning have become arbitrary in our cultures. This arbitrariness splits the subject from his or her body. Meaning ought to express the body and the flesh, not cut itself off from them" (1993:159).

[7] The oral differs from the visual in its relationship to time. Walter Ong (1982:31-32) writes:

> All sensation takes place in time, but sound has a special relationship to time unlike that of the other fields that register in human sensation. Sound exists only when it is going out of existence. It is not simply perishable but essentially evanescent, and it is sensed as evanescent.

Speech, at least in live performance, can never be reproduced in exactly the same way. It exists only in performance, while it is witnessed. It is experienced in the moment, always for the first time. It marks a passage of time, and then it vanishes: "If I stop the movement of sound, I have nothing – only silence" (Ibid.).

it happens, lives only fleetingly and always in the present moment.[7]

My last extract illustrates this. It is taken from scene 12, the trial. The doctor has been captured by The Furies and is questioned by them about his actions. His character is split into two adversaries, X1 and X2, who argue with each other, laying the blame on each other. The Furies are the prosecution counsel, attempting to prove that a crime was knowingly committed by deconstructing the veiled language of the lawyers.

1    X2: Crime? Qui parle de crime?
     Jusqu'ici on disait homicide!
     Ai-je voulu tuer? A-t-il voulu tuer?!
     X1: Ai-je jamais touché à un cheveu d'une tête?
5    Je n'ai jamais administré à personne ni, remède, ni poison.
     MAITRE BRACKMAN: Oui, qui peut dire et jurer: il a voulu tuer
     Et cependant ne pas mentir?
     LES ERINYES: Voulutuer, en voilà un autre mot!

     . . . . . . . . . . . . . .

     Les phrases commencent droit et finissent de travers,
10   Il n'y a pas de rime.
     Mais vous ne m'échapperez pas. Bon, je retire crime. Mais je garde tuer.
     Donc, vous avez tué
     Même si vous n'avez pas voulutué.
     Et en quoi vous avez tué, je vais vous le dire:
15   Vous n'avez rien fait pour nous éviter la mort.

     . . . . . . . . . . . . . .

     Oui. Et ne pas tuer ce n'est pas ne pas tuer,
     Ne pas tuer c'est tout faire pour ne pas tuer.
     Est-ce que vous avez tout fait pour ne pas tuer?
     Non. Avez-vous *voulu ne pas* tuer?
     (Cixous 1994:122)

1    X2: Crime? Who said crime?
     Until now it was homicide!
     Did I want to kill? Did he want to kill?!
     X1: Did I ever touch a hair on a head?
5    I never administered either remedy or poison to anyone.
     BRACKMAN: Yes, who can say and swear: he wanted to kill
     Without telling a lie?
     THE FURIES: Wantedtokill, now there's a word!

     . . . . . . . . . . . . . .

The sentences begin straight and finish upside down,
10  There's no rhyme.
But you won't get away with it. Fine. I'll withdraw crime. But I'll stick with
kill.
So, you killed
Even if you didn't wanttokill.
And as to how you killed, I'll tell you:
15  You did nothing in our eyes to prevent death.

.....……….

Yes. And not to kill is not not to kill,
Not to kill is to do everything not to kill.
Did you do everything not to kill?
No. Did you *want not to* kill?

This passage demonstrates both the playfulness and the seriousness of language. While playing with words itself, it exposes language as a way of avoiding the truth. Again the passage is overtly oral and improvisational, with its spontaneous tongue twisters rattled out by the furious Furies, in stark contrast to the carefully and coldly worded defence of the doctors and their lawyers.

The text refers to itself (in the comment on rhyme in line 10), emphasizing a sense of immediacy. It is responsive to itself, to its audience, and between speakers. There is a sense of playfulness, even in this most serious of moments of the play. The argument form, as well as the plural voices of the Furies, lends itself to spontaneity. As the text accelerates, each speech launching itself from the last, triggering a response, building like a call and response, it builds on what has come before and shifts inexorably towards a climax.

Improvisation works through the principle of creating structures and then playing with them and within them. Like games, there are rules, less or more complex, which create the framework within which play can happen. Our most familiar experience of an improvised form is musical – particularly jazz, although improvised music can be traced right back through time, and across all continents. Singing is probably the oldest form of all.

In the case of Cixous' text, and supported by her theoretical writings, as a translator I feel she is giving me licence in a very direct, even directed sense, through her own writing technique, which is playful and improvised. If I can understand the overall pattern and the basic parameters, follow her lead, then I too can improvise, in mutual sympathy with her text but in my own language, tuneful to its sounds and assonances, to its rhythms and breaths. I can approach her work through this experience of *jouissance*, which gives me an overall strategy without feeling bound to follow the stresses of each line or the position of each word.

As my three extracts have demonstrated, translation of Cixous' text is necessarily participatory and performative. It is also creative, as I listen to her tongues and respond with mine, improvising with a different but nonetheless faithful sense of timing, breath, rhythm. Translation of drama is a creative performance of the original script in collaboration with its textual directors. Translation of Cixous involves even more directly an attentiveness to instants of re-enactment, listening to changes, to silences, to her multitude of voices and her pregnant words.

## References

Cixous, Hélène (1987) *L'Indiade, ou l'Inde de leurs rêves: et quelques écrits sur le théâtre*, Paris: Théâtre du Soleil.

------ (1994) *La Ville parjure ou le réveil des érinyes*, Paris: Théâtre du Soleil.

------ and Catherine Clément (1975) *La jeune née,* trans. Betsy Wing (1986) as *The Newly Born Woman*, Minneapolis: University of Minnesota Press.

Hervey, S. and I. Higgins (eds.) (1992) *Thinking Translation: A Course in Translation Method: French>English*, London: Routledge.

Irigaray, Luce (1987) *Sexes et Parentes*, Paris: Les Editions de Minuit; trans. Gillian C. Gill (1993) as *Sexes and Genealogies*, New York: Columbia University Press.

MacCannell, Juliet Flower (eds.) (1990) 'The Two Countries of Writing: Theater and Political Fiction', in *The Other Perspective in Gender and Culture: Rewriting Women and The Symbolic,* New York: Columbia University Press.

Ong, Walter J. (1982) *Orality and Literacy: The Technologising of the Word*, London and New York: Methuen.

Venuti, Laurence (1995) *The Translator's Invisibility: A History of Translation*, London: Routledge.

## Acknowledgement

I would like to acknowledge Professor Mary Orr, Exeter University, for her invaluable support in the writing of this paper.

# C.  SOURCES OF RESISTANCE

# 9     Getting the Word Out
## Issues in the Translation of Latin American Theatre for U.S. Audiences

KIRSTEN NIGRO

*Abstract*. While Latin American theatre has gained increased attention in the English-speaking world in the last few decades, it is still essentially absent from stages in the United States. The reasons for this are many and complex, not least among them that not enough valuable, stageworthy plays are translated, despite the existence of various festivals dedicated to Latin American theatre, a few theatres dedicated to promoting Spanish-English bilingual theatre, and growing academic interest in the subject. Important topics considered here include: reasons for the marginalization of Latin American theatre; cultural and linguistic challenges in translating it for US audiences; the role of the translator as cultural mediator; issues of majority and minority cultures, mainstream and Hispanic stages; 'political correctness' as an inhibiting factor; the need for translations to be workshopped. Cultural bias is something to be overcome, and this translator is reluctant to relocate on the grounds that this encourages the marginalization of Latin American theatre.

The myths that once grounded our identity have become bankrupt. Sixties-era pan Latinoamericanism, *la mexicanidad* (unique, monumental, undying), and Chicanismo (with thorns and a capital C) have all been eclipsed by processes of cultural borderization and social fragmentation. Like it or not, we are now denationalized, de-mexicanized, trans-chicanized, and pseudo-internationalized. (Guillermo Gómez-Peña 1996:172)

We can begin to see that the project of translating culture within the politics of identity is not a quick fix. (Gayatri Spivak 1992:794)

The way we imagine translation is changed by the fact that the worlds it seeks to bridge are already to some extent informed by plurality, are *already* saturated with a logic of translation. (Sherry Simon 1996:165)

To enter into a discussion about the translation of Latin American theatre is in many ways to be catapulted into a kind of combat zone of competing political, cultural and aesthetic projects, one where identity politics and postmodern deconstructions meet, often clash and sometimes negotiate. It is, to borrow from the critic Mary Louise Pratt, to cross over into a bordered in-between place where, ironically, borders continuously dissolve and reconfigure themselves (Pratt 1991). As a postcolonial entity, all of Latin America can be considered such a place, where for over five centuries the European and the autochthonous have met and battled, negotiated or retrenched. But Latin America is also a contact zone with its sometimes good neighbour to the North, whose point of entry is the over two thousand miles of border between Mexico and the United States. This in turn has produced yet another in-between-space which, as some calculate it, extends about fifty to seventy-five miles into each country, the so-called *fronterizo* area shared by Anglos and Mexicans in complex, often economically inequitable but also culturally rich ways. By other calculations, however, the United States, once conceived of as an impervious 'melting pot' of European peoples, has itself become a contact zone, a kind of porous 'salad bowl', to liberally rework a current metaphor, made of ingredients from all over the world which are tossed together, their flavours accenting, yet never overpowering, each other. In this mixture, the Latin American diaspora has become a basic component. Thus the often-heard reference to the *Latin Americanization* of the United States, something which calls for a reconsideration of both entities, where they start and where they end.

The problematics of defining Latin America are not new, of course. The name itself is a misnomer, a colonial invention, with America in honour of the explorer Americo Vespucci, and Latin a qualifier added by Napoleonic France as an act of solidarity with Spanish and Portuguese-speaking America, and more importantly, as a way of combatting English cultural and political hegemony. But the designation is also problematic for the way it homogenizes numerous nations, many of which are artificial creations, carved out according to political or geographical, rather than cultural criteria. While the concept of *a* Latin America often has made geopolitical sense, especially when the world was divided into blocks of superpowers, it also has made no sense of the great diversity of these countries, within and among themselves. While this diversity has produced a splendid cultural richness, it also has resulted in internecine wars, armed conflicts between nations and state-run programmes of extermination which would erase difference, especially that embodied by indigenous populations. Perhaps one of the biggest conundrums for many Latin American countries today is their push to enter into the free flow of a postmodern world, with its supposedly unhindered, borderless circulation of goods and people (including cultural ones such as theatre and the individuals who produce it), while at the same time their unease at relinquishing the national, regional and local identities that have provided a measure of autonomy, in addition to some defence against economic and cultural imperialism from without and repression or extermination from within.[1]

These contradictions about names and identities, about borderless and bordered zones, about difference and homogeneity all have a significant bearing on the task of translating Latin American theatre for a majority English-speaking audience in the United States. They underscore the positionality not only of the

---

[1] I would only have readers recall such recent events as the aptly named Dirty War in Argentina, the Pinochet era in Chile and the continuing Zapatista rebellion in Chiapas, Mexico.

translator vis-à-vis the work to be translated, but also of the text itself, in a site where art and culture, politics and economics meet in complex and challenging ways; in short, in yet another kind of contact zone. In this essay I will look at the nature and some of the consequences of this encounter, for the translated playtext, as all other texts, is in the words of Edward Said, 'wordly' ('The World, the Text and the Critic' in Said 1983). It circulates and takes on a life of its own as it enters into contact (and possibly combat) with casual readers, theatre practitioners, critics, audiences. That is to say, it is consequential on *and* off stage. As a mediator of words, texts and cultures, the translator plays no small role in setting the stage for these consequences.

In the United States, however, this stage is still rather empty. For despite the growing influence of Latin America in our language, food, architecture, arts and economy, the Latin American is noticeably absent in film, television and especially the theatre. So, while aspects of Latin American culture do insinuate themselves into our daily lives, the Latin American, him or herself, is not necessarily there to be seen. Indeed, one of the complaints repeated in survey after survey of Latinos in this country is that they are invisible to Anglos and so, they rarely see reflections of themselves in the national media and arts. And when they do, it is too often as illegals, drug lords, gang members, criminals, over-sexed males and hot mamas.[2]

As with all generalizations, there are exceptions to this one too. In the theatre, the Chilean Ariel Dorfman had a stunning hit with *Death and the Maiden* (the film version was less well-received), and the Argentine Manuel Puig's *The Kiss of the Spiderwoman*, first a novel, then a play and movie, was later adapted into a successful Broadway musical that, in an interesting twist, was exported to Latin America. Other playwrights, like José Triana (Cuba/France) and Griselda Gambaro (Argentina) have had some resonance on university and alternative stages. Several high-visibility events have been dedicated to Latin American theatre, such as the now-defunct Joseph Papp Latino Festival, and the annual festival organized by the Teatro Avante in Miami, which receives generous corporate support in no small measure because of the economic and political clout of the Cuban-American community. In addition there are various venues in the United States now dedicated to promoting Spanish-speaking and Spanish/English bilingual theatre: INTAR and the Repertorio Español in New York, Teatro Gala in Washington D.C., Teatro Dallas, South Coast Repertory Company and the Bilingual Foundation for the Arts in the Los Angeles area, to name but a few of the more prominent ones.

---

[2] For a better sense of this situation, see Rodríguez (1997). Just this last fall (1999) there was a call for a Latino boycott of the major television networks in the United States because in their new season of shows there was a noticeable absence of Latino characters and actors. The columnist Ed Morales has an excellent and pointed editorial on this in the September 27, 1999 issue of *The Nation*.

These exceptions notwithstanding, Latin American theatre in English translation simply has little presence on the U.S. stage. Granted, our theatre is
notoriously insular, but given the growing number of Latinos, who will be our
second largest minority by the year 2005, one should ask why this absence. The
least complicated explanation is that Latin American theatre does not circulate
widely in published form. Even within Latin America it travels little from country to country, and within its own national boundaries it can have limited market
appeal in the face of European and especially U.S. imports (these, not surprisingly, have no trouble getting translated and sometimes even playing concurrently
in New York and major cities like Buenos Aires and Mexico City; the free flow
of cultural goods turns out to not be so free after all, with North to South traffic
by far the heaviest). For those of us interested in translating Latin American
plays, being up-to-date on the theatre scene is certainly the first major hurdle to
overcome. Travel, word-of-mouth, websites, e-mail, a network of well-placed
contacts in numerous theatre communities – these are our necessary resources
for finding out, as best we can, what is 'out there' playing well in Latin America
and which might have some chance of doing likewise in the United States.[3]
Which plays these might be is subject to a host of variables, not the least of them
being the general ignorance, lack of awareness and/or disdain of things Latin
American shared by many in the United States. A long history of tense political
and economic relations with our 'neighbors to the South', our generally (Northern) Eurocentric set of cultural values, the prejudice against peoples of mixed
race and the recent immigration backlash have all conspired to make difficult
the promotion of Latin American cultural products. Granted, a handful of novelists and poets have made a breakthrough (the obvious examples being Pablo
Neruda, Octavio Paz, Jorge Luis Borges, Carlos Fuentes, Gabriel García
Márquez, Mario Vargas Llosa, Isabel Allende), but the fact still remains that
most readers are unaware of or uninterested in Latin American writing, assuming
– incorrectly – that it is too exotic or of inferior quality (meaning usually 'too
political'). For Latin American playwrights the situation is made more difficult
by the performance dimension, with its production, casting and monetary pres-
sures. In matters of dollars and cents, Latin American theatre seems a risky
business, the assumption being that it will *not* play well to English-speaking
audiences, who supposedly might be bored or perplexed by, or perhaps even
hostile to it. As one experienced translator of Latin American plays has cau-
tioned, when trying to promote our translations, we should put *Latin American*
in lower case or leave it out altogether, for the moment it is mentioned, the eyes
of potential producers may well begin to glass over.

Alternatively, there is sometimes an opposite phenomenon: the push to stage

---

[3] It should be noted, however, that Dorfman's *Death and the Maiden*, so embraced by
English-speaking audiences on both sides of the Atlantic, fared rather poorly in his
native Chile and elsewhere in Latin America, where it did not resonate politically or
artistically.

Latin American theatre *because* of its 'otherness'. Stereotypes are equally at play here, especially the one about magical realism, which conjures up images of a world where the improbable becomes the everyday; where nature, politics, art, love and sex are lived in the extreme, a world rich with lessons to be learned by outsiders from a more tired and spent European culture. This rather ethnographic view of Latin American theatre was the spark for a quite heated debate at a meeting I attended in Paris soon after the fall of the Berlin Wall. At a time of mixed emotions for many of those in attendance – euphoria at the liberation of the Eastern bloc and uncertainty about the future of the Left's political project – there was an anxiety voiced about a perceived trend in Latin American theatre away from its political commitment and its experimentation with alternative performance styles. This supposed change in direction was anxiety-producing because it depleted a rich mine of inspiration for European playwrights who were then in the process of recharging and redefining themselves. The reaction from many Latin Americans in the audience, especially from one noted dramatist, was strong and immediate: that their theatre was not some exotic resource for European 'exploitation', that neither he nor his other colleagues at the meeting were noble savages in twentieth-century dress, and that the lived experience of Latin American political reality was quite distinct from the virtual and romanticized sense of it many Europeans have. Although in this instance *Latin American* was written in upper case, perhaps with the best of intentions, the effect was not so different from writing it small: an essentializing that reduces this theatre to a cultural activity marginal for its inferiority or irrelevance, or to an exotic, idealized cultural practice whose relevance depends on its remaining marginal.

This precarious position of Latin American theatre helps explain why many (myself included) who translate it see ourselves not only as mediators between languages and theatrical traditions, but also between the cultures in which these are embedded. Certainly cultural considerations have always been inherent to all translation. But whereas one tradition has posited culture as essential and enduring, there is a growing consideration of it as an unstable and contested site, and the translation/circulation of artistic artefacts as ideologically (in an Althusserian sense) motivated. Thus I see my choice to translate Latin American theatre as having both creative *and* political ramifications whose direction is immediately plotted by the plays I choose to translate. For, as Nicole Ward Jouve has stated, we make culturally-marked choices that are far from innocent or inconsequential: "[T]he translation process implies untold selections, omissions, enlargements that have as much to do with the translating culture, its needs and projections, as they have to do with the writing that is being translated" (Jouve 1991:91, quoted in Simon 1996:88). Earlier I spoke of seeking texts with potential for successful stagings; as a translator I certainly do not want my work to go unnoticed or unrewarded (although sadly often it does).[4]

---

[4] Most of us who do translations of Latin American theatre do so without pay; our hope

Success can be had in community, university and regional theatres and off-off-Broadway, of course, but as everyone knows, *real* success is measured in big box-office revenues. Not surprisingly, then, Latin Americans with name recognition fare better than those without it: Carlos Fuentes, Gabriel García Márquez, Octavio Paz, Mario Vargas Llosa, Antonio Skármeta, José Triana, Griselda Gambaro (a list that seems to keep repeating itself!). Working with authors of such prestige certainly can help open doors to publishing houses and stages that usually are closed to Latin American playtexts.[5] And one open door can lead to others. Still, with the exception of Triana and Gambaro, these individuals are novelists or poets who have written the occasional and sometimes successful play. To promote only them is to distort the reality of the stage in Latin America, where some quite extraordinary people are devoted to and produce extraordinary theatre, but who have not been discovered, packaged and sold by and to the theatre establishment in the United States. I choose to translate these dramatists above all because I believe in their work, but also because of a commitment to their status as *professional*, not occasional, *Latin American* writers for the stage. However, I recognize the contradiction here in my translation project: on the one hand I am eager to break down essentialisms that make difficult the promotion of the works I translate; on the other hand, I am building them back up by underscoring the global qualifier *Latin American* in an effort to draw a less distorted picture of the major players in the contemporary theatre of Spanish-speaking America. I do this while recognizing that this picture is itself another kind of distortion, for it suggests a homogenous subject matter when in fact it is anything but that. Speaking within the context of feminism, Gayatri Spivak has suggested the practice of a strategic essentialism which, while resisting and deconstructing the essentialization of Woman in ways egregious to women, allows for that same essentializing when it can be beneficial (as it so often can be in questions of the law) (see Spivak 1987, especially 'Subaltern Studies: Deconstructing Historiography' and for an extended study of the question of essentialism in feminist thinking, Fuss 1989). It seems to me that such a strategy is very much in order in translation projects as well, where we are constantly having to erase, yet set boundaries, and where we are always walking a high wire between cultural territorialization and de-territorialization. The constant awareness of this helps me to not fall off that wire, by mistaking a *strategic* essentialism for an *essential* one. So, while knowing full well the dangers in speaking of *Latin American theatre*, to do so can often be advantageous. Choos-

---

is ultimately to get some royalties if and when our translated plays are staged. This situation seemed to greatly surprise (or amuse; I could not really tell by his expression) one translator of Shakespeare into French who attended the *True to Form* translation conference at the University of Hull in 1997. I would venture to say that translators of all non-hegemonic theatre would not have been so surprised, if at all; they certainly would not have been amused.

[5] I have in mind here Doggert (1997) and Holt and Woodyard (1986).

ing when to depends on where I am positioned at any given moment in my project, and I think the consequences of that choice can be as significant as any I make in the actual course of translating a specific playtext.

How I come to be translating that specific playtext is also the consequence of a choice made, one that in turn can have far-reaching consequences if and when that translation is staged. I have taught various university-level courses that deal with the images and stereotypes that we have in the United States of Latin Americans. I have seen how unaware my students can be that these ways of seeing are socially constructed and not essential realities: for too many of them, the lazy Mexican with his *sombrero* dozing under a cactus becomes The Mexican, a *mythology* in the words of Roland Barthes.[6] And this despite all the statistics that show that Mexicans are one of the hardest working minorities in the United States. This naturalization of human-made signs makes me extremely nervous about playtexts which might – wittingly or unwittingly – confirm our more negative or wildly exotic view of Latin Americans. Consequently, I try to choose playtexts that do not obviously run this risk and so, in my own small way, I am hoping to filter which aspects of Latin America to make accessible to U.S. theatre audiences.

In this, I may seem to act very much like the border patrol of which I can be so censorious in other contexts. I also recognize that ultimately border patrols fail in their attempt to keep so-called unwanted elements from crossing over to the other side, and that sometimes these very elements, these Barthean mythologies, can be just the right stuff for a lively night at the theatre. For example, I am interested in possibly translating a Mexican text that deals with a pathological case of *machismo* that masks a father's sexual desire for his son. The play is intense, almost delirious in parts and extremely violent; the two men in many ways seem to confirm the stereotype of Mexican men as pistol-crazy and sexually overcharged. Nevertheless, this is a carefully wrought text, with two powerful, meaty roles, a small supporting cast and simple staging needs – things that will matter very much to potential producers. There are translation choices for me that might deflect the play's stereotypical *Mexicanness*; for example, in the language. Rather than trying to reproduce as closely as possible the regional slang, expletives and class-specific terms in the very Mexican Spanish spoken by the characters, I could use a regional American English equivalent. I could delete specific references to things Mexican, in an effort to universalize the play, or replace them with recognizable U.S. referents in an effort to transpose the play geographically. But these are choices that would in my estimation diminish the original text, whose appeal and richness ironically lie in its depiction of a *machismo* that is distinctively Mexican. I say ironically because here again the translator is caught between the specific and the general, the reductive and the expansive, the fact that what is *other* about the original playtext is its plus

---

[6] Barthes (1957) looks at a variety of phenomena in popular culture, in order to unmask them as artificial signs that masquerade as reality.

*and* its minus: in this case, the Mexican *macho*, a figure often so very bold and theatrical in real life, and therefore so compelling on stage, but also the source of partial, distorted and denigrating perceptions of Mexicans in the United States.

In opening the present discussion, I quoted the Mexican/Chicano *border brujo* (border shaman) Guillermo Gómez-Peña, who has made a career of deconstructing these kinds of categorizations of his people, insisting on the one hand that in a globalized world, national borders have been erased and replaced with liminal, magical spaces where any identity is possible. On the other hand, Gómez-Peña sees borders and boundaries going up all around him (figuratively and literally, with proposals to build walls between the U.S. and Mexico), which isolate and fragment by highlighting supposedly dangerous differences. His own performance art seems to me to struggle with this contradiction, especially with regards to his positionality as a Mexican male. Aggressive in playing up his dark, Latino sexuality, Gómez-Peña means to awaken desire of the forbidden in Anglo audience members, to then frustrate it by showing the lie behind the mythology. His method here is to trigger the dynamic of attraction and repulsion that has defined the relationship between colonizers (Anglo Americans) and colonized (Mexicans), so that he can then bracket it off for deconstruction. However, once aroused, desire is not always so easily turned off; the image that too often can linger and thrill is precisely the one Gómez-Peña says he hopes to shatter: the one that distils the Mexican male into a sinister and violent Other driven by unbridled sexuality.[7]

The above underscores three fundamental and contradictory issues I find myself constantly negotiating in my translation work: 1) the importance of postcolonial relationships between the United States and Latin America, the difficulties in surpassing it and the dangers of ignoring it; 2) the recognition that whatever control I might have in the choice of playtexts compatible with my personal positioning as a translator is ultimately undermined by the impossibility of totally controlling actual audience reception; 3) and the fact that often it is the Barthean mythologies that have the best chance of making an impact in an iconographic medium whose very nature is to be elliptical and reductive. As I set about to *translate* Latin America through its theatre into North American consciousness, I find myself forced to work both with and against a gaze hardset by U.S. colonialism, and no matter what choices I make, my project is limited by forces ultimately beyond my control (on the question of how culture is or is not translatable, see Budick and Iser 1996). Indeed, I may even find myself having to negotiate with my own project, as I select incompatible texts because of their chance for theatrical success with an English-speaking audience; such

---

[7] Gómez-Peña is best known for his performance pieces *Border Brujo*, *The Couple in the Cage* (with Coco Fusco) and *The Temple of Confessions: Mexican Beasts and Living Santos* (with Roberto Sifuentes). Those unfamiliar with his work should read his *The New World Border. Prophecies, Poems & Loqueras for the End of the Century*, as well as *Warrior for Gringostroika*.

would be the case were I to translate the text I have referred to, whose characters embody cultural and gender-specific traits that cause me personally, as a feminist, great discomfort and even anger. For in my capacity as translator, I am not just making choices about which *scenes* from Latin America hopefully might be enacted on the U.S. stage; I also am an intermediary who can clash culturally with the text I translate, even in spite of an overall love of that culture and a real attraction to the text as potential theatre.

In such a situation, I could resist by not translating the text, but this might not be the wisest choice if my long-term goal is to get as much interesting Latin American theatre as possible produced in the United States. To refer back to and elaborate (rather freely) upon the quotation from Gayatri Spivak at the beginning of this essay, identity politics may not always be the best locus from which to translate culture, for it may mean not translating it at all. The better solution seems to me to translate *and* somehow resist at the same time. I say somehow, because I am not quite sure there is any one recipe for doing this. In her excellent study *Gender in Translation. Cultural Identity and the Politics of Transmission*, Sherry Simon speaks of various ways to assume gendered positions in translation theory and practice, such as the use of prefaces, addenda and footnotes, strategies that seem more suited to prose and poetry than to theatre, where written commentary is lost in performance (although there can be creative ways to include it there, and space for it can be made available in hand programmes). Simon also discusses the potential for resistance in the translator's understanding of, relationship to and handling of the engendered and culturally-marked characteristics of language in the original text. While she speaks mainly of women translating woman-authored texts with which they mostly feel an affinity and ones whose use of language is itself already resistant to patriarchy, this approach can work with male-authored texts as well, especially if the translator is positioned as a creator and activist whose engagement with and against the text unapologetically and openly reconfigures its rhetorical base.[8] While such a strategy is appealing, I do not know how far it would go in furthering my goal of making Latin American (I am essentializing yet again!) theatre present in the United States, since the secondary text would be far more distant from its original context, far more deformed, if you will, than all translations inevitably are.

But then, I must also consider to what degree this making present can be done without the translator's engaging with, contextualizing and problematizing the cultural values of the source text with respect to his or her own, and to those of the translation's target audience. This brings me back again to questions of wanting to exert some control over audience reception; or as some might say, of so-called political correctness. I suppose my hesitancies about *machismo* and

---

[8] Judith Fetterly (1978) is one of the first to theorize a feminist reading strategy around resistance. Gayle Austin (1990) follows the example with regards to the reading and mounting of dramatic texts, while Sherry Simon (1996) applies it to translation theory.

other stereotypes *is* a kind of p.c., and sometimes it probably does cloud my judgement. But at others, it can set off danger signals that, by working in conjunction with the playwright, produce textual changes that might help assure the play's positive reception. For example, in the first version of my translation of *Muerte súbita* ['Sudden Death'] by the Mexican Sabina Berman, I worried that her lead female character would be problematic for U.S. audiences, especially university ones where the play would get its first reading and then full staging, and where there can be a rather naive belief that women who are beautiful but not particularly brilliant, perhaps even a bit spacey and who rely too much on men for their sense of identity, cannot possibly be positive, sympathetic stage characters. In Berman's play, Gloria is all of these things, but as I feared, she was perceived by many as being just stupid and weak. For some female audience members there was even distress at what they saw as yet another example of Anglo actors representing Latinas as vapid sex objects.[9] The p.c. *s*ensors and *c*ensors were picking up all manner of messages that I and the playwright knew to be wrong. After much lively discussion about cultural differences (in the play's original 1988 staging Mexicans – male and female – did not react to Gloria in this way) Berman wrote two more drafts for the English version, with some far-reaching changes in the character of Gloria, ones which in turn led the playwright to make other, significant rewrites. My own feeling is that these have strengthened the playtext overall for future U.S. audiences, and may have something to do with the play's two subsequent stagings in Mexico City (1998 and 1999) playing to packed houses.

As I look back on what I have written, it may sound as if the lady protests too much, that I have complicated overly a rather straightforward activity: that of sitting down, dictionaries at the ready, and translating a worthy Latin American playtext from its Spanish ideolect into an appropriate American English. Is not the bottom line here a question of excellence – of the original and of its translation? Is not the latter's excellence a matter of linguistic playability in ultimately theatrical terms? And, if we live in an already translated world, as my opening quote from Sherry Simon suggests, why so much bother about possible cultural misunderstandings? My answer is that in the end, of course, it is a matter of me and the text at hand, and the outcome of our relationship depends on the worthiness of us both: the text as theatre and I as translator. However, we each bring to this relationship our own textuality, the history that has led us to this encounter. In the case of Latin American theatre, the route there has been a complicated and difficult one. And in the case of the United States, while theatregoers may

---

[9] My translation of *Sudden Death* has had a staged reading and full production at the University of New Mexico. It has also been staged at the Vortex Theatre in Albuquerque, New Mexico, as well as the University of Kansas. Ironically, the person who commented about Anglo actors and Mexican stereotypes failed to notice that the actress in the role of Gloria in the University of New Mexico production was of Mexican heritage.

themselves be translated beings (to borrow rather loosely from Homi K. Bhabha), far too many are oblivious to this fact, while others who are not, resist it mightily. May they lose the battle.

## References

Austin, Gayle (1990) *Feminist Theories for Dramatic Criticism*, Ann Arbor: University of Michigan Press.

Barthes, Roland (1957) *Mythologies*, Paris: Editions du Seuil; trans. Annette Lavers (1972) as *Mythologies*, London: Jonathan Cape.

Budick, Sanford and Wolfgang Iser (eds.) (1996) *The Translatability of Cultures. Figurations of the Space Between*, Stanford: Stanford University Press.

Doggert, Sebastian (1997) *Latin American Plays. Stage Labyrinths*, London: Nick Hern Books.

Fetterly, Judith (1978) *The Resisting Reader. A Feminist Approach to American Fiction*, Bloomington: University of Indiana Press.

Fuss, Diana (1989) *Essentially Speaking. Feminism, Nature and Difference*, New York and London: Routledge.

Gómez-Peña, Guillermo (1993) *Warrior for Gringostroika*, Saint Paul, Minnesota: Graywolf Press.

------ (1996) *The New World Border. Prophecies, Poems and Loqueras for the End of the Century*, San Francisco, California: City Lights Books.

Holt, Marion Peter and George W. Woodyard (eds and trans) (1986) *Drama Contemporary. Latin America*, New York: PAJ Publications.

Jouve, Nicole Ward (1991) *White Woman Speaks with Forked Tongue: Criticism as Autobiography*, London and New York: Routledge. Quoted in Sherry Simon.

Morales, Ed (1999) 'We Ought to Be in Pictures', *The Nation* 269 (9): 9.

Pratt, Mary Louise (1991) 'Arts of the Contact Zone', *Profession 91*, New York: Modern Language Association: 33-40.

Rodríguez, Clara E. (ed.) (1997) *Latin Looks. Images of Latinas and Latinos in the U.S. Media*, Boulder, Colorado: Westview Press.

Said, Edward (1983) 'The World, the Text, and the Critic', in *The World, the Text, and the Critic*, Cambridge: Harvard University Press: 31-53.

Simon, Sherry (1996) *Gender in Translation. Cultural Identity and the Politics of Transmission*, London and New York: Routledge.

Spivak, Gayatri Chakravorty (1987) 'Subaltern Studies: Deconstructing Historiography', in *In Other Worlds: Essays in Cultural Politics*, New York and London: Methuen: 197-221.

------ (1992) 'Acting Bits/Identity Talk', *Critical Inquiry* 18: 770-803.

# 10   The Irrepressible in Pursuit of the Impossible
## Translating the Theatre of the GDR

ANTHONY MEECH

*Abstract.* This study of the uniquely significant role played by the theatre of the German Democratic Republic during the forty years of that state's existence attempts to identify how the translation and adaptation strategies adopted by GDR theatre writers and practitioners informed their theatre practice. Relocation in particular was a vital technique for defeating the censors. The essay considers whether the particular qualities of the drama of the GDR might be rendered intelligible to a West-European democratic audience. The conclusion reached is that, if such translation were possible, it might aid not only the understanding of the potential of theatre in a totalitarian state, but also offer a stimulus to theatre to better define its role in a democracy.

For four decades the German Democratic Republic constituted an anomaly in the centre of Europe. With its borders decided on an almost accidental basis, and its capital divided, it represented a unique environment, astride The Iron Curtain, the defining structure in Europe during the forty years of its existence. It was difficult, if not impossible, to generate elsewhere in the so-called Eastern Bloc the particular *frisson* one felt when, abandoning the many West Berliners waiting to change underground trains on the platform at Friedrichstrasse station (itself deep under the centre of East Berlin), one headed up the shabby stairs to the *Grenzübergangsstelle* [Border Crossing Point]. The abruptness of the culture shock served to bring home the very separate identities of the two Germanies, despite their common language and history. Looking back from the end of the 1990s, it all seems like a lost world; and a world, which if it is to be rendered in translation to a non-German speaking audience, living in a stable democratic system, will make very specific demands on any translator. These demands will extend beyond the merely linguistic into the cultural and the contextual.

We must accept that no translation can convey all the resonances of the original. Even as simple a word as *Frau* presents difficulties for the translator of German, meaning as it does both *woman* and *wife*. We also recognize that a word cannot be rendered in isolation. The meaning of words or phrases generally depends on the context in which they are used. These two arguments, or defences, are, of course, two sides of the same question, and may be seen to apply for any translator. But both of these perennial problems have, I believe, a peculiarly, if not uniquely powerful resonance for anyone attempting to render the theatre of the GDR into English. If this is the case, why bother trying to translate plays from the GDR at all, now that the régime has been consigned to history after the re-unification of Germany?

I believe that the forty years of GDR offer an arguably unique opportunity of researching how a theatre speaks to its audience; how it responds to and expresses the aspirations and concerns of that audience. In the authoritarian and highly politicized GDR there were few opportunities to question, let alone criticize the government in print. Only the church rivalled the theatre as a forum for discussion, a place where the concerns of society could be aired. Where the theatre scored over the church was in its mimesis. Characters on stage could adopt roles in real time. Points of view could be embodied and enlivened. Positions held, in particular those held by the authorities, could be interrogated and frequently exposed as ridiculous. It is this melding of the artistic and political, and its immediate reference and relevance to its audience that gives the theatre of the GDR its fascination.

Two elements fundamental to the functioning of the theatre in the GDR made it inevitable that it would find itself at the forefront of the debate on how GDR society did and should function.

The first is the pan-German assumption of the role of the theatre in a society. Born out of the theoretical writings of Schiller at the start of the nineteenth century, the Germans regard the stage as a forum for serious moral, ethical and political debate. Neither the government, nor the population would have expected the theatres to have supplied simply 'culinary' entertainment.

The second was the GDR government's commitment to high levels of spending on theatre, both on personnel and material. Immediately at the end of the War (while the West Berlin theatres were commandeered by the Allies to provide entertainment for their troops) the Soviet occupying forces dispatched cultural commissars to their zone of occupation to discuss the resurrection of the theatre for the German population. Whatever problems it might pose for the authorities, it was always regarded as an essential cultural institution. For the duration of the GDR generous funding and the régime's full employment policy ensured that theatres had the wherewithal to remain at the forefront of the country's cultural expression.

This generosity of support attracted the country's leading writers,eager to exploit such a public means of debate. However there was a heavy price to pay for the government's subsidy. Until the early 1970s the Ministry of Culture acted as censor, keeping close control on scripts presented on stage. It was during these years that directors often turned to adaptation (what might be called internal translation) or elected to stage classic and therefore unexceptionable texts, but with a particular slant.

German directors on both sides of the Wall had a habit of indulging their flights of interpretative imagination in a way unfamiliar to English audiences. Under the cover of a 'concept' production, it had long been the practice in Eastern Europe to stage plays from the classical canon, injected with a contemporary political relevance. *Hamlet* or *Julius Caesar* needed little in the way of adaptation to present all too familiar images of tyranny for a politically aware East German audience. No wonder Stalin banned productions of Shakespeare's plays in pre-War Russia.

Such authoritarian action was not, however, an option for the GDR Ministry of Culture in the 1970s and 1980s, without giving the unfortunate impression to the outside world of artistic repression on a grand scale. The game of bluff between theatres and the authorities was very sophisticated, and depended on the totality of the translation of the foreign or classic German text into stage production. It was not enough for a censor to check a play's script on paper. The offensive component frequently appeared only when the text was realised on stage. Where any newly written text had to be submitted for approval – or censorship – it was a much trickier affair for the authorities to raise objections to a classic playtext before it went into production. Representatives of the Ministry would feign interest in the director's work and ask to sit in on rehearsals. On occasion they were compelled to wait until the first night of a production before deciding whether the bad publicity which would result from imposing a ban on a production of, say, *Julius Caesar* in which a latex mask made the tyrannical Caesar look uncannily like Party Secretary Honnecker, was preferable to the impact the production might have on its audiences, if allowed to continue in the theatre's repertoire, perhaps for several years.

Audiences were wise to the power of the theatre as an ephemeral and mutable form of communication. The control of the translation of a foreign play into a performance on the GDR stage, unlike the publishing of a foreign novel was a matter of trade-offs in real time. It was this aspect of the theatre's staging of recognized foreign or established German texts which placed it in a uniquely powerful position both at the forefront of the interrogation of the régime and as a platform for ideas from outside and within the GDR. Where a novel is generally read – and can be banned – in private, the theatre is nothing if not a public activity. A thousand people in one place applauding a comment spoken by an actor is a powerful force. What matter if that comment might, in the context of the play, refer to a foreign dictator, perhaps in the distant past?

The best known of these strategic classics from the German canon was undoubtedly Schiller's *Wilhelm Tell* [*William Tell*], in which audiences insisted on wilfully misunderstanding the word *Pass*, which means in German both *mountain pass* and *passport*. Whenever a character in this early nineteenth century classic said he was seeking a 'pass', audiences habitually cheered their agreement that they too were seeking a 'passport'. In this, and many other examples, we can see evidence of the unique bond which existed between stage and audience, and the ingenuity and humour which characterized the culture of dissent in the GDR.

The problems of translating contemporary foreign language plays could often work to the advantage of a theatre company. Presenting the *Volkspolizei* [People's Police] on stage was a potentially hazardous enterprise, but presenting policemen wearing the uniforms of the Volkspolizei in the translation of a fashionable Italian play was acceptable. How else was a director to costume policemen in a play to be performed in German translation to citizens of the GDR? It would be ludicrous to go to the trouble of dressing actors in accurate costumes as Italian policemen. How many of the audience, none of whom had the opportunity to travel to Italy, would recognize the uniform of an Italian policeman? After all, wasn't Dario Fo a member of the Italian Communist Party, struggling to try to initiate in that country the kind of state enjoyed by the audience of *Can't Pay, Won't Pay* at the Berliner Ensemble in 1985? Who could object to such a reasonable production device? The fact that the audience at the Berliner Ensemble drew just the inference which the company intended from the appearance of the '*Vopos*' (representing as they did the Italian Police) – that they were incompetent and oafish, but nonetheless dangerous, precisely because of their stupidity – was, of course, an unfortunate coincidence. The atmosphere in the auditorium when the lights went on and we were questioned about the sugar which we had a moment before been passing down from the back of the seating to the stage was electric, another example of flexibility in translation to evade the claws of the censor.

The cases of overt censorship of contemporary German writing are well known. Perhaps the most renowned, Brecht's struggle with the authorities over the opera *Lucullus*, has been comprehensively documented by Joachim Lucchesi (1995:13-21). The decision of many artists to leave the GDR for the West (whether voluntarily or involuntarily), is also a significant element in the story, but is not what gives the practice of theatre in the GDR its particular interest. It is far more those artists who had the opportunity to leave, but chose to stay, preferring what Brecht called the invitation into the kitchen to the invitation into the dining room. It is the product of the creative tension between these artists and the régime which constitutes the GDR's unique contribution to contemporary drama, and one which justifies attempts at its communication to an English-speaking audience.

These artists were neither able nor willing to remain aloof from their audiences. It was a fascinating experience to attend after-show discussions at the biennial Werkstatt-tage of GDR theatre, where writers such as Heiner Müller, Christoph Hein and Volker Braun were prepared to enter into debate with younger writers and audience members from the theatre profession. The often heated discussions tended to centre on how the play we had just seen could, and should have better served its socialist society. By which the audience did not, of course, mean support the status quo. What of this excitement and involvement can be carried over into another culture and language? After the curtain comes down on the production at the Staatstheater, and the discussions, however vibrant, are over, all the translator is left with is the language on the page.

The German language has had a particularly troubled history. Not until the mid-nineteenth century was the Rhineland dialect chosen as the official national language. But even before this the *Burschenschaften* (groups of revolutionary students) were attempting to rid the German language of 'ungermanic elements' and to return to the language of Luther's Bible. This has been a continual process in the development of High German. The Nazis in their turn made concerted attempts to purge the language of non-German words and expressions. The often awkward replacement formulations, as well as those words specifically linked to the 'Hitler Time' still carry a resonance of the dark period of their inception.

Brecht was the master of the flexible translation. He, more than most dramatists, was aware that the nuance which might offer an interesting diversion in a translation class, could prove dangerous or even fatal for him. Before the House Committee on un-American Activities on 30th October, 1947, he invoked the Library of Congress translator to support his contention that the title of his play *Die Massnahme* should not be translated as 'disciplinary measures' but instead should be rendered as 'measures or steps to be taken', and that a crucial line, "Du musst die Führung übernehmen" in his poem *Lob des Lernens* [*In Praise of Learning*] from the play *Die Mutter* [*The Mother*] would be more properly rendered as 'You must take the lead' instead of 'You must be ready to take over'(Brecht 1988:290). Such arguments as this would later dog him and many other original writers throughout the forty years of the life of the GDR.

The GDR régime was itself supreme in its arcane use of language and in exploiting German's facility for formulating jargon. Highlighting and ridiculing this affliction was one of the roles willingly undertaken by the theatre.

One example of this occurs in a play which was extremely popular in the late 1980s in East Germany, at the time when each of the Germanies was attempting to claim Martin Luther as a precursor and validator of its political system. The play *Die Preussen Kommen* [*The Prussians Are Coming*] was written by Klaus Hammel, and is set in the 'PRI' or 'Assessment Centre for the Reintegration of Historical Personalities' where Martin Luther is discussing with Frederick the Great the relative roles allotted to them in what Johannes Küpper calls the "unvarnished, all but brutal political orchestration of historical facts" by the official East German historians (Weidenfeld 1987:167). Central to this brazen rewriting of history is the discourse employed by the authorities, and familiar enough to cynical GDR audiences to stimulate the laughter of instant recognition. Martin Luther has to memorize from a state history book that he was, "... instrumental in the promotion of the social and cultural advancement of humanity in a situation of intensified societal contradiction at the onset of the transition from feudalism to capitalism" (Hammel 1988, my translation).

It is the Professor in charge of the Centre who points out to Luther that he gave the Germans their language, to which he replies, "And what have you made of it? You can't read a newspaper, or a scientific book, and as for the utterances of the politicians ..." (Ibid.)

This text was rapturously received by audiences in the GDR, and is an important example of the use of the deadly weapon of comedy, the ridiculing of the authorities in this most authoritarian of states, but it must remain of parochial relevance, and (in spite of its interest for the student of GDR theatre) would not repay translation for the English stage. So too, mentions of the organs of state in a production would frequently generate what a theatre company might be able to claim was an unexpected, disrespectful response. The reference to *Neues Deutschland* [*New Germany*], the party daily paper, in Heiner Müller's

masterly *Wolokolamsker Chaussee* [*The Road to Volokolamsk*] produced jeers
in Leipzig in 1988; while the introduction of the red kerchief of the Young
Pioneers and the blue shirt of the Free German Youth, as essential ingredients in
the making of the perfect citizen, at the start of the 1986 Berliner Ensemble
production of Georg Seidel's *Jochen Schanotta* brought the house down. Again
these are elements essential for a full understanding of the theatre of the GDR,
but which must be explained to a reader in footnotes and will be lost in a stage
translation.

What can be carried over from the GDR is writing which contains the particular insights that were generated by the peculiarly close relationships in society
and the microcosmic quality of East German life. These are most commonly
expressed in a kind of wry humour rarely found elsewhere in the canon of German literature. When I drew Christoph Hein's attention to this characteristic of
his writing, he replied, "You need a sense of humour to live in a state like this".[1]

The artistic élite in the GDR was a small grouping, cut off from intellectual
contact with the West (although nightly able to receive its television), but in
close, frequent and productive interaction with each other. Their use of their
society as an Absurd paradigm does offer us distilled images which, while remaining specific to the GDR and not pretending to universal relevance, can
speak to us. It is this that I believe constitutes a valuable and perhaps unique
quality in GDR playwriting, which deserves and demands translation for performance on the English-speaking stage.

As an example of this I would like to compare two extracts on the function
and role of the police in perfect societies. These two extracts are the products of
a society with a particular and sophisticated relationship to its police force, which
had a very different reputation from the 'friendly copper' image of the British
police.

The first is a vision of a primitive pre-socialized state from Christoph Hein's
*Die Wahre Geschichte des Ah Q* [*The True Story of Ah Ku*]. The play is set in
pre-Revolutionary China, and in Scene Six a discussion takes place between the
ragged philosopher Wong and the Policeman Masker (with one interruption
from Ah Ku).

> WONG: In the past we knew many things ... we didn't need police or Gra-
> cious Lords. Everyone had enough, and nobody too much. We needed no
> laws, no state, no wars. What is the point of violence, anyway? Where there
> is violence you can't truly live, you can't know what it is: life.
> AH KU: There were Anarchists like us, though, Fungus Face, weren't there?
> WONG: You idiot. Why should there be Anarchists? They had everything.
> MASKER: How come there were no police?
> WONG: What for?
> MASKER: And the regulations?

---

[1] Christoph Hein in conversation with the author, East Berlin, 1988.

WONG: Weren't any. That's why they were truly alive.

MASKER: Must have been a fine old pickle. Murders and muggings.

WONG: Why should they cave each other's skulls in? There was enough for all.

MASKER: I know people.

WONG: And what sort of people do you know? Lords and servants, yes, exploiters and exploited, but not real people.

MASKER: Don't you preach at me, Fungus Face, I'm educated. I know my way about. No police; they'd be at each other's throats.

WONG: And now you're at their throats.

MASKER: According to regulations. All right and proper.

(Hein 1984:113-4, my translation).

Compare this with the contemporary policeman's nightmare: the perfection of society. Such would be the logical outcome of the development of the GDR under the benign hand of socialism, a system which, serving the best interests of all its inhabitants, renders crime a logical absurdity. Heiner Müller offers us this vision at the start of the fourth section of *Wolokolamsker Chaussee*, a play which in its five sections charts the history of the GDR (Müller 1986. Unpublished translation by Julian Hammond as *The Road to Volokolamsk*, section IV).

I had a dream/ It was a nightmare/
I woke up and everything was in order/
Comrade Chief everything is in order/
No incidents and no infringements or crimes
Committed/ Our people act according to
The models set out in books and in the paper ....

... The game is called cops and robbers
The game has rules/ Rule number one is One
Hand washes the other /And I'd like to see
The man who can wash his hand with one hand/
In short cops and robbers are a dia
Lectical unity ....

... Who needs us when everything is
In order /I can make matches from my desk
And start a fire with the training squad files/
We can take off our uniforms
And hang them on the nail/ And us ourselves
There and then/ but only if the nail will hold/
What are you doing.

        Taking off my uniform.

You are on duty and not on a nudist beach ...

            ... Being
Determines consciousness in pre-history/
It's the other way round in socialism/
A different fire is what is needed here
To what a desk can make hacked up to bits/
Or a washing basket filled with files/
And when you have corrected your mistake
You won't need to hang yourself after work/
The medal and the premium will be yours/
Now go over the crossroads on red/
Over the crossroads on red.
            Me.
                And in
Your uniform/ And that is an order/
Over the crossroads on red in uniform.

The other theme typical of the later writing of the leading dramatists of the GDR is a wry, world-weariness, a sense of being part of a brave experiment which is bound to fail. This atmosphere permeates the evocative masterpiece *Die Übergangsgesellschaft* [*Society in Transit*], written by Volker Braun while he was working as script consultant on a production of Chekhov's *Three Sisters* at the Maxim Gorki Theater in Berlin. Retaining the same cast of characters, he set the action in contemporary East Germany. The transfer works exceptionally well. The agonizing sense of futility and of the impossibility of escape resonates from a group of characters trapped within a doomed society.

    Two other examples will complement this literature of the final chapter of the GDR's history. Both texts conclude with a clash of generations; the perceived failure of the father lent an added piquancy by our awareness of the imminent collapse of the GDR régime. In the final section of *Wolokolamsker Chaussee* the party worker, who has suffered imprisonment at the hands of both the Nazis and the GDR government, faces his rebellious son who despises his sacrifice and the cause to which he has dedicated his life. As the father faces the agonising decision whether to report his son to the authorities for his anti-social behaviour, the play concludes:

FORGOTTEN AND FORGOTTEN AND FORGOTTEN
The last thing I heard was his crying and
His voice that tried to scream against the tears
You should be shot you Nazi bastard
You should be shot like a dog
Then the sound of the telephone as he
Picked up the receiver and dialled the number. (Ibid., section V).

At the end of Christoph Hein's prophetic play *Die Ritter der Tafelrunde* [*The Knights of the Round Table*] a very different father and son confront each other and the failure of the dream to which the father has devoted his life. King Arthur speaks to his son Mordred:

> ARTHUR: ... We don't understand you. We don't understand what you want.
> MORDRED: I don't know that myself. But all this, I don't want this.
> ARTHUR: It's not a bad table. I'm glad to sit at it. Do you really plan to smash it?
> MORDRED: I plan to move it to a museum.
> ARTHUR: Yes, that's what I thought. And will that help you? Will that make anything clearer?
> MORDRED: It will make room. Breathing space, Father.
> ARTHUR: I'm scared, Mordred. You'll destroy so much.
> MORDRED: Yes, Father. (Hein, trans. Robinson 1995:123).

Indeed much has been destroyed along with the Wall. The theatre no longer fulfils the vital function it did during the four decades of the GDR. Seats are available now anywhere in theatres which used to play to 100% houses six nights a week. Little is left of what the theatre meant to its audience then but the texts. It is my contention that, despite all the difficulties inherent in the enterprise, these deserve translation and determined attempts, against all the odds, to present them on stage to English-speaking audiences on both sides of the Atlantic.

But it would be hard to overestimate these odds. It might be maintained, with some justification, that the qualities which joined to make the theatre of the GDR as successful as it was on every level, are all absent on the English-speaking professional stage on both sides of the Atlantic. Nobody with even a cursory knowledge of the traditions of these theatres could realistically hope for the introduction of the changes necessary for the ready acceptance of GDR theatre texts in London's West End or on Broadway.

The problems are both cultural and logistical. The British mainstream theatre has since the time of Shakespeare been regarded primarily as a commercial institution. The commercialism of the American theatre is even more complete. It might have been expected, or at least hoped, that the introduction of the subsidized sector in Britain after the Second World War would have allowed for the staging of significant works from world theatre, irrespective of their likely commercial success. The steady erosion of funding in real terms to the British national companies has, however, led them to adopt a defensive stance. These companies feel themselves compelled by financial exigency to rely on productions of the tried and tested classics and musicals with high production values, rather than attempt to introduce their audiences to the unfamiliar.

Heiner Müller's major plays might have been staged for more than a decade throughout Europe, but have yet to receive a production by either of the British national theatre companies. And Müller's case is far from being an isolated one on the British stage. Apart from Brecht, who should be regarded as a special case, plays by East German writers were not welcomed by British theatres in receipt of national subsidy throughout the forty years of the GDR.

Perhaps British audiences would have been more receptive to plays from East Germany, had they been given the opportunity to see them. The primary reason why so few reached the stage is the ignorance of British theatre practitioners of German, indeed non-English language theatre in general. British theatres are not, as their German counterparts, blessed with dramaturgs, part of whose function is to research foreign theatre. Where GDR plays have reached the British stage, it has usually been as a result of the enthusiasm of an individual director. Müller's plays have been seen on the fringe in London, through the work of the director Marc von Henning. But it is significant that the Müller production to receive most critical attention was Robert Wilson's *Hamletmachine* imported to the Almeida Theatre in 1988, with an American cast.

Those London theatres which took the initiative to stage GDR plays in the 1980s (the Almeida, the Royal Court and the Gate) received generous support from the Goethe Institute, which has played a crucial role in supporting German theatre on British stages. Their recent introduction of the *Theaterbibliothek* series of play translations should make contemporary German theatre texts more readily available to British and American theatres. Whether such an initiative, had it been taken by the GDR régime, would have resulted in a greater awareness in Britain and the USA of the riches of East German theatre, must remain an open question.

The GDR has now been consigned to history, but the plays, documents of a unique period in European theatre history, remain. They deserve translation as a study resource of an era during which the theatre had a significance in its society which practitioners in the English-speaking world can only dream of. Many of the texts have much to offer actors and audiences alike, and deserve performance. Productions in the non-commercial environment of universities and colleges could be expected to realize both these aims, and enrich the experience of future generations of theatre practitioners.

The fact that something might be impossible has never been a good reason not to attempt it. It was after all Brecht's Herr Keuner who, when asked what he was working on, replied: "I'm having a lot of trouble: I'm preparing my next mistake" (Brecht, trans. Kapp 1961:124).

## References

Brecht, Bertolt, trans. Yvonne Kapp (1961) 'The Exertions of the Best People', in *Tales from the Calendar*, [*Kalendergeschichten*], London: Methuen.

------ (1988) *Stücke: Drei*, Berlin: Aufbau-Verlag (Berliner und Frankfurter Ausgabe).

Hammel, Klaus (1988) *Die Preussen Kommen*, Berlin: henschelSCHAUSPIEL typescript.

Hein, Christoph (1984) *Die Wahre Geschichte des Ah Q. – Stücke und Essays*, Darmstadt: Luchterhand.

------ (1988) *Die Ritter der Tafelrunde*, trans. David W. Robinson (1995) as *The Knights of the Round Table*, in *Contemporary Theatre Review* 4(2).

Küpper, Johannes (1987) 'Das Geschichtsbewusstsein in der DDR', in W Weidenfeld (ed.) *Geschichtsbewusstsein in Deutschland*, Cologne.

Lucchesi, Joachim (1995) 'From Trial to Condemnation: The Debate over Brecht/ Dessau's 1951 Opera *Lucullus*', *Contemporary Theatre Review* 4 (2).

Müller, Heiner (1986) *Wolokolamsker Chaussee*, Berlin: henschelSCHAUSPIEL typescript.

# 11 Translating the Untranslatable
## Edward Redliński's *Cud Na Greenpoincie* [*Greenpoint Miracle*] in English.

SZCZĘSNA KLAUDYNA ROZHIN

*Abstract*. This translator/director discusses the difficulties of drama translation from Polish into English, taking as an example her translation of Edward Redliński's *Greenpoint Miracle*. The essay focuses on realia and cultural context; describes possible strategies for dealing with such problems and analyzes the strategy finally adopted. She also introduces a notion of concepts and argues whether these are what make Polish drama untranslatable. Lastly, she considers a specific problem encountered while translating *Greenpoint Miracle*: the problem of dialect. She presents her attempts to preserve it in production, so avoiding cultural relocation, and demonstrates to what extent they were successful.

*Greenpoint Miracle* by Edward Redliński was first published in the Polish theatre magazine *Dialog* in December 1995. In less than a year, the play opened in a number of repertory theatres around the country and won the Best New Play award. I chose to translate it not only because I thought it was an excellent play, but also, paradoxically, a perfect example of 'the untranslatable'.

The **cultural context** as well as **realia** seem to be the most difficult problems in translating drama from Polish into English. In this section I want to discuss both of them, looking at possible solutions and using examples from my translation of *Greenpoint Miracle*.

The cultural context of the play is a framework built of objects, processes, institutions, customs and ideas, peculiar to one group of people, among which the play is set. In the case of modern Polish plays, the cultural context is usually very strong and inseparable from the plot. In the works of Mrożek, Redliński or Głowacki, all the events and all the characters' experiences are a consequence of a certain social or political situation, that is, of the cultural context. Stripping the play of its references and allusions deprives it of its raison d'être. Patrice Pavis in his essay 'Problems of translation for the stage' (1989:37) says: "By [...] maintaining the source culture by refusing to translate its terminology [...] we could isolate the text from the public" and "[w]e would run the risk of incomprehension or rejection on the part of target culture: by trying too hard to maintain the source culture, we would end up by making it unreadable". I believe, however, that such a risk is worth taking. The text will be isolated from the public only when the public isolates itself from the text. Certainly, if no effort is taken on the part of the target audience to prepare themselves for the 'journey towards otherness', Polish plays might as well be treated as culturally untranslatable.

It is said that Chekhov was so worried about his plays being misunderstood in foreign tongues, that he regretted not being able to prevent their translation and production abroad. And coincidentally it is Chekhov who so often falls victim to sophisticated translations that abandon the source culture and transplant the play to a target culture. Those 'versions', as they are sometimes called, cannot be treated as translations, rather as adaptations that create a new piece on the basis of an original, usually ignoring the importance of its social and historical context.

In my translation of *Greenpoint Miracle* I did not change the context, but by providing a glossary as well as some historical information, I tried to create a 'manual' to the play for potential directors and actors. But what about the audience? Background reading or at least studying the programme notes prior to the show would be an ideal preparation. This, however, is wishful thinking. In reality, I think problems of context in this particular case are impossible to overcome. The play will either be 'lost', when the context changes, or will be incomprehensible and rejected when it remains untouched.

Another major problem in drama translation from Polish into English, is the problem of realia. Realia (from the Latin *realis)*, are words and combinations of words denoting objects and concepts characteristic of the way of life, the culture, the social and historical development of one nation and alien to another. Newmark calls them cultural words (1988:94). Since they express local and historical colour, they have no exact equivalents in other languages and cannot be translated in the conventional way. Examples would be English *scones*, Hungarian *puszta*, or Polish *barszcz*. Eastern European scholars use the term realia to describe "... those elements or concepts in the original that are intimately bound up with the universe of reference of the original culture ..." (Florin 1993:122). However, since the universe of reference of one culture never totally overlaps with that of another, the problem of realia always remains unsolved. There are some strategies offered by theorists of translation to deal with this problem, none of them thoroughly successful.

The first one is **transcription** or, as Newmark calls it, **transference** (1988:81). It is said to be the easiest method and involves transferring a source language word or lexical unit into the target language text by graphic means (in some cases it might involve transliteration). This method works successfully in narrative texts, as it can be accompanied by a footnote. However, this is impossible in drama. The only other solution, when realia are too important to be discarded, is to provide a glossary (the solution I adopted in *Greenpoint Miracle*) of all terms alien to the target audience or readers. Such a glossary could be incorporated into the programme – the strategy often practised by Polish theatres when they present a play from a foreign culture. This, I think, gives the audience a chance to broaden their knowledge and makes their theatre experience more exciting through their discovery of the unknown. Unfortunately, not everyone will be willing to accept the 'otherness' of such a production. Transcription then, carries the risks of making the text incomprehensible. Still, because in the majority of Polish dramas, realia and context are crucially important and unchangeable, it seems the only acceptable strategy.

All other strategies introduce realia by means of **substitutions**. One of them is called **approximate translation**. In this case only a general content of realia is communicated. In drama translation from Polish, this strategy will always result in the loss of local colour or, even worse, in the loss of subtexts and hidden meanings. In Nicholas Bethell's translation of Mrożek's *The Martyrdom of Piotr Ohey* (Mrożek 1967:26), Johnny, Piotr's son, is playing soldiers, whereas in the original he is playing the Priest Kordecki. The difference is substantial. Playing soldiers has no more meaning than playing ball or cowboys, while impersonating Kordecki – who was a Polish patriot and spiritual leader at the time of the partitions – gives a clear idea of the values that are preserved in Ohey's home and the atmosphere in which Johnny is growing up. This way of treating realia simplifies the play and does not give the audience the chance to discover the true depth of the text.

**Deletion** of stretches of text, especially metaphors and intensifiers, can be another method of approximate translation of the cultural vocabulary. Ruthless as it is, this strategy brings an immediate and easy solution to problems caused by phrases alien to the target culture.

Another approximate strategy is **neutralization**, which involves introducing a culture-free functional or descriptive equivalent (*Sejm* becomes *Polish Parliament*). In this case, the translator wants to achieve a reaction in the reader of the translation similar to that of the reader of the original. The alien concepts are substituted by familiar ones: one kind of flower, dish, name of a place is substituted for another. Again, the local colour as well as subtexts are usually lost and, as Newmark (1988:83) points out, it is "... deculturalising a cultural world." In *Greenpoint Miracle* the word *akademia*, meaning a communist celebration involving the obligatory participation of school pupils or factory workers, was translated as *festivity*. I realize that the terms are poles apart, but it seemed to me that there was no other way of preserving the mood of this sentence and achieving similar reactions on the part of the reader or spectator.

Alternatively, a cultural equivalent may sometimes be found, but this again changes the climate of the text, as well as the concept, because the content of the term – even considered as cultural equivalent – is hardly ever the same as that of the original. For example in *Greenpoint Miracle* Surfer talks about *imieniny* [Saint's Day party]. The cultural equivalent I used was *birthday party*, which of course does not mean the same, as the nature of Polish Saint's Day parties is totally different from that of English birthday celebrations. However, a literal translation as *Saint's Day party* would certainly create a feeling of "the third language" (Duff 1981:124).

**Literal translation** (known also as **loan translation**, **calque** or **through-translation**) which often results in introducing neologisms is another way of dealing with realia. Each component of the phrase is substituted. In this way *Kolumna Zygmunta* becomes *Sigismund's Column* and *Długi Targ* becomes *Long Marketplace*. Often those calques look and sound odd; sometimes, however, they become assimilated or adapted into the target language. In drama translation this strategy has the advantage of not neglecting or changing realia, but calques, although comprehensible, do not provide any information about the nature of the original term or its associations in the source culture. For example, in *Greenpoint Miracle*, Surfer talks about *first communions* (in Polish: *pierwsze komunie*). Although the English translation will probably be understood, it does not bring those immediate connotations and images in the minds of English readers or audiences, which it does for Polish people.

There is one more strategy: **contextual translation**. In this case the content and meaning of the translated words are communicated by suitably transforming the context. This method, once widely used by communist censors, now seems to be popular in English-language 'versions' of foreign classics. In most Polish drama, the cultural context is crucially important and changing it would irreversibly change the nature of the play. If the translator decided to set *Greenpoint Miracle* among, for example, Irish rather than Polish immigrants, s/he would have to remove all the cultural references and allusions, and, as a result, create a totally different play.

None of the strategies presented above guarantee complete success in the treatment of cultural words. Deciding what strategy to use, the translator has to take into account the importance of realia in the original and the character of the text.

As communication is the first priority, the translator should choose a strategy that will make realia comprehensible. In *Greenpoint Miracle* realia are extremely important in creating the character and atmosphere of the text. As in my translation the context remained unchanged, ideally they should all have been transcribed into the English text. Unfortunately, this would have rendered the text unreadable and totally incomprehensible. I therefore used a combination of strategies to ensure that the target audience would understand the play, but at the same time, to preserve as much of the original character as possible. Methods of approximate translation involving substitution and deculturalizing of the text were rarely used. All the proper names (*Kraków*, *Zakopane*) were transcribed, although some of them have recognized English equivalents, as were socio-cultural terms (*gastarbeiter*). Some terms were translated literally (through-translated): *Solidarity* – for *Solidarność* , as the English term is recognized and used as widely as the Polish. Also the term *Party* was introduced in place of the original *Partia* [Communist Party] to make it easier to understand. For all the transcribed terms as well as those translated literally, I provided a glossary with some basic information about the places, people and organizations mentioned in the text. Not all the cultural words, however, were transcribed or translated literally. Some, like *gorzała* [slang term for vodka] were neutralized and a functional equivalent, *vodka* was used. The same happened to the terms *komuna* [slang term for Communism] – which was neutralised to *communism* and *partyjny* [an active member of the Communist Party], for which a descriptive equivalent, *active in the Party* was used. Cultural equivalents were used for terms: *adwokat* – *attorney*, *gospodarstwo* [smallholding] – *farm* and *akademia* [a communist celebration] – *festivity*. Unfortunately, deletions were also used occasionally, when the term in the source culture was regarded as untranslatable.

Metaphors created a problem of their own. The text is full of expressions that do not exist in Polish dictionaries, but are used by the author to 'colour' the text. They are perfectly understandable for source language readers, however, in literal translation they would be meaningless. For some of them cultural equivalents were found – always bleaker and less expressive: *łże jak z nut* [he lies as if he was reading the notes] was translated as *he lies through his teeth*, *twarz jak klawiatura* [face like a keyboard] as *you keep a poker face*. Some had to be replaced by descriptive equivalents: *skoczyć w bok* [to jump aside] was translated as *to have an affair*; *przysmrodził* [he gave off a stink] as *he couldn't hold his tongue*. A metaphor: *szczurować* [literally: to rat] which appears in the text several times turned out to be linguistically untranslatable (the English meaning of this verb is completely different) and was replaced by its descriptive equivalent: *to live like rats*. In my opinion, the fact that most of the metaphors are either linguistically or culturally untranslatable causes greater loss of the character, spirit and colour of the original than any other untranslatable cultural concept.

The translation of drama from Polish into English presents further problems, alongside those of context and realia, which make successful cultural transfer difficult, or even impossible. Realia are virtually untranslatable because they do not exist in the universe of reference of the target culture. Strategies that can be adopted to deal with realia work on the basis of finding a close equivalent or describing the problematic term. There are, however, a number of troublesome terms, or **concepts**, that are not regarded as realia, because, as J.C. Catford (1965:32) says: "... a relevant situational feature ..." in the target language culture exists for them. In other words, they can be easily translated literally into the target language. What then is the problem? The problem has its roots in the different traditions, histories and religions of Poland and England – in all that creates the cultures of the countries and influences their languages. This results in concepts not covering exactly the same field of meaning in both languages. The content of the concepts is different, so that they bring different associations and induce different emotions among the target audience. Let me present some examples from *Greenpoint Miracle*: Surfer, at one point, talks about the *reżim* [régime]. For a Polish reader or spectator, this term evokes immediate and very strong images of the days when the Communists were in power: empty shelves in the shops and lies on the news. For an English person, the term might have some vague associations with the political situation in some distant country, but it definitely will not create such clear and vivid pictures. *Pilgrimages* may serve as another example. For us Poles, the word creates in our minds a colourful picture of crowds marching along a country road, singing and stopping the traffic. Every Pole has taken part in a pilgrimage or, at least, seen one. Examples can be multiplied: *boycotts*, *crisis*, *opposition*. All are linguistically translatable but as concepts they differ in the source and target cultures. Sometimes, the spectrum of associations that a given concept brings is wider in the target culture. In the source culture (Polish – in this case), all the terms I gave as examples carry unequivocal associations. *Crisis* – for a Pole is always the crisis of the 80's. *Boycotts* – are those in which most of us participated also in the 80's. Nobody reading or listening to those words in a certain context (as in *Greenpoint Miracle*) will search for any other connotations – the play is therefore unmistakably clear.

The concepts so far presented as examples are all connected with political and historical events. But even the simple and universal concept of *wedding* has a different content in Polish and English cultures. The associations involve different smells, colours and sounds. Is 'unity' in reading such concepts so important? Should the translator aim at narrowing the scope of interpretation? I think that in a play like *Greenpoint Miracle* s/he must. No room is given in the text for describing concepts. They are meant to create slide-like images in the mind of the reader or spectator. These images, in turn, create a picture of Poland. To be able to fully understand the dilemmas, dreams and uncertainties of the characters, one has to see this picture in the same colours as they do.

There are many examples of Polish dramas where, as in *Greenpoint Miracle*, a precise understanding of concepts is required (Mrożek's, Głowacki's, some of Różewicz's works). In such cases, successful cultural transfer is difficult to achieve. In translation, nuances of the language are lost and the message the author conveys can be misunderstood or, even worse, pass unnoticed.

The problem of **dialect** presented a crucial dilemma while working on my translation of *Greenpoint Miracle*. Dialect can be seen as "... a self-contained variety of the language not a deviation from standard language ..." (Newmark 1988:195). Its purpose in drama is to show a slang use of the language, to stress social class contrasts, or to indicate local cultural features. Dialect in translation can be dealt with by transferring it into neutral language, which results in the text suffering a loss of individual character; or by replacing it with another dialect as a cultural equivalent. However, translation into dialect runs the risk of being antiquated (ibid.:195) and of distorting the meaning of the original. Polish plays have suffered greatly when translated into English, due to the loss of their particular dialect features. The problem is especially difficult when, while translating a play, we decide on preserving the cultural context of the original. This causes the dialect-replacement strategy to be inadequate and the only remaining one – transferring into neutral language, does not do the translated text any favours.

The dialect in *Greenpoint Miracle*, because of its character, creates a difficulty which, in English translation, cannot be solved successfully. The characters of the play are Polish immigrants in New York; some of them left Poland quite recently, others years ago. All speak the immigrants' dialect, which is a peculiar mixture of Polish and English. English words (mainly nouns) with Polish endings are introduced into sentences constructed according to the rules of Polish grammar. It is full of neologisms and has unlimited potential for development. Justified as it is in America, this language phenomenon occurs more and more frequently in the everyday speech of Polish people in their home country. Polish names on shop-signs are replaced with English ones; bars selling beer are all called *pubs*; garages – *car centres*; computer shops – *computerlands*. No longer do girls wear *makijaż* – they wear *make-up*, and treat their hair with *conditioner* rather than with *odżywka*. It has become quite hard to survive in Poland for any unfortunate individual who does not speak English. As Aniela Korzeniowska (1994:52) observes:

> ... this presence of English in the Polish domestic context has more to do with the social and political aspirations of the people than with the country's economic or cultural realities. For some, the presence of English in public life is a symbol of Poland's break with the communist past and return to democracy, while for the others, it symbolises modernity, technological advancement and the Western way of life.

Coming back to *Greenpoint Miracle*, one can successfully apply Korzeniowska's theories to find the roots of the immigrants' dialect and explain why it develops so quickly and is so widely used. English, representing freedom, wealth and a 'better life' is eagerly adopted by the characters in the play and incorporated into their native language. Living in America they are surrounded by English; some terms existing in American culture do not have equivalents in Polish – no wonder they become part of everyday speech. The dialect is unique, potent and rich – without it the language of the play is dull and bleak. It would not be a problem to translate the play into French, Hungarian or Swedish. The target language could still be combined with English inserts to create the same effect. With English however, this does not work. There was no question of finding a replacement. The context of the play remained unchanged; thus, no other dialect could be introduced.

   My first idea was to preserve the author's idea of 'the mixture', leaving in the element of Polish to the largest possible extent. In the original, English words are mainly nouns (*job*, *green card*, *air-conditioner*) with Polish declension endings. Verbs, adjectives and adverbs are mostly Polish. In my English translation I decided to reverse it, hoping that this would create the effect of 'the mixture' without distorting comprehensibility. I translated most of the verbs into English, giving them Polish inflections (*kidnappli, messuję, movnąć*). The same with nouns and adjectives – they became English but with Polish endings (*boozerze, pimpa, peoplów*). What remained Polish were prepositions, conjunctions, pronouns, all cultural words and the word order. As a result, I created a new dialect, my own representation of Redliński's original.

> ASBESTOS: Kto? Jak? Po co?
> POTATO: *(sits on the chair, breathes heavily)* Oni mnie kidnappli! Undressli mnie i jak byłem naked to, oh Jesus!... naked ...

PROFESSOR: Zbeatli Cię? Rapnęli?
POTATO: ...koło churcha mnie chucknęli, tam gdzie people!
PROFESSOR: Ale who?
POTATO: To twoja fault, ty boozerze!
PROFESSOR: Moja?
POTATO: Kto tu broughtnął tego pimpa i jego daughter?
PROFESSOR: To był him?
POTATO: A who else? Ja tu z nikim nie messuję!
ASBESTOS: Calmuj down, Ignac.
POTATO: Blocknijcie doory! I zaboltujcie. Cały jestem scared! Jaki shame!

I doubt if my 'invention' is used anywhere by anyone, but for the purposes of translation I thought it could work. It certainly gave the effect of being a mixture of Polish and English and that was my aim. However, I did not apply this strategy for translating to the whole play as 'my' dialect turned out to have disadvantages of its own. Firstly, in reading the translated passages great problems are caused for the actors in terms of pronunciation. I used English spelling combined with Polish spelling for Polish words. Actors without any knowledge of Polish tended to pronounce Polish words according to English pronunciation rules. The effect was meant to be the reverse. Not only should the Polish words be pronounced properly but also the English words should be pronounced in a Polish accent. This problem could possibly be worked out during a long and painstaking rehearsal process, but still I doubt whether the effect would be achieved with an English-speaking cast. Secondly, the dialect turned out to be too Polish for an English audience to understand. Those who were listening to the readings said that Polish endings and word order, as well as an abundance of Polish words significantly affected comprehensibility.

Those were the arguments against 'my' dialect. Every translation has, above all, to be speakable for the actors and understandable for the audience. If those aims are not achieved, the translation fails. I decided to reduce the degree of 'Polishness' by producing the exact reverse of the original: instead of a Polish text containing English words, it was an English text containing Polish words. In this way, I thought I would make it understandable and preserve the idea of a 'mixed' dialect. I used Polish words in metaphors or idioms, where there were no literal English equivalents, as those elements more than any other add individual character to the language. Also in situations when the characters were excited or emotional (*mnie gołego!, to ja!* meaning *me naked, it's me!*), Polish seemed more natural for them to use. I also introduced Polish for cultural terms like church (*kościół*) – because such words are habitually used in the mother tongue even by those who use a second language on an everyday basis.

ASBESTOS: Who? Why? What for?
POTATO: *(sits on the chair, breathes heavily)* They kidnapped me! Undressed! And then, mnie – gołego ... gołego, oh Jesus!.. gołego ...
PROFESSOR: They beat you? Raped?

> POTATO: ... they chucked me off pod kościół, among the people!
> PROFESSOR: But who?
> POTATO: It's your fault – pijaku!
> PROFESSOR: My?
> POTATO: Who brought that pimp with his daughter here?
> PROFESSOR: Was it him?
> POTATO: Who else? I didn't mess up with anyone here!
> ASBESTOS: Calm down, Ignac.
> POTATO: Block the door! And bolt it! I'm scared! Ale wstyd!

Unfortunately, as the readings proved, the language was still not clear enough. Polish words – which sound foreign and are completely meaningless for English audiences – passed unnoticed, adding nothing to the character of the text. In the original, the situation was different. English terms incorporated into the dialect are either functioning in the Polish language, or even if not, the majority of spectators know English well enough to understand them. The strategy turned out to be useless. Polish words did not add any character or colour to the text because they were simply meaningless for the audience. Worse still, the information they carried was lost. I decided to abandon this strategy and look for another solution.

I realised that the presence of Polish in the English translation had to be reduced to a minimum. Understandability was my priority. This time I decided to keep the text English (using Polish only in proper names) but create the effect of foreign-English by simplifying the grammar and making all the mistakes that a Polish immigrant speaking English would probably make. The omission of articles, use of wrong tenses and word order and a very limited vocabulary are quite common characteristics for Polish speakers of English.

> ASBESTOS: Who? Why? What for?
> POTATO: *(sits on the chair, breathes heavily)* They kidnapped me! Undressed! And then, me – naked ... naked, oh Jesus! ... naked ...
> PROFESSOR: They beat you? Raped?
> POTATO: ... they chucked me off by church, among people!
> PROFESSOR: But who?
> POTATO: It's your fault – you boozer!
> PROFESSOR: My?
> POTATO: Who brought that pimp with his daughter here?
> PROFESSOR: Was it him?
> POTATO: Who else? I not mess up with anyone here!
> ASBESTOS: Calm down, Ignac.
> POTATO: Block door! And bolt it! I'm scared! What shame!

This version did not have the disadvantage of being only a translator's invention. Recent immigrants both in England and America do speak 'bad' English, so I thought it could be used effectively in *Greenpoint Miracle*. However, after further consideration I realized that the whole idea of simplifying the language and introducing 'bad grammar' was flawed. Translating the play into English I am creating a wholly artificial world of Poles speaking to each other in English. The English language becomes only a medium, which carries information to a foreign audience. It becomes a gate through which the audience can enter the world of Potato, Professor and the others. Why then should they speak bad English? They certainly do not speak bad Polish. The whole idea now seemed to be illogical. The dialect was lost anyway, and introducing 'bad' English only to suggest that the characters on the stage are Polish immigrants was not reasonable. The set, the costumes, as well as the way actors move and speak (Polish accents) would be enough to suggest who the characters are. The idea was abandoned altogether. I decided to use 'standard' English and reduce the presence of Polish to proper names.

> ASBESTOS: Who? Why? What for?
> POTATO: *(sits on the chair, breathes heavily)* They kidnapped me! Undressed! And then, me – naked ... naked, oh Jesus! ... naked ...
> PROFESSOR: They beat you? Raped?
> POTATO: ... they chucked me off by the church, among the people!
> PROFESSOR: But who?
> POTATO: It's your fault – you boozer!
> PROFESSOR: My?
> POTATO: Who brought that pimp with his daughter here?
> PROFESSOR: Was it him?
> POTATO: Who else? I didn't mess up with anyone here!
> ASBESTOS: Calm down, Ignac.
> POTATO: Block the door! And bolt it! I'm scared! What shame!

After several unsuccessful attempts to preserve the immigrants' dialect, I produced a version virtually free from Polish words, free from 'bad' English and strange neologisms. I neutralized the dialect, and by doing this undoubtedly deprived the language of the play of its unique character and colour. In the case of *Greenpoint Miracle*, however, I decided that no other strategy was effective. I hope that with the final version I achieved the main aim of my translation and produced a text that is understandable for an English audience.

Translating drama from Polish into English is not an easy task. Serious dilemmas are caused by context, realia and other aspects of cultural transfer. Here, no straightforward or wholly successful solution can be found. Compromises have to be made and the result achieved rarely retains the quality of the original. My translation of *Greenpoint Miracle* stripped the original of the unique dialect and the colourful slang as well as numerous metaphors and idioms. It was the price that had to be paid for making the play understandable to foreign audiences. That was my priority, and that is why I decided to provide background information in the glossary. In so doing I was able to preserve the realia and the cultural context. I realize that this information can only be helpful to the reader, whereas the potential audience would have to cope with the cultural 'otherness' of the play. However, I strongly believe that if the director and the actors have a thorough understanding of the play and a detailed knowledge of its cultural background, they will be able to draw the audience into the world of Greenpoint immigrants by giving it a real-life quality.

Although the context and realia of the play remained unchanged, the strategy I adopted neutralized the text, inevitably losing some of its character. Hopefully this made the play more accessible to the target audience. The reverse strategy – preserving the dialect and other unique language features – could distort the understanding of the play and communication with the audience. There is no perfect solution. After all, as Humboldt (in Savory 1968:75) said: "All translations seem ... to be simply an attempt to solve an insoluble problem." I think this is true. Especially in the case of Edward Redliński's *Greenpoint Miracle*.

## References

Catford, J. C. (1965) *A Linguistic Theory of Translation*, Oxford: Oxford University Press.

Duff, Alan (1981) *The Third Language*, Oxford: Pergamon Press.

Florin, Sinder (1993) 'Realia in Translation', in Palma Zlateva (ed.) *Translation as Social Action*, London: Routledge.

Korzeniowska, Aniela and Piotr Kuhiwczak (1994) *Successful Polish-English Translation*, Warszawa: PWN.

Mrożek, Sławomir (1967) *Six Plays,* London: Jonathan Cape.

Newmark, Peter (1988) *A Textbook of Translation*, London: Prentice Hall International Ltd.

Pavis, Patrice (1989) trans. Loren Kruger, 'Problems of translation for the stage: interculturalism and post-modern theatre', in Hanna Scolnicov (ed.) *The Play Out of Context*, Cambridge: Cambridge University Press.

Savory, Theodore (1968) *The Art of Translation*, London: Jonathan Cape.

# 12 A Samovar Is A Samovar Is A Samovar. Hopes and Failures of the Author as the Object and Subject of Translation

ANDRÁS NAGY

*Abstract*. The contention here is that the relocation of language involves the fragmentation of the entire play. From his unique perspective as translated playwright as well as adapter of plays, Nagy first explores the translational processes of adaptation, interpretation, paraphrasing, contemporization, and most importantly, understanding, that combine to create meaning in the theatre. He assesses theatrical attempts to cross the cultural frontier that still encloses Eastern Europe. Discovering, in an attempt to 'transplant' *Three Sisters* to Hungarian soil, that Chekhov's samovar is a unique and untranslatable cultural phenomenon, he draws a parallel with the role and significance of the whole cultural-historical-spiritual milieu of Hungary, closed behind linguistic and historical barriers. Drawing on this experience and his stage adaptations of *King Lear*, *Anna Karenina*, and Kierkegaard's *The Seducer's Diary*, he concludes that it is holistic context rather than discrete text that poses the real challenge to the translator for performance.

## A rose is a rose is a rose.

But is it then true that *a rose* is *eine Röse* is *egy rózsa*? Is the famous sentence of Gertrude Stein valid when talking about translation and likewise, necessarily, about interpretation, adaptation, understanding? Roses are probably too fragile for such an exercise.

*Samovars* are much more resistant. Regardless of time, space, cultural context, Chekhov's *samovar* is a *samovar* is a *samovar*. At least this was the conclusion of my experiences, being on both sides of the mirror, as the object and subject of translation.

I wonder whether translation is really the best word to describe everything that is involved where translating and theatre are concerned. But is there any better word to express what happens to a text when it is changed to suit different needs?

Hesitating in using a word is already a very familiar situation for anyone who has ever been involved in translation. Or in writing. Or in theatre. Translation for theatre focuses our attention on the very complexity of the problems.

The conclusion above is the result of my experience on stage, the consequence of some very concrete processes that I am going to describe. To be concrete however, I should first make clear in what sense I am going to use categories, references, words even at the risk of restating certain commonplaces.

1. Theatre is a **language**, and everything performed on stage should be translated into it. It has its own grammar, its dialects, its elements and even its
   neologisms. This language is the condition of communication with the audience and this communication is necessarily non-verbal in its essence.
2. Time is always **suspended** on stage. In the over-arching present everything
   will be necessarily contemporized. Understanding is always contemporary,
   regardless of whether the events on the stage refer to ancient Greece or 19th
   century Russia. Our presence transforms everything into the time of our reception. This is unalterable fact.
3. Every understanding is **misunderstanding**, when talking about art. There is
   no 'authentic' performance or interpretation, even of classical works – should
   we need masks now to perform *Electra* or a handsome boy to play Juliet
   Capulet? The language of theatre may have been born out of a long process
   but the actualization is always the performance itself, in the present cultural
   context. Philology can only be a *voyeur* of acts on stage never a judge, and
   not even a witness.

In order to be concrete in thinking about interpretation I have briefly to refer to
two very un-theatrical – but nonetheless appropriate – geniuses when considering language, interpretation and understanding, in a more theoretical way.

Firstly, it was Ludwig Wittgenstein who defined the limits of our thinking as
the limits of the language itself. Within these limits in theatre there is also theatrical imagination and expression. Everything, translated for the stage is limited
by the language established and used in theatre. "The rest", as we well know, "is
silence", being beyond the reach of language.

Secondly, it was Martin Heidegger who referred to the wisdom of language.
An authentic perception of the world is deeply hidden in language. Linguistic
archaeology, or rather philosophical etymology, may reveal the lost meaning of
words, which have become heavily corrupted in everyday use. In theatre however we may intimate the lost authenticity by questioning the use of theatrical
expressions, a familiar process in experimental productions.

Both geniuses were questioning language itself, that seemed to be a given to
many thinkers before them. Who would question language as often and as des-
perately as someone involved in translation – in both senses: translating for the
stage and translating the text itself?

This 'double desperation' is very familiar for us Hungarians. Having a won-
derful and hopelessly isolated language in the centre of the continent, a language
that is hardly penetrable for anyone not born Hungarian, our culture is necessarily bound to translation. Furthermore we live at a crossroads of different traditions,
cultural influences, zones of interests – all of which make our history both exciting and hard to survive, and moreover bring about permanent interactions,
forced or wilful communications, cross-fertilizations. During our history, which
has included often dramatic 'interactions' with Mongols, Turks, Austrians,
Germans, Soviets, Americans (who next?), our culture as well as our language

has been opened up to foreign influence, which has in turn been quickly transformed (translated) into a very special Hungarian experience. The combination of receptivity on one side and isolation on the other has greatly shaped the nature and function of our theatre, as one of the 'main stages' for such cultural interaction.

But translating from (as well as into) Hungarian immediately raises the problem of the **communicability** of our very own experiences. How could we reveal that which is deeply embedded within the language: the prints of our collective personality? How could we share with anyone outside our culture the very unique (the very Hungarian) experience that inspired the text itself?

As a playwright I tried to experiment with two-way communication, often simultaneously, translating into Hungarian (or to be exact: onto the Hungarian stage) some major works of European literature and interpreting the Hungarian experience in the framework of a foreign cultural context. For this reason I experimented with the *lingua franca* of theatre, to transcend our cultural isolation, to find common experiences expressed across frontiers, in order to reinterpret them on stage. My attempt was somehow 'modelled' on ancient Greek mythology, the theatrical *lingua franca* for authors using a given plot, familiar characters, unchanging gods, when translating their unique experience into the shared language of the wider community and onto the stage.

In my view a new, secular mythology has replaced that historical-anthropological common knowledge. I therefore experimented in reinterpreting the myths that I found expressed in the narratives of modern novels, literary works, even essays of the last few centuries (i.e. during the process of the secularisation of mythology). I was happy to cross borders of literature, philosophy, and fairy tales, in order to find the best 'raw material' for this common knowledge.

In this way for example I recycled the myth of the social career of Julien Sorel (from Stendhal's *Le Rouge et le noir* [*The Red and the Black*]), something that was archetypally familiar and yet common experience from the social changes and chances that had arisen since 1989. I told on stage the mythical story of marital infidelity of *Anna Karenina* (based on Tolstoy's novel), in the context of changing intimate human relationships, when the smell of freedom was already in the air. In another play I experimented with the myth of Don Juan, focusing on manipulation, charismatic strength and secularized morality, later trying to mirror it in the extreme eroticism of *Nana* (borrowed from the novel of Zola), and concluding in the birth of the 'sexual animal'. In another work I translated for the stage Don Juan's younger and Nordic brother: Johannes from Kierkegaard's *The Seducer's Diary*, as an example of initiating the 'human experience', something many of us went through in history.

The challenge of *King Lear*, when we started to work on its translation in a very complex sense, was the very impossibility of interpretation. Or, to put in another way: the impossibility of communicating what is most important. The tragic error committed by the old king was to force his daughters to translate into words something that can hardly ever be expressed in any form, and particularly not by talking – love. The whole plot can also be understood as the conflict between an authentic and an inauthentic sense of love. This is the basis of the choice the daughters make when reacting to their father's request.

The historical milieu, although greatly influential for Shakespeare's play, necessarily faded away in our reading of it, which focused on the contradictions of communication when verbalizing love. Our project with *King Lear* was to focus on those living in Hungary, whose drama of communication in a wider sense may be fundamentally and fatally the same as it was for Lear. We decided to recreate the story from a very special and yet 'archaic' angle: that of the Gypsies living in Hungary. The largest ethnic minority, victims of social changes, cursed with prejudices and contradictions, the Gypsies experience a historical transition, as did the medieval king. Theirs might be different in its motifs and causes, but it is similar at the point where archaic segments and rules of society start to disappear, in a way that affects very close human relationships.

When 'translating' *King Lear* into the story of the old horse-trader Gypsy, called Lóvér, we kept the structure of the play intact but significantly altered many of its details. The father's request for a verbal confession of love started the dramatic process, fuelled by the daughters' confusion over communication. The price for the confession was not the kingdom, but the sum of money the old Gypsy was offered when his home in the 'ghetto' was destroyed by the local authorities and a new area was reassigned for him and the other Gypsies to build houses in. Lóvér's wandering started after he distributed his money between the older girls (as the youngest refused to answer his question), and the wandering was the same for an old Gypsy in Eastern Europe as it was for the court and for the king in the middle ages – a way of life. The Fool expressed the same irrationality of fate as in the original drama and the impossibility of revealing love was every bit as painful as it had to be. While our work led us farther and farther from the Shakespearean play, incorporating motifs from Gypsy customs and details from fairy tales, the whole text expressed much more about authentic choices and conflicts than we had expected, and this not in any historical sense, but in the language of the theatre.

The audience realized the very essence of our idea when we performed it in the first Hungarian Gypsy Theatre (Napház – Khamorro). Again, when the play was turned into a film script and the film was produced, a larger public received it very sensitively. In the depth of the drama we confronted traditions that had remained unconditional for centuries, as changes started to occur and new forms of expression (communication) modified earlier ones. When recreating the main characters, we tried to follow Shakespeare in presenting different choices for life, but for life in present-day Hungary. Thus three 'alternatives' were described in the daughters: the oldest one decided to give up her very identity as a Gypsy in order to be accepted by the Hungarian majority. The second daughter locked herself into the strict and dated traditions of the Gypsies, as she wanted to be a part of a world where she could be accepted unconditionally. Meanwhile 'Cordelia' represented a way of keeping her identity while at the same time being part of a larger socio-cultural context, even if this proved ultimately self-destructive.

The unchangeable part of the play, the *'samovar'* of this drama, was the lack of communication where love is concerned: a *silence* is a *silence* is a *silence*, even if a patriarch orders this silence to be broken by the expression of something profound and obvious.

The impossibility of translating love into words was probably the insoluble tragic conflict for *King Lear*, but for Chekhov's *Three Sisters* the absolute impossibility of communication seemed to be the inspiring element. Again, the hidden or indirect possibility of communication that invites translation, often serves to make clear the very impossibility of understanding, of translating anything from personal experience into the language of collectivity.

Our project was to translate Chekhov's masterpiece thoroughly: not only by finding the necessary words in the Russian-Hungarian vocabulary, but rather to find an adequate way of expressing the complexity of communication that goes beyond words, beyond vocabulary, beyond the text itself. The whole world of the play should be recreated.

The idea behind the project was that no one can understand Chekhov from the surface. And simple translation may only scratch the surface. The complexity of meanings, of associations, of references, will necessarily be eliminated from the translated text or even worse: they will be substituted with a turn-of-the-century Russia of our simple imagination. Our idea was to recreate the *whole* context of the play, to discover and include what lay beyond the textual communication and in this way to make understood the necessarily untranslatable parts of the context – which had obviously been clear to Chekhov's original audience.

In the process of discovering this complexity we were immediately confronted with the extremely large number of references, including hidden references to things like habits, customs, types of behaviour, quotations, etc. – a whole world lay beneath what we thought was the 'real' and only world. We needed serious and scientific assistance to aid our understanding: this included the author's correspondence, the philology of the origin of the play, memoirs of contemporaries, colleagues and actors involved, Russian encyclopaedias, poems, newspapers, popular songs. Everything that Chekhov had touched or referred to, was investigated in the reconstruction of a universe which was still present in the original text.

We soon came to a dramatic realization that nothing was accidental in Chekhov's play, and that each line was loaded with different layers of simultaneous meaning. The trees in blossom at the beginning had their very special (erotic) atmosphere – just like the trees to be cut down at the end (with strong male references to Russian folk tales, so that Natasha's gardening ideas similarly included symbolic castration). The food being served, the news the Doctor reads, the fragment of the poem Masha quotes, as well as each further segment were all extremely meaningful; and the drama of this communication was to explain, to ironize, to oppose or to emphasize the flow of events in the communication on the 'main stage'.

These references incorporated into the meaning of the play were obvious in its original socio-cultural context, so unconditionally clear for its contemporary audience, and yet empty or just ornamental for historical latecomers and outsiders like us. How could we get closer to the authentic meaning if translation was obviously not enough? We decided to recreate also the language of references, to regain the lost meaning by substituting for Chekhov's details elements that are communicative for us in the same way as the ones in his play were for the contemporary audience.

Thus we embarked upon a difficult and risky process. We substituted Hungary for fin de siècle Russia, hence the *pirog* could become the well known *pogácsa*, the poem by Lermontov became the lines of a similar Hungarian poet, the names of characters had to carry the same funny overtones as in Russian, etc. We carefully went into all details, from military ranks to ethnic differences, from references to Moscow to the character of the seasons. During our work we immediately realised how little we had understood of Chekhov before, and while enjoying the richness of the text revealed before our eyes, we had to consider whether translating it could ever be possible. And then, just when we were nearly done with all the substitutions, and all the references had been changed in an 'equivalent' way – we came to the *samovar*. To the gift the Doctor gives to Irina for her birthday and to a symbol of home, marriage, family life (and an accepted present for a wedding anniversary). This simultaneously refers to the Doctor's unhappy love for the sisters' mother and mocks Irina's unmarried status. Meanwhile this ultimately Russian object is full of references to fire, tension, steam, boiling – an easy metaphor for anyone familiar with passion as well as tea-making! What could ever substitute for a samovar? Would a kettle or a coffee-maker do? Should we think in terms of lamps, or a huge clock? After endless hours of hesitating we had to confess – such efforts are hopeless. A *samovar* is a *samovar* is a *samovar*. And even if we understand hardly anything of Chekhov's hidden references, his contextual meaning, his indirect quotations and hints, this non-understanding is part of the richness of the play, and we have no chance of altering it, by taking it out of the context in which it was conceived. A paradox is a paradox is a paradox.

After all these experiences it seemed obvious that I should experiment directly with paradoxes on stage. Not only on a practical level, as part of a problem that I realized I couldn't solve – but also theoretically, talking about paradoxes and acting them out in the form of a play. My ambitious experiment necessarily included the genius of paradoxes, the Danish existentialist thinker, Søren Kierkegaard. In terms of translation, a paradox can also be defined as one impossibility translated into another impossibility.

My striving towards impossibility started with a stage interpretation of Kierkegaard's philosophical essay masquerading as a novel and paraphrasing the Don Juan myth: *The Seducer's Diary*. The play I wrote based on the novel and on some other writings of Kierkegaard (including his journals and papers, other essays and letters), in spite of its appealing title and the serious cultural references, is first and foremost about **interpretation** – as a basic condition of communication. And yet, the crucial point of Kierkegaard's ideas as well as my interpretation on the stage was that interpretation often negates, hides, or even blocks communication. Particularly when love is interpreted in an indirect way, as is necessary for a sophisticated seduction, then for breaking off the relationship, later to regain the passionate love on a much higher level, as Johannes the seducer had planned it. The protagonist thus became a genius of incognitos, of personalities made-up (interpreted) as appropriate to fulfil his wishes. The Latin word for mask is *persona*, well known also from the origins of theatre. Writing about seduction, confessing and hiding his passion toward his seduced and abandoned fiancé, using scripts and communicating with pseudonyms, Kierkegaard necessarily invokes 'pseudo-persons', something fundamentally theatrical. I had to realize on stage something that was a basic concept for the author.

Meanwhile Johannes' seduction doesn't focus only on love but on eroticism in a much larger sense, including political excitement as well as religious passions. The victims of his early 'seductions' therefore became politician, priest, and so on, differentiated by interpreting different sides (masks) of the totality of his thinking – again a very familiar and very theatrical method of interpretation. As soon as these are personified they may and do become involved in concrete interactions with Johannes. The interpretations begin to invade the space of ideas, or rather the space of theatre: the stage.

But when love comes into the picture, unexpectedly growing over the frames of manipulation, then the manipulator of significations and interpretations gets trapped in his own plan. The limits of communication become obvious, just as the use of an incognito becomes a burden when the very essence of personality is involved. The manipulator finds himself manipulated by the very fragile power of love, and the virtuoso of meanings will be mute when communication transcends the verbal – the territory of his once absolute power. The unhappy ending on stage pointed to the poverty of interpretation as long as only words are involved, and the lack of action was more eloquent than the brilliantly sophisticated sentences of Johannes.

This was my interpretation of Kierkegaard's work (and his ideas, his personality and life) that was later re-interpreted in another language. The translation turned into interpretation, as the translator, in close collaboration with the author (myself) understood that the set of (Hungarian) theatrical traditions can be neither altered nor translated but only substituted by the traditions of another one: *The Seducer's Diary* was adapted to the British stage. The process of adaptation was revealing of many aspects of theatrical interpretation. The richness of the language was restricted to pure communication and actions became more 'talkative' than originally planned. Cultural and historical references, both explicit and hidden (extremely important in a country surviving totalitarianism and learning to use 'newspeak') had to be cut out or explained on stage. All the unsolved details that in Hungarian were cloaked by the captivating use of our metaphorical language were revealed in their nakedness in English, and had to be reworked, but only for the British audience. By the end the play was a version of my original drama, that I could easily have imagined re-translating from English and adapting for the Hungarian stage – starting the process anew, understanding the seducer's paradox that in order to remain faithful, one needs to be unfaithful.

And probably this paradox was the *samovar* of my play: something that was deeply rooted in our traditions, in our historical experience, and which nothing could replace. These paradoxes have to be interpreted by other paradoxes, that are part of the culture of the interpreters, otherwise the very essence is lost. You can make tea in a kettle, in a pot, even in a ball, but *a samovar* is a *samovar* is a *samovar*.

## References

### Essays

Heidegger, Martin (1989 [1927]) 'A beszéd időbelisége' ['The temporality of Speaking'], in Lèt ès idő [*Sein und Zeit*, or *Being and Time*], Budapest: Gondolat Kiadò: 569-571. See also his lectures on Parmenides.

Wittgenstein, Ludwig (1974 [1921]) *Tractatus Logico-Philosophicus*, Budapest: Gondolat Kiadò: para. 4. 121; 132.

### Plays and adaptations

Nagy, András (1990) *Anna Karenina Pályaudvar* [*The Anna Karenina Railway Station*], a theatre version of Tolstoy's novel, performed at the Radnóti Theatre, Budapest.

------ (1991a) *A csábító naplója* [*The Seducer's Diary*], a play based on the philosophical novel of Kierkegaard, performed in the Budapesti Kamaraszínház, Budapest; Gárdonyi Géza Theatre, Eger (1994); staged readings and guest performances in Berlin 1992; Iowa 1993; Washington 1993; Copenhagen 1994. Translated and adapted to the British stage by Julian Garner (1996), *The Seducer's Diary* is published by Nick Hern Books, London.

------ (1991b) *Magyar Három Nővér* [*A Hungarian Three Sisters*], a 'Hungarisation' of Chekhov's masterpiece, performed at the Játékszín, Budapest.

------ *Nana* – a play based on Zola's novel, in (1993) *Drámák – Dramas*, Budapest: Prológ.

------ (1994) *Vörös és Fekete* [*The Red and Black*], a play based on Stendhal's novel *Le Rouge et le noir*, performed at the National Theatre of Győr.

------ (1997a) *Don Juan*, performed at the Merlin Theatre, Budapest.

------ (1997b) *Romani Kris – Cigánytörvény* [*Gipsy Lore*], a film based on Shakespeare's *King Lear*, produced by the Satellitfilm Gmbh and Hungarian Television; the play was performed at Napház – Khamorro, the First Hungarian Gypsy Theatre, Budapest, 1997.

# Notes on Contributors

**MARK BATTY** is a lecturer in Theatre Studies at University of Leeds. His areas of interest are twentieth-century French theatre, contemporary Swedish theatre, the role of the director and non-verbal drama. In the course of his work, he translates plays for class discussion and for production. He is currently working on the translation of a series of Swedish plays, and has been invited to present one of them at the Huddersfield Festival of Contemporary European Plays in 2000. His book, *Writers and their Work: Harold Pinter,* is forthcoming.

**LINDSAY BELL** is a PhD candidate at the Graduate Centre for the Study of Drama, University of Toronto, having completed her Master of Arts degree in Drama at the University of Alberta. She has worked in professional theatre as a playwright and dramaturg in Alberta, Toronto and the Shaw Festival. Her adaptation of Virginia Woolf's novel *To the Lighthouse* will have its première at the Shaw Festival (August 2000) and on CBC Radio Drama (February 2001).

**MARTIN BOWMAN** is a native of Montreal of Scots parentage. He teaches English at Champlain Regional College, St. Lambert, Quebec. With Bill Findlay, he has co-translated into Scots seven plays by Quebec dramatist Michel Tremblay: *The Guid Sisters*, *The Real Wurld?*, *Hosanna* (all Tron Theatre); *The House Among the Stars* (Traverse Theatre and Perth Theatre); *Forever Yours, Marie-Lou* (LadderMan/Tron Theatre); *Albertine in Five Times* (Clyde Unity Theatre); and *Solemn Mass for a Full Moon in Summer* (Traverse Theatre, 2000). Findlay and Bowman have translated a number of other Québécois plays, including Jeanne-Mance Delisle's *The Reel of the Hanged Man* (Stellar Quines Theatre Company, 2000). With Montreal playwright and director Wajdi Mouawad, Bowman has co-translated into French *Trainspotting* by Harry Gibson, adapted from Irvine Welsh's novel, and *Disco Pigs* by Enda Walsh.

**DERRICK CAMERON** is a lecturer at Staffordshire University, following a period of research into Black British Theatre at Liverpool John Moores University. He is the writer of *Black Sheep* (Temba Theatre Company, 1988), *Different Decks* (Splash Theatre Company, Humberside Tour, 1990), and *Hello Lunch* (rehearsed reading, Soho Theatre, 1994). His paper 'Better a Bad Night in Toxteth: Black British Popular Theatre' was published in *Popular Theatres?* (Liverpool John Moores University). Other research interests include sexuality and performance.

**KATE CAMERON** has an MA in French Literary Translation from Exeter University, and a first degree in Theatre Studies. She has worked as a performer and choreographer on several projects in London, Devon and abroad. She has also lectured at Dartington College of Arts in theatre, choreography and visual performance.

**EVA ESPASA** holds a PhD on drama translation, on the processes of transposing translated written texts into performance. She is a translation lecturer at the University of Vic (Spain), and has studied translation at Essex (U. K., 1989-1990) and at Leuven (Belgium, 1992). Her current research interests include drama translation, audio-visual translation and gender studies. She is presently completing a book on drama translation.

**BILL FINDLAY** is a lecturer in the Department of Drama, Queen Margaret University College, Edinburgh. He is editor of *A History of Scottish Theatre* (Edinburgh: Polygon, 1998), *Scottish Plays of the Seventies* (Edinburgh: Scottish Cultural Press, forthcoming 2000) and *Frae Ither Tongues: Essays on Modern Translations into Scots* (Clevedon: Multilingual Matters, forthcoming 2001). He has adapted into Scots Gerhart Hauptmann's *The Weavers* (Dundee Rep Theatre), Pavel Kohout's *Fire in the Basement* (Communicado Theatre Company), and Teresa Lubkiewicz's *Werewolves* (Theatre Archipelago). With co-translator Martin Bowman, he has translated for the Scottish stage ten plays from Quebec French into Scots (see above).

**TERRY HALE** is British Academy Research Fellow in the Performance Translation Centre at the University of Hull. He was formerly director of the British Centre for Literary Translation and has been editorial director of a publishing house specializing in translation. He has translated and edited more than twelve books, most recently the *Dedalus Book of French Horror: The 19th Century*. He is currently working on a new translation of J.K. Huysman's *Là-bas*.

**DAVID JOHNSTON** is Professor of Hispanic Studies at Queen's University, Belfast. He has written extensively on Spanish theatre and has translated a number of plays for both theatre and radio. His translation of Valle-Inclán's *Bohemian Lights* won the LWT Plays on Stage Award for 1993. He is also editor of *Stages of Translation – Essays and Interviews on Translating for the Stage*.

**ANTHONY MEECH** is a senior lecturer and head of the Department of Drama at the University of Hull. He has published translations of plays from all periods of German drama (including Christoph Hein and Botho Strauss) as well as articles on Brecht and contemporary German theatre, in particular that of the former GDR. Many of his translations have been professionally staged in London and elsewhere.

**ANDRÁS NAGY** is a playwright, essayist and academic. Starting out as a fiction writer, he published stories, novels and essay-novels. Later he turned to theatre; many of his dramas and adaptations have been performed and published in Hungary and abroad. He is also involved in documentary as well as feature filmmaking. Besides his activity in literature and theatre, he teaches in a number of universities including the University of Veszprém, and has a special interest in philosophy (particularly Existentialism and Kierkegaard's oeuvre). Founder of the Kierkegaard Cabinet, an independent research centre in Budapest, he was appointed President of the Hungarian Centre of the International Theatre Institute in 1998.

**KIRSTEN NIGRO** is Professor of Spanish and Latin American Literature at the University of Cincinnati. Her specialisms are Mexican theatre, theory and women's literature. She received her doctorate from the University of Illinois and has also taught at the Universities of Arizona and Kansas, and Arizona State University. She sits on the editorial boards of *Latin American Theatre Review* and the *Latin American Research Review*. She has published over thirty articles and book chapters and is the editor of three books. She has translated plays from Chile, Mexico and the Caribbean, and is currently working on a long-term project in the translation and promotion of Mexican theatre, supported by the US/Mexico Fund for Culture, which is funded by the Rockefeller Foundation and the Mexican Ministry of Culture.

**KLAUDYNA ROZHIN** trained at the University of Maria Curie-Skłodowska in Lublin, Warsaw Theatre Academy and the University of Hull, where she completed an MA in Theatre Production. As a director she has worked for the Young Vic, the Theatre Royal Plymouth and Salisbury Playhouse and the Osterwa Theatre Lublin, Poland. Her translations into Polish include *Beauty and the Beast* by Laurence Boswell, *Chess* by Tim Rice, Benny Andersson and Bjorn Ulvaeus, *The Weir* by Conor McPherson, *The Beauty Queen of Leenane* by Martin McDonagh, David de Silva's *Fame*, *Deceptions* by Paul Wheeler, *Joseph and the Amazing Technicolor Dreamcoat* by Andrew Lloyd Webber and Tim Rice, *Moments of Weakness* by Donald Churchill, and *Blood Brothers* by Willy Russell. Other works include adaptations of *The Ghost of Atlantis* by Jaroslaw Abramow-Newerly and *The BFG* by Roald Dahl. Currently, she is involved in a project for the Royal National Theatre in London researching and translating Russian folk tales.

**CAROLE-ANNE UPTON** is a lecturer in Drama and co-founder of the Performance Translation Centre at the University of Hull. In 1997, she organized the *True to Form: On Stage Translation* Conference in Hull, which gave rise to this collection. Amongst her other interests are modern Irish theatre, French theatre and directing. She has also published articles on African and Caribbean theatre, and is translating a series of contemporary plays from Burkina Faso.

# Select General Bibliography

I have tried here to indicate a range of texts which focus centrally on the issue of translating for performance in another culture. With a few exceptions, I have excluded from this list the many articles which deal with issues specific to one particular playwright or event. It is also worth noting that the complexities of translating a given text for performance are often clearly addressed in a prefatory note to the published translation of the play itself. Such introductions are obviously too numerous to list here. Only works published since 1980 have been included, in the intention of providing some kind of overview, by no means exhaustive, of the development of the subject in recent years.

## 1. BOOKS AND SPECIAL ISSUES

Aaltonen, Sirkku (1996) *Acculturation of the Other. Irish Milieux in Finnish Drama Translation*, Joensuu: Joensuu University Press.

------ (2000) *Time-Sharing on Stage. Drama Translation in Theatre and Society*, Clevedon: Multilingual Matters.

Banu, Georges (ed.) (1982) 'Traduire', *Théâtre/Public* 44.

Brisset, Annie (1990) *Sociocritique de la traduction: théâtre et altérité au Québec (1968-1988)*, Montreal: Préambule, trans. Rosalind Gill and Roger Gannon (1996) as *A Sociocritique of Translation: Theatre and Alterity in Quebec (1968-1988)*, Toronto: University of Toronto Press.

Burger, Brigitte (ed.) (1994) *Traduire le Théâtre II*, Lausanne: Université de Lausanne, Centre de traduction littéraire.

Bharucha, Rustom (1990) *Theatre and the World – Performance and the Politics of Culture*, London: Routledge.

Déprats, Jean-Michel (ed.) (1996) *Antoine Vitez – le devoir de traduire*, Montpellier: Editions Climats and Maison Antoine Vitez.

*Donaire* 11 (1998) (Special issue on translations of Lorca).

Donaldson, Ian (ed.) (1983) *Transformations in Modern European Drama*, London: Macmillan, in association with Humanities Research Centre, Australian National University, Canberra.

'Dossier: Traduction théâtrale' (1990) *Jeu* 56.

Fischer-Lichte, Erika (et al, eds.) (1988) *Soziale und theatralische Konventionen als Problem der Dramenübersetzung*, Tübingen: Narr.

*German Life and Letters* XLIII (4) (July 1990) (Special issue on translation).

Heylen, Romy (1993) *Translation, Poetics and the Stage – Six French 'Hamlets'*, London: Routledge.

Johnston, David (ed.) (1996) *Stages of Translation: Essays and Interviews on Translating for the Stage*, Bath: Absolute Press.

Lenschen, Walter (ed.) (1993) *Traduire le Théâtre: Je perce l'énigme mais je garde le mystère*, Lausanne: Université de Lausanne, Centre de traduction littéraire.

Merino Alvarez, Raquel (1994) *Traducción, tradición y manipulación. Teatro inglés en*

*España, 1950-1990*, León: Universidad de León, Secretariado de Publicaciones.

*Modern Drama* XLI (1) (Spring 1998) (Special issue on translation).

Paul, Fritz and Brigitte Schultze, (eds.) (1991) *Probleme der Dramenübersetzung 1960-1988 – eine Bibliographie*, Tübingen: Narr.

Pavis, Patrice, trans. Loren Kruger (1992, reprinted 1995) *Theatre at the Crossroads of Culture*, London: Routledge.

------ (ed.) (1996) *The Intercultural Performance Reader*, London, USA and Canada: Routledge.

Peacock, Noël A. (1993) *Molière in Scotland 1945-1990*, Glasgow: University of Glasgow French and German Publications.

Perridon, H. and H. Van Der Liet (eds.) (1998) *TijdSchrift voor Skandinavistiek: Transposing Scandinavian Drama*, Jaargang 19 nummer 1.

*Platform Papers 1. Translation* (1989) London: National Theatre (Michael Frayn, Christopher Hampton and Timberlake Wertenbaker in a discussion chaired by Colin Chambers).

Schultze, Brigitte (et al, eds.) (1990) *Literatur und Theater. Traditionen und Konventionen als Problem der Dramenübersetzung*, Tübingen: Narr.

Scolnicov, Hannah and Peter Holland (eds.) (1989) *The Play out of Context – Transferring Plays from Culture to Culture*, Cambridge: Cambridge University Press.

*Sixième assises de la traduction littéraire (Arles 1989): Traduire le théâtre* (1990), Arles: Actes Sud.

Tőrnqvist, Egil (1991) *Transposing Drama. Studies in Representation*, Basingstoke: Macmillan.

Vigoureux-Frey, Nicole (ed.) (1993) *Traduire le Théâtre aujourd'hui?*, Rennes: Presses universitaires de Rennes, Collection "Le Spectaculaire".

Zuber, Ortrun (ed.) (1980) *The Languages of Theatre: Problems in the Translation and Transposition of Drama*, Oxford: Pergamon.

Zuber-Skerritt, Ortrun (ed.) (1984) *Page to Stage – Theatre as Translation*, Amsterdam: Rodopi.

## 2. ESSAYS AND ARTICLES

Aaltonen, Sirkku (1997) 'Translating plays or baking apple pies: A functional approach to the study of drama translation', in Mary Snell-Hornby, Zuzana Jettmarová and Klaus Kaindl (eds.) *Translation as Intercultural Communication – Selected Papers from the EST Congress – Prague 1995*, Amsterdam/Philadelphia: John Benjamins: 89-98.

Anderman, Gunilla (1998) 'Drama Translation', in Mona Baker (ed.) *The Routledge Encyclopedia of Translation Studies*, London: Routledge:71-74.

Bassnett, Susan (1980a) 'An Introduction to Theatre Semiotics', *Theatre Quarterly* 10 (38):47-55.

------ (1980b, revised 1988) 'Translating Dramatic Texts', in *Translation Studies*, London: Methuen:120-132. (Revised edition 1991, London: Routledge, reprinted 1996).

------ (1985) 'Ways through the Labyrinth: Strategies and methods for translating theatre texts', in Theo Hermans (ed.) *The Manipulation of Literature: Studies in*

*Literary Translation*, London: Croom Helm:87-103.

------ (1990) 'Translating for the Theatre: textual complexities', *Essays in Poetics* 15 (1), April:71-83.

------ (1991) 'Translating for the theatre: the case against 'performability'', *Traduction, Terminologie, Rédaction: Etudes sur le texte et ses transformations* 4 (1):99-111.

------ (1998) 'Still Trapped in the Labyrinth: Further Reflections on Translation and Theatre', in Susan Bassnett and André Lefevere *Constructing Cultures – Essays on Literary Translation*, Clevedon: Multilingual Matters, Topics in Translation 11:90-108.

------ (2000) 'Theatre and Opera', in Peter France (ed.) *The Oxford Guide to Literature in English Translation*, Oxford: Oxford University Press:96-103.

Cant, Sarah E. (1999) 'In Search of "Lessness" – Translation and Minimalism in Beckett's Theatre', *Forum for Modern Language Studies* XXXV (2), April:138-157.

Griffiths, Malcolm (1985) 'Presence and Presentation: Dilemmas in Translating for the Theatre', in Theo Hermans (ed.) *Second Hand. Papers on the Theory and Historical Study of Literary Translation*, ALW-Cahier 3:161-182.

Hale, Terry (2000) 'Romanticism and the Victorian Age', in Peter France (ed.) *The Oxford Guide to Literature in English Translation*, Oxford: Oxford University Press:64-73.

Johnston, David (1996) 'Text and Ideotext: Translation and Adaptation for the Stage', in Malcolm Coulthard and Patricia Anne Odber de Baubeta (eds.) *The Knowledges of the Translator*, Lewiston, Queenston and Lampeter: Mellen Press:243-258.

------ (in press) 'Translation for the Stage as Intercultural Activity', in Christopher Shorley (ed.) *Reading Between the Lines*, Dublin: Royal Irish Academy.

Jónás, Erzsébert C.S. (1996) 'The Ageless Chekhov. Text Modality as a Key to Three Hungarian Chekhov Interpretations', in Kinga Klaudy, José Lambert and Anikó Sohár (eds.) *Translation Studies in Hungary*, Budapest: Scholastica:149-156.

Kohlmayer, Rainer (1997) 'From saint to sinner: The demonization of Oscar Wilde's *Salomé* in Hedwig Lachmann's German translation and in Richard Strauss' opera', in Mary Snell-Hornby, Zuzana Jettmarová and Klaus Kaindl (eds.) *Translation as Intercultural Communication – Selected Papers from the EST Congress – Prague 1995*, Amsterdam/Philadelphia: John Benjamins:111-122.

Koustas, Jane (1988) 'Traduire ou ne pas traduire le théâtre? L'approche sémiotique', *Traduction, Terminologie, Rédaction: Etudes sur le texte et ses transformations* 1 (1):127-138.

Lefevere, André (1985) 'What is Written Must Be Written. *Julius Caesar*. Shakespeare, Voltaire, Wieland, Buckingham', in Theo Hermans (ed.) *Second Hand. Papers on the Theory and Historical Study of Literary Translation*, ALW-Cahier 3:88-105.

------ (1998) 'Acculturating Bertolt Brecht', in Susan Bassnett and André Lefevere, *Constructing Cultures – Essays on Literary Translation*, Clevedon: Multilingual Matters, Topics in Translation 11:109-122.

Mateo, Marta (1997) 'Translation strategies and the reception of drama performances: a mutual influence', in Mary Snell-Hornby, Zuzana Jettmarová and Klaus Kaindl (eds.) *Translation as Intercultural Communication – Selected Papers from the EST Congress – Prague 1995*, Amsterdam/Philadelphia: John Benjamins: 99-110.

Peacock, Noël A. (1994) 'Translating Molière for the English stage', in Stephen Bamforth (ed.) *Molière – Proceedings of the Nottingham Molière Conference 17-18 December 1993*, University of Nottingham: Nottingham French Studies, 33 (1), Spring:83-91.

Primavesi, Patrick (1999) 'The Performance of Translation: Benjamin and Brecht on the Loss of Small Details', *The Drama Review*, 43 (4), Winter:53-59.

Schultze, Brigitte (1987) 'Theorie der Dramenübersetzung – 1960 bis heute: ein Bericht zur Forschungslage', *Forum Modernes Theater* 2:5-17.

Snell-Hornby, Mary (1984) 'Sprechbare Sprache – Spielbarer Text: zur Problematik der Bühnenübersetzung', in Richard J. Watts and Urs Weidmann (eds.) *Modes of Interpretation: essays presented to Ernst Leisi*, Tübingen: Narr:101-116.

Valló, Zsuzsa (1996) 'Translating an American Comedy for the Hungarian Stage', in Kinga Klaudy, José Lambert, Anikó Sohár (eds.) *Translation Studies in Hungary*, Budapest: Scholastica:134-148.

Verma, Jatinder (1998) "Binglishing' the stage: a generation of Asian theatre in England', in Richard Boon and Jane Plastow (eds.) *Theatre Matters – Performance and Culture on the World Stage*, Cambridge: Cambridge University Press:126-134.

Worthen, W.B. (1995) 'Homeless Words: Field Day and the Politics of Translation', *Modern Drama* XXXVIII (1), Spring:22-41.

# Index

Abbensetts, Michael, 23

accent, 20-21, 28, 30, 70, 94, 96, 146, 148, *see also* Dialect

acculturation, 60

Ackland, Rodney, 6

'actability', 50

actors, 6, 9, 18, 19, 21, 24, 30, 49-51, 53, 55-58, 61, 63, 67-68, 70, 80, 82, 91, 98, 101, 103, 109, 140, 146, 148-149, 155

adaptation, 2, 4, 5-7, 9, 10, 17, 20, 25, 27, 28-29, 30, 50-51, 57, 69, 73-83, 85, 117, 127, 128, 140, 151, 153-158

Addison, Joseph, *Cato*, 3

Aeschylus, 35, 104

Akalaitis, JoAnne, 69, 70

Albee, Edward, 87

Albery Theatre (London), 6

Allende, Isabel, 118

Almeida Theatre (London), 5, 6, 136

America: American setting, 144-145, 147; House Committee on Un-American Activities, 131; American theatre 4, 5, 9, 25, 69, 70, 135-136, 115-125

Amyot, Jacques, 2

approximate translation, 32, 141, 142

Arrabal, Fernando, 87

Asian (British) theatre, 17-24

authenticity, 10, 18, 38, 40, 44, 152, 154, 156

authorship, 57, 63-72, 73, 82-83, 101

Baker, Houston A. Jr., 59-60

Bandele-Thomas, Biyi, 23

Barthes, Roland, 121-122

Bassnett, Susan, 9-10, 49, 50, 53, 55-59

BBC, 91

Beaumarchais, 35

Beckett, Samuel, 9, 63-72, 89; *Endgame*, 66-68, 69; *Footfalls*, 69; *Krapp's Last Tape*, 66; *Mercier et Camier*, 65; *Waiting for Godot*, 64-66, 69, 70

Berliner Ensemble, 130, 132

Bethell, Nicholas, 141

Berman, Sabina, *Muerte súbita* [*Sudden Death*], 124

Bhabha, Homi K., 125

Bharucha, Rustom, 18-19, 22, 24

Bilingual Foundation for the Arts (Los Angeles), 117

bilingual theatre, 115

*Binglish*, 20-24

Bird, Antonia, 80, 82

black British theatre, 17-24

Blin, Roger, 65-67, 70

Bolt, Ranjit, 5, 7

Borges, Jorge Luis, 118

Boswell, Laurence, 86

Braun, Volker, 130; *Die Übergangsgesellschaft* [*Society in Transit*], 134

**breathability**, 49-50

Brecht, Bertolt, 8, 21, 35, 50, 55, 90, 102, 131, 135, 136; *Lucullus*, 130

Brewster, Yvonne, 23

Bridie, James, 5

Broadway (New York), 70, 117, 135

Brook, Peter, 18, 24

Bulgakov, Mikhail, *Flight*, 5-6

Calderón de la Barca, Pedro, 85, 95

**calque**, 141-142

Canadian theatre: 5, English-speaking, 73-83; French-speaking, 17, 25-33, 36

Catalan theatre, 51, 54, 55

censorship, 2, 8, 124, 127, 128-130, 142

Cervantes, Miguel de, *Don Quijote*, 85

Césaire, Aimé, *Une Tempête*, 6

Chaucer, 2

Chekhov, Anton, 3, 5, 28, 139-140; *The Cherry Orchard*, 4; *Three Sisters*, 17, 22, 134, 151, 155-156; *Uncle Vanya*, 5, 6

Cibber, Colley, 3

Cixous, Hélène, *La Ville parjure ou le réveil des érinyes*, [*The Perjured City or the Awakening of the Furies*], 8, 101-112

Clark, Sally, *Moo*, 77

class (social), 26-29, 35-37, 43-44, 144, 154

Cognates, 32, 38